First World War
and Army of Occupation
War Diary
France, Belgium and Germany

55 DIVISION
166 Infantry Brigade
Prince of Wales's Volunteers (South Lancashire Regiment)
1/5th Battalion
1 December 1915 - 31 July 1919

WO95/2929/2

The Naval & Military Press Ltd
www.nmarchive.com
Published in association with The National Archives

Published by

The Naval & Military Press Ltd

Unit 10 Ridgewood Industrial Park,

Uckfield, East Sussex,

TN22 5QE England

Tel: +44 (0) 1825 749494

www.naval-military-press.com

www.nmarchive.com

This diary has been reprinted in facsimile from the original. Any imperfections are inevitably reproduced and the quality may fall short of modern type and cartographic standards.

Contents

Document type	Place/Title	Date From	Date To
Heading	WO95/2929/2 1/5 Bn. 5th Lancs Regt Jan 1916-July 1919		
Heading	55th Division 166th Infy Bde 1-5th Bn Sth Lancs Regt Jan 1916-Jly 1919		
Heading	1/5 S Lancs Regt Vol 4		
Heading	1/5 S Lancs Regt Jan Vol I		
War Diary		06/01/1916	27/05/1916
War Diary	Talmas	02/05/1916	31/06/1916
War Diary		04/06/1916	20/06/1916
Heading	166th Brigade 55th Division 1/5th Battalion South Lancashire Regiment July 1916		
Heading	War Diary Of The 1/5th South Lancashire Regt 166th Infantry Brigade 55th (West Lancashire) Division For The Period 1st July 1916 To 31st July 1916 Vol VII		
War Diary		01/07/1916	30/07/1916
Heading	166th Brigade 55th Division 1/5th Battalion South Lancashire Regiment August 1916		
Heading	War Diary Of The 1/5th South Lancashire Regt For The Period 1st August To 31st August 1916 Vol 8		
War Diary		01/08/1916	31/08/1916
Heading	War Diary Of 1/5th S. Lancs. R. 1st September To 30th September 1916 Vol 9		
War Diary		01/09/1916	30/09/1916
Heading	War Diary Of 1/5th S. Lancs. Regt. For The Period 1st To 31st October 1916 Vol 10		
War Diary		01/10/1916	31/10/1916
Heading	War Diary Of 1/5th S. Lan. R. For Period 1st November To 30th November 1916 Vol XI		
War Diary		01/11/1916	30/11/1916
Miscellaneous	Report On A Raid carried Out By The 1/5th South Lancashire Regt		
Miscellaneous	55th Division No. 676 G	06/11/1916	06/11/1916
Heading	War Diary Of 1/5th S. Lan. R. for Period December 1st-31st 1916 Vol 12		
War Diary		01/12/1916	31/12/1916
Heading	War Diary Of The 1/5 S. Lan. R. For The Period 1/1/17 To 31/1/17 Vol 13		
War Diary		01/01/1917	28/02/1917
Heading	War Diary Of 1/5 S Lan. R. for the Period 1st To 28th February 1917 Vol 14		
Heading	War Diary Of The 1/5th S. Lan. R. For The Period 1st To 31st March 1917 Vol 15		
Miscellaneous	J 1143	03/04/1917	03/04/1917
War Diary		01/03/1917	31/03/1917
Heading	War Diary Of 1/5th S. Lan. R. For The Period April 1st To 30th 1917 Vol 16		
War Diary		01/04/1917	30/04/1917
Heading	War Diary Of 1/5th S. Lan. R. For The Period May 1st-31st 1917 Vol 17		
War Diary	Wieltje Sector	01/05/1917	09/05/1917

War Diary	L Camp	10/05/1917	18/05/1917
War Diary	Ypres Ref. Trench Map Zillebeke 1/10000	18/05/1917	26/05/1917
War Diary	Railway Wood	26/05/1917	31/05/1917
Heading	War Diary Of 1/5th S. Lan. R. For The Period June 1st To June 30th 1917 Vol 18		
War Diary	Railway Wood	01/06/1917	30/06/1917
Miscellaneous	55th Division No. 656 I. G.	06/06/1917	06/06/1917
Miscellaneous	55th Division No. 690 G	09/06/1917	09/06/1917
Miscellaneous	55th Division AQC. 594	11/06/1917	11/06/1917
Miscellaneous	Messages And Signals		
Heading	War Diary Of 1/5th Battalion South Lancashire Regiment From 1st July 1917 To 31st July 1917 Vol 19		
War Diary	Esquerdes	01/07/1917	30/07/1917
War Diary	Wieltje	31/07/1917	31/07/1917
Miscellaneous	Scheme For Operations	14/07/1917	14/07/1917
Miscellaneous	Instructions For Operations	14/07/1917	14/07/1917
Miscellaneous	Appendix I Administrative Details		
Miscellaneous	Appendix II Signal Communication		
Diagram etc	Diagram No. 1 Lines		
Miscellaneous	Diagram No. 2 Wireless		
Diagram etc	Diagram No. 3 Visual		
Diagram etc	Diagram No. 4 Runners		
Miscellaneous	Appendix III Traffic Control Wieltje		
Miscellaneous	Appendix V Medical		
Miscellaneous	Appendix VI Stragler Posts		
Miscellaneous	Appendix VII Liaison Officers Etc		
Map	Map No. 1		
Map	Map No. 2		
Map	Map No. 3		
Miscellaneous	X/Y Night		
Operation(al) Order(s)	166 Infantry Brigade Order No. 88	23/07/1917	23/07/1917
Operation(al) Order(s)	166 Infantry Brigade Order No. 89	24/07/1917	24/07/1917
Operation(al) Order(s)	All Recipients 166 Infantry Brigade Order No. 89	27/07/1917	27/07/1917
Miscellaneous	All Recipients 166 Infantry Brigade Order No. 88	28/07/1917	28/07/1917
Map	Map		
Heading	War Diary Of 1/5th Battalion South Lancashire Regiment From 1st August 1917 To 31st August 1917 Volume 31		
War Diary	Capricorn Trench (1000 yd SSE St Julien)	01/08/1917	02/08/1917
War Diary	Wieltje	02/08/1917	05/08/1917
War Diary	Nr Poperinghe	05/08/1917	22/08/1917
War Diary	Tournehem	23/08/1917	31/08/1917
Operation(al) Order(s)	55th (West Lancashire) Division Special Order Of The Day 3rd August 1917	03/08/1917	03/08/1917
Heading	1/5 S. Lancs. Regt. Vol 21		
Heading	War Diary Of 1/5th Battalion South Lancashire Regiment From 1st September 1917 To 31st September 1917 Volume 37		
War Diary	Tournehem	01/09/1917	13/09/1917
War Diary	Audruicq	13/09/1917	13/09/1917
War Diary	Ypres N. Area	13/09/1917	13/09/1917
War Diary	Wieltje Forward Area	14/09/1917	19/09/1917
War Diary	Ypres North Area	19/09/1917	19/09/1917
War Diary	Wieltje	19/09/1917	23/09/1917
War Diary	Ypres N. Area	23/09/1917	23/09/1917
War Diary	Watou No. 2 Area	24/09/1917	26/09/1917

War Diary	Bapaume	27/09/1917	30/09/1917
War Diary	Epehy (Sheet 62 France)	30/09/1917	30/09/1917
Miscellaneous	55th Division Instruction No. 5	16/09/1917	16/09/1917
Miscellaneous	5th R. Lanc. R.	17/09/1917	17/09/1917
Miscellaneous	Amendment No 1 to 166th Infantry Brigade Appendix 1		
Miscellaneous	Herewith Map Referred To In Para 2 Appendix 1	17/09/1917	17/09/1917
Miscellaneous	Administrative Instructions	17/09/1917	17/09/1917
Miscellaneous	Articles To Be Carried By Each Battalion		
Miscellaneous	166 Infantry Brigade Instruction For Operations	17/09/1917	17/09/1917
Miscellaneous	Instructions For Signal Communications		
Diagram etc	Diagram Of Communication		
Operation(al) Order(s)	166th Infantry Brigade Order No. 97	17/09/1917	17/09/1917
Miscellaneous	Issued With 166 Inf. Bde. Order No. 97		
Operation(al) Order(s)	Inborn Operation Order No. 114	18/09/1917	18/09/1917
Miscellaneous	A Form Messages And Signals		
Miscellaneous	166 Infantry Brigade Appendix 6 To 0/1 Medical Arrangements	18/09/1917	18/09/1917
Miscellaneous	Fifth Army I/2/40 A.	18/09/1917	18/09/1917
Map	Map		
Operation(al) Order(s)	166 Infantry Brigade Order No. 98	18/09/1917	18/09/1917
Miscellaneous	Addendum No.1 Movement Table	18/09/1917	18/09/1917
Map	Map		
Miscellaneous	Message Form		
Diagram etc	Diagram		
Miscellaneous	Addendum No. 1 To Appendix 2 To 0/1	18/09/1917	18/09/1917
Miscellaneous	Addendum No. 1 To Appendix 9 To 0/1	19/09/1917	19/09/1917
Miscellaneous	A Form Messages And Signals		
Miscellaneous	166th Infantry Brigade Appendix 2 To 0/1		
Operation(al) Order(s)	Inborn Operation Order No. 116	19/09/1917	19/09/1917
Miscellaneous			
Miscellaneous	A Form Messages And Signals		
Miscellaneous	Police Arrangements For Straggler Posts	19/09/1917	19/09/1917
Operation(al) Order(s)	Operation Order No. 115 by Lieut Colonel C.P. James D.S.O. Commanding 1/5th South Lancashire Regiment	19/09/1917	19/09/1917
Miscellaneous	Burials During Heavy Fighting	19/09/1917	19/09/1917
Miscellaneous	1/5th Battalion South Lancashire Regiment Narrative Of Operations		
Miscellaneous	C Form Messages And Signals		
Miscellaneous	A Form Messages And Signals		
Miscellaneous	C Form Messages And Signals		
Miscellaneous	A Form Messages And Signals		
Miscellaneous	55th (West Lancashire) Division Order Of The Day	21/09/1917	21/09/1917
Miscellaneous	55th (West Lancashire) Division Order Of The Day	22/09/1917	22/09/1917
Miscellaneous	55th (West Lancashire) Division Order Of The Day	23/09/1917	23/09/1917
Operation(al) Order(s)	55th (West Lancashire) Division Order Of The Day	24/09/1917	24/09/1917
Miscellaneous	Smoke Signal From Counter Attack Aeroplanes Without The Makings Of Contact Aeroplanes		
Miscellaneous	Employment Of R.E And Pioneers		
Miscellaneous	Prisoners Of War		
Miscellaneous	166 Infantry Brigade Artillery		
Miscellaneous	Action Of Massed Machine Guns		
Heading	War Diary Of 1/5th Battalion South Lancashire Regiment From 1st October 1917 To 31st October 1917 Volume38		
War Diary	Epehy Sheet 62c France	01/10/1917	13/10/1917
War Diary	Tincourt	13/10/1917	22/10/1917

War Diary	Right Sub-Sector	22/10/1917	31/10/1917
Operation(al) Order(s)	Operation Order No. 120 by Major W.N. Pilkington D.S.O. Commanding 1/5th South Lancashire Regiment	21/10/1917	21/10/1917
Operation(al) Order(s)	Operation Order No. 121 by Major W.N. Pilkington D.S.O. (Comdg)	26/10/1917	26/10/1917
Operation(al) Order(s)	Operation Order No. 122 by Major W.N. Pilkington D.S.O. Commanding 1/5th South Lancashire Regiment		
Operation(al) Order(s)	Operation Order No. 123 by Major W.N. Pilkington D.S.O. Commanding 1/5 South Lancashire Regt	27/10/1917	27/10/1917
Heading	War Diary Of The 1/5 S. Lan. R. For The Period 1st To 30th November 1917 Vol 23		
War Diary		31/10/1917	30/11/1917
Miscellaneous	Amendment To O.O 123		
Heading	War Diary Of The 1/5th S. Lan. R. For The Period 1st To 31st December 1917 Vol 24		
War Diary		01/12/1917	31/12/1917
Heading	War Diary Of The 1/5th S. Lan. R. For The Period 1st To 31st January 1918 Vol 25		
War Diary	Field	01/01/1918	31/01/1918
Heading	War Diary Of The 1/5th S. Lan. R. For The Period 1st To 28th Feb. 1918 Vol 26		
War Diary		01/02/1918	28/02/1918
Heading	War Diary Of 1/5th S. Lan. R. For Period 1st To 31st March 1918 Vol 27		
War Diary		01/03/1918	31/03/1918
Heading	1/5th Battalion South Lancashire Regiment April 1918		
Heading	War Diary Of 1/5 S. Lan. R. For Period 1st To 31st May 1918 Vol 29		
War Diary		01/04/1918	30/04/1918
Miscellaneous	1/5th Battn. South Lancashire Regt.	18/04/1918	18/04/1918
Miscellaneous	Operations April 9th to 14th/15th	17/04/1918	17/04/1918
Miscellaneous	Narrative Of Events Affecting Letter 'A' Company	01/08/1918	01/08/1918
Miscellaneous	Brief Account Of The Part Taken By "B" Coy.		
Miscellaneous	Report On Action From April 9th To 16th		
Miscellaneous	Narrative Of Events Affecting No. 4 Platoon 'A' Company		
Miscellaneous	Diary Of Events		
Miscellaneous	Summary Of Events	18/04/1918	18/04/1918
Miscellaneous	Operations 9th/13th April 1918		
Miscellaneous	Operations 9th/14th April		
Miscellaneous	Account Of Operations April 9th-14th 1918	01/08/1918	01/08/1918
Miscellaneous	B Company		
Miscellaneous	D Company	01/08/1918	01/08/1918
Miscellaneous	Diary Of Events	01/08/1918	01/08/1918
Miscellaneous	'X' Company Operations Against Enemy	15/04/1918	15/04/1918
War Diary	In The Field	01/05/1918	31/05/1918
Heading	Raid On Enemy Trenches North Of Givenchy On June 19th 1918		
Heading	War Diary Of 1/5 S. Lan. R. For Period 1st To 30th June 1918 Vol 30		
War Diary	In The Field	01/06/1918	30/06/1918
Miscellaneous	166th Inf. Bde. No. G. 11/54	09/06/1918	09/06/1918
Miscellaneous	166th Inf. Bde. No. G. 11/54/1	16/06/1918	16/06/1918
Miscellaneous	166th Infantry Brigade	17/06/1918	17/06/1918
Operation(al) Order(s)	166th Infantry Brigade Order No		
Operation(al) Order(s)	55th (West Lancashire) Division Order No. 197	18/06/1918	18/06/1918

Operation(al) Order(s)	166th Infantry Brigade Order No. 165	18/06/1918	18/06/1918
Operation(al) Order(s)	5th S. Lancs. R. Order No. 30		
Operation(al) Order(s)	Account Of Minor Operation	19/06/1918	19/06/1918
Miscellaneous	166th Inf. Bde. No. G.11/67/3	19/06/1918	19/06/1918
Miscellaneous	Reference Map Willow Road	18/06/1918	18/06/1918
Operation(al) Order(s)	I Corps Counter Battery Order No. 85	18/06/1918	18/06/1918
Miscellaneous	55th Division	20/06/1918	20/06/1918
Miscellaneous	166th Infantry Brigade	20/06/1918	20/06/1918
Map	Map		
Miscellaneous	List Of Honours And Awards		
War Diary	In The Field	01/07/1918	31/07/1918
Miscellaneous	Patrol Operation	20/07/1918	20/07/1918
Operation(al) Order(s)	5th S. Lan. R. Order No. 37	19/07/1918	19/07/1918
Heading	War Diary Of 1/5 S. Lan. R. For Period 1st To 31st August 1918 Vol 32		
War Diary	In The Field	01/08/1918	31/08/1918
Miscellaneous	2nd Lieut. Dodds Reports		
Operation(al) Order(s)	Patrol Order A		
Miscellaneous	166th Infantry Brigade	06/08/1918	06/08/1918
Miscellaneous	Report By Sergeant Carr.		
War Diary	In The Field	01/09/1918	30/09/1918
Miscellaneous	5th South Lancashire Regiment Operation	20/09/1918	20/09/1918
Miscellaneous	Addendum To Narrative Of Operations	23/09/1918	23/09/1918
Map	Map		
Heading	War Diary Of 1/5 S. Lan. R. For Period 1st To 31st October 1918 Vol 34		
War Diary		01/10/1918	31/10/1918
Heading	War Diary Of 1/5th S Lan R for the Period 1st-30th November 1918 Vol 35		
War Diary	In The Field	01/11/1918	30/11/1918
Heading	War Diary Of 1/5 S. Lan. R. For Period 1st To 31st December 1918 Vol 35		
War Diary	In The Field	01/12/1915	31/12/1915
Miscellaneous	B Company	06/11/1918	06/11/1918
Heading	War Diary 1/5th S. Lancs. R. January 1919 Vol 37		
War Diary	Fort Jacko Brussels	01/01/1919	31/01/1919
Heading	War Diary 1/5th S. Lancs. R. February 1919 Vol 38		
War Diary	Brussels	01/02/1919	31/03/1919
Miscellaneous			
War Diary	Boulogne	01/04/1919	30/04/1919
War Diary	Ostrohove Camp Boulogne	01/05/1919	31/07/1919

WO 95 2929/2

1/5 Bn. 5th Lancs Regt

Jan 1916 - July 1919

55TH DIVISION
166TH INFY BDE

1-5TH BN STH LANCS REGT

JAN 1916-JLY 1919

FROM 4 DIV 12 BDE

55

1916

1/5 S Lancs Regt

Vol 4

Instructions regarding War Diaries and Intelligence Summaries are contained in F. S. Regs., Part II. and the Staff Manual respectively. Title Pages will be prepared in manuscript.

WAR DIARY
or
INTELLIGENCE SUMMARY
(Erase heading not required.)

Army Form C. 2118

1/5 South Lancashire Regt.

Place	Date	Hour	Summary of Events and Information	Remarks and references to Appendices
	1916 Jan 16th		Left 36th Division and marched to MERELESSART to join 55 (West Lancs.) Division. Together with 5 Kings Own, 10th Liverpool Scottish, and 5 Loyal North Lancs to form 166th Inf. Bde. Training resumed, special attention being given to Musketry Instruction, Grenade Instruction and open fighting tactics.	
	Jan 20th		Left MERELESSART and marched to fresh billets at METIGNY and LALEU. Training resumed under Brigade arrangements.	

1875 Wt. W593/826 1,000,000 4/15 J.B.C. & A. A.D.S.S./Forms/C. 2118.

Instructions regarding War Diaries and Intelligence Summaries are contained in F. S. Regs., Part II. and the Staff Manual respectively. Title pages will be prepared in manuscript.

WAR DIARY

or

~~INTELLIGENCE SUMMARY~~

(Erase heading not required.)

Army Form C. 2118.

Hour, Date, Place	Summary of Events and Information	Remarks and references to Appendices
Feb 4th 1916	Marched from METIGNY to DOMART and went into billets at night	
5th	Marched to BEAUMETZ and resumed training under Brigade arrangements. Chiefly occupied with musketry, Bayonet exercises and attack practice.	
10th	Marched to AMPLIER and went into huts for the night. 55 Division moving up to take over from French. Spent next day in huts.	
12.	Marched to BERLES-AU-BOIS and spent night in billets.	
13	Marched at 3am from billets and relieved French troops in support at BELLACOURT. Brigade dispositions 1/5 Loyal North Lancs Regt and 1/10 L'pool Regt in front line 1/5 K.O.R. Lancs Regt and 1/5 South Lancs Regt in support. Battalion going into front line previous day got shelled in BELLACOURT and lost 30 men. Our transport was sent up before us during night and relief completed without any shelling. ~~[illegible]~~ Day left to 1/10 L'pool Regt in front line to make them up to necessary strength. Trenches in very bad condition. No drainage system and no revetting along Parapet too low and very thin in places [illegible].	
17	Relieved 1/5 Loyal North Lancs Regt in front line. Trenches knee deep in mud and impossible to clean in short period. Men served out with gum boots thigh which	

Instructions regarding War Diaries and Intelligence Summaries are contained in F. S. Regs., Part II. and the Staff Manual respectively. Title pages will be prepared in manuscript.

WAR DIARY
or
INTELLIGENCE SUMMARY
(Erase heading not required.)

Army Form C. 2118.

Hour, Date, Place	Summary of Events and Information	Remarks and references to Appendices
Feb 21st 1916	Several cases of frostbite and trench feet. Line got diminished we hold WILLOWS and OSIERS with two Coys. 1 Coy in support in SOUTIENS and one Coy in village. Trenches still very bad and made worse by heavy falls of snow.	
26/27	Line shortened by [illegible] Inf Bde taking over between [illegible] Inf Bde and [illegible] Inf Bde. We now only hold WILLOWS with 1 Coy and 1 Coy in support. Remaining 2 Coys in BELLACOURT.	
Feb 27th to March 14th	Battalion relieved itself by Coys doing 4 days in front line, 4 days in support and 8 days in village. Snow still continued and trenches became almost blocked, men stood extremely well, casualties very light, only about 25 being evacuated to hospital. Since taking over from French troops the enemy have been very inactive opposite us. Their guns being nearly always silent except for light shelling by Field guns. No enemy patrols seen and very little enemy sniping. Our artillery much more active with good results. Patrols out each night and snipers busy whenever targets seen.	
March 14/15th	Relieved by 1/[illegible] Regt and marched 8 miles to rest billets at SAULTY. 1 Coy left in BELLACOURT to supply working parties.	

1247 W 3299 200,000 (E) 8/14 J.B.C. & A. Forms/C. 2118/11.

Instructions regarding War Diaries and Intelligence Summaries are contained in F. S. Regs., Part II. and the Staff Manual respectively. Title Pages will be prepared in manuscript.

WAR DIARY
or
INTELLIGENCE SUMMARY
(Erase heading not required.)

Army Form C. 2118

Place	Date	Hour	Summary of Events and Information	Remarks and references to Appendices
			While out resting, special courses started for Bombers, Lewis Gunners and Signallers.	
March	22/23rd	1916	Relieved 1/5 Loyal North Lancs in Right Sub Sector. Trenches in very good condition and all boarded. Work chiefly directed to strengthening and revetting parapets.	
"	30/31st		Relieved by 1/5 Loyal North Lancs Regt and after relief relieved 1/10 L'pool Regt in Centre Sub Sector.	

1875 Wt. W593/826 1,000,000 4/15 J.B.C. & A. A.D.S.S./Forms/C. 2118.

Instructions regarding War Diaries and Intelligence Summaries are contained in F. S. Regs., Part II. and the Staff Manual respectively. Title Pages will be prepared in manuscript.

WAR DIARY
or
INTELLIGENCE SUMMARY
(Erase heading not required.)

Army Form C. 2118

Place	Date	Hour	Summary of Events and Information	Remarks and references to Appendices
March 31st	to April 15th		Held centre sub sector with one company in front line, one Company in support and two companies in Bellacourt, relieved every four days. Worked chiefly on improving fire trenches and wire. Line much strengthened enemy very passive.	2
April	15th/16th		Relieved by 1/10th Lpool Regt and march to rest billets at Saulty. D Coy left in Bellacourt for work.	
April	17th		B Coy went into huts at Gouy, to prepare same as rest camps.	
April	23rd/24th		Relieved 1/5th Loyal North Lancs Regt in right sub sector.	
April	24th/May 3rd		Held right sub sector with two coys in front line and two Companies in support in Bellacourt, relieved Coys in line every four days. Worked chiefly on building Lewis Gun positions, observation posts and reclaiming disused trench. Both enemy artillery and snipers very inactive, no enemy Patrols seen or heard during the tour. Our snipers doing very good work.	

[illegible]
Capt & Adjt
1/5th South Lancs Regt.

1875 Wt. W593/826 1,000,000 4/15 J.B.C. & A. A.D.S.S./Forms/C. 2118.

1/5 South Lancs Regt 56

Army Form C. 2118.

Duplicate 1/5 S Lancs Regt Vol 6

WAR DIARY or INTELLIGENCE SUMMARY

(Erase heading not required.)

Instructions regarding War Diaries and Intelligence Summaries are contained in F. S. Regs., Part II. and the Staff Manual respectively. Title Pages will be prepared in manuscript.

Place	Date	Hour	Summary of Events and Information	Remarks and references to Appendices
May 3rd/4th		1916	Relieved by 1/10th Lpool Regt in GRANGE and 1/5th Loyal North Lancs Regt in PARK. Battalion placed in Brigade Reserve BELLACOURT. Line re-allotted by 164 Infy Bde taking over OSIERS and 166th Infy Bde taking over LANDAFF & LANARK from 4th Div. One battalion holds WILLOWS & GRANGE. One battalion PARK LANDAFF & LANARK. One battalion in brigade reserve BELLACOURT & one battalion resting in Divisional Reserve.	
May 11th			Relieved 1/5th Loyal North Lancs Regt in LANARK LANDAFF & PARK (right Sub-sector). Enemy very quiet & passive, good work done by our snipers and rifle batteries.	
May 19th			Relieved by 1/5th Loyal North Lancs Regt & march to rest camp GOUY. Spent week training. Attention chiefly given to smoke Helmet drill, musketry & bayonet fighting.	
May 27th			Relieved 1/5th Loyal North Lancs Regt in right sub-sector. enemy slightly more active but quietened by our snipers.	2/12

2449 Wt. W14957/M90 750,000 1/16 J.B.C. & A. Forms/C.2118/12.

Instructions regarding War Diaries and Intelligence Summaries are contained in F. S. Regs., Part II. and the Staff Manual respectively. Title pages will be prepared in manuscript.

WAR DIARY
or
INTELLIGENCE SUMMARY.
(Erase heading not required.)

Army Form C. 2118.

1/5 S Lancs Rel
Vol 5

Place	Date	Hour	Summary of Events and Information	Remarks and references to Appendices
TALMAS	2 5/16		Draft arrived from base of 13 other ranks.	
	13 5/16		Draft of 1 Officer & 8 other ranks arrive from Base. Officer 2Lt Dymond, who left the Battalion at OISSY in Jany. 16 to go into hospital.	
	14 & 15th		Drafts arrived of 2 Officers & 48 O.R. Hon Lieut & Qr Mr W. B. Douthwaite and 2nd Lieut. R.F. Woodroofe from England	
	17th		2nd Lt. F. K. Robinson is transferred to 148/2 T.M. Battery from this date.	
	22		Capt. H. P. Smith takes up duties of Town Major of NAOURS, and O.C. Divisional Salvage Section.	
	28th		2nd Lieut. B. C. Alldrone joins Battalion from England.	
	29th		7 Officers, names as follows, join Unit on this date, 2nd Lieuts. J.F. Marshall C.H. Clegg. A.F.H. Peal. S. Day. J. Wrigley. F. Waring. W.G. Storm.	
	31st		Whole time devoted to training, attacks on trenches, consolidation of trenches, attack and defence of woods, and village fighting.	
			Strength of Battn. 34 Officers 820 O.R.	

W Mendall Lieut Col. Cmdg.
1/5th York Lancaster Regiment

1577 Wt. W10791/1773 500,000 1/15 D. D. & L. A.D.S.S./Forms/C. 2118.

1/5 South Lancs Regt

Army Form C. 2118.

Instructions regarding War Diaries and Intelligence Summaries are contained in F. S. Regs., Part II. and the Staff Manual respectively. Title Pages will be prepared in manuscript.

WAR DIARY
or
INTELLIGENCE SUMMARY

(Erase heading not required.)

255 Vol 6

Place 1916	Date	Hour	Summary of Events and Information	Remarks and references to Appendices
June	4th		Relieved by 1/5th Loyal North Lancs Regt & placed in Brigade Reserve BELLACOURT. during the week the whole battalion was used for working parties each day.	
June	12th		Relieved 1/5th Loyal North Lancs Regt in right sub sector. Enemy inactive but very alert, good work done by our patrols.	
June	30th		Relieved by 1/5th Loyal North Lancs Regt & marched to rest camp GOUY. Training chiefly concentrated on company in attack and smoke helmet drill.	

213

166th Brigade.

55th Division.

1/5th BATTALION

SOUTH LANCASHIRE REGIMENT

JULY 1916

W.O.C.* / VIII

214

166 / 55

War Diary
of the
1/5th South Lancashire Regt.
166th Infantry Brigade
55th (West Lancashire) Division
for the period
1st July, 1916 to 31st July, 1916.

Summaries are contained in F. S. Regs., Part II. and the Staff Manual respectively. Title pages will be prepared in manuscript.

INTELLIGENCE SUMMARY

(Erase heading not required.)

Hour, Date, Place	Summary of Events and Information	Remarks and references to Appendices
July 1st 1916	Marched from Camp at GOUY & took over billets from 6th Liverpool Regt at BEAUMETZ	
July 2nd 1916	Returned to Camp at GOUY & 6th Liverpool Regt returned to billets at BEAUMETZ.	
July 5th 1916	Relieved 1/5th Loyal North Lancs Regt in right sub sector of brigade line BELLACOURT.	
July 6/10th 1916	Very active patrolling & bombing of enemy saps each night. Enemy quiet but very alert; very little hostile shelling.	
July 11th/12th	Relieved by 1/6th Sherwood Foresters, 46th Div. and marched to billets at BEAUMETZ	
July 12th/13th	Relieved 1/8th Liverpool Regt. 164th Bde in trenches in front of AGNY. Dispositions of 166th Bde. 1/5th South Lancs Regt in front line right sub sector, 1/5th K.O. (Royal Lancaster) Regt in left sub sector. 1/10th Liverpool Regt in support in AGNY. 1/5th Loyal North Lancs Regt working for 165th Infy Bde in BRETENCOURT.	
July 14th	Discharged smoke at 3am and heavily bombarded enemy's lines. Retaliation was prompt but not heavy	

1247 W 3299 200,000 (E) 8/14 J.B.C. & A. Forms/C. 2118/11.

Instructions regarding War Diaries and Intelligence Summaries are contained in F. S. Regs., Part II. and the Staff Manual respectively. Title pages will be prepared in manuscript.

WAR DIARY
or
~~INTELLIGENCE~~ SUMMARY
(Erase heading not required.)

Army Form C. 2118.

Hour, Date, Place	Summary of Events and Information	Remarks and references to Appendices
	Wind blew most of smoke back over our own lines.	
	Casualties 1 Killed 2 wounded.	
July 16th/17th	Relieved by 1/6th York & Lancaster [illegible] 11th Division,	
	and marched to billets at BEAU[illegible]	
July 18th	March to billets at GRAND RULLE[illegible]	
20th	fresh billets at NEUVILLE	
21st	RIBEAU[illegible] [illegible]	
22nd/24th	Trained & refitted the battalion. Draft 1 officer 200 O.R. arrived: 87 OR of these belonged to 6 Cheshire Regt & were attached to 1/5th K.O. (Royal Lancaster) Regt	
July 25th	Marched to CANDAS entrained 12 30 pm. Detrained MERICOURT 5 30 pm, marched to billets at VILLE SOUS CORBIE.	
July 27th	Marched to bivouacs at SANDPIT E 18 D	Trench Map 62 d NE 1/20000
30th	Moved further forward to bivouacs E 16 B F 17 A	

E.P. James Lt Col
Cmdg 1/5th South Lancashire Regt

1247 W 3299 200,000 (E) 8/14 J.B.C. & A. Forms/C. 2118/11.

166th Brigade.
55th Division

1/5th BATTALION

SOUTH LANCASHIRE REGIMENT

AUGUST 1 9 1 6

215

War Diary

of the

1/5th South Lancashire Regt.

for the period

1st August to 31st August

1916.

1/5th SOUTH LANCS REGT

Instructions regarding War Diaries and Intelligence Summaries are contained in F. S. Regs., Part II. and the Staff Manual respectively. Title Pages will be prepared in manuscript.

WAR DIARY

~~or~~

~~INTELLIGENCE~~ SUMMARY

(Erase heading not required.)

AUGUST

Army Form C. 2118.

Place	Date	Hour	Summary of Events and Information	Remarks and references to Appendices
August	1. 1916		Moved forward from MANSEL COPSE F16b F17a to reserve trenches at. OXFORD COPSE A14 A15 (Sheet 62c NW 1/20.000)	
"	2. 1916	8 A.M.	Valley shelled by 8" Howitzers for 15 minutes. and again at 2 p.m. Casualties 15 Killed 17 Wounded.	
"	3/5 "		Supplied working parties to 164 Inf Bde holding front line. Chiefly employed digging communication trenches, and clearing Brigade area. Casualties for 3 days. 6 Killed. 21 wounded.	
"	6 "		Moved back to Bivouacs (62D NE 1/20000) F22A near Citadel	
"	8 "		55th Division attacked GUILLEMONT. 165 Brigade attack B1C 20.85 to T25 A30.20. 164 Brigade attack T25 B10.15 to Railway T19b 0.0.30. First wave get their objective, but supports unable to get across.	
"	8 "	5 P.M	166 Inf Bde warned to attack morning of the 9th to relieve 164 Inf Bde hung up in GUILLEMONT.	
"	8	12 midnight	Operation orders for attack received and Btn moves forward to get into position for an attack. 166 Inf Bde ordered to attack as follows:- 1st Objective. Enemy front line from T25b 1.5 through T25a 3.3 to S24d 65.75 2nd do The capture of GUILLEMONT and of a line on the eastern side of the Village from T25b 15 to the railway T19b 0.3 10th Liverpool Scottish to attack on the right. and 5th Loyal North Lancs Regt on the left. The boundary between being TRONES WOOD –	

2449 Wt. W14957/M90 750,000 1/16 J.B.C. & A. Forms/C.2118/12.

Army Form C. 2118.

Instructions regarding War Diaries and Intelligence Summaries are contained in F. S. Regs., Part II. and the Staff Manual respectively. Title Pages will be prepared in manuscript.

2

WAR DIARY
or
INTELLIGENCE SUMMARY
(Erase heading not required.)

Place	Date 1916	Hour	Summary of Events and Information	Remarks and references to Appendices
August	8		GUILLEMONT Road, as far as T.25 a 0.8. Thence a straight line running North East, through the Church to the GUILLEMONT – LEUZE WOOD Road, to 5th Loyal North Lancs Regt. 5th South Lancs Regt, to support the right Bn.	
			Zero hour. 4.20 AM.	
			In moving up valley was found blocked with troops and transport.	
	9	2 AM	Commanding Officer with Adjutant arrived at proposed Bn Hqrs. A 5 d 8 9. and found 2 Bns 165 Inf Bde (5th and 7th Kings Liverpool) in possession. Informed 166 Inf Bde Hqrs, and were told to move up to Sunken Road. T 30 c	
		3 AM	Established Hqrs in Sunken Road. Company Officers warned of changed Hqrs. and sent for to explain changed scheme of attack, as issued in operation orders. No time to go into detail, or for Coy Comdrs to explain to Coy Officers and N.C.O's as attack was timed for 4.20 AM. Owing to all N.C.O's and Bn and Coy runners having no idea of the Country, and the sunken road being crowded with men of 164 Bde, great delay was caused in getting the Coys out in position.	
		3.55 AM	North Lancs just arriving and Officer in Command said he had only just heard they were going to attack.	
		4.15 AM	Our Guns opened a Heavy Barrage and the Germans dropped their Barrage within 3 minutes. Their back barrage line being on sunken road. Companies not all in position had to move thro Barrage. Those in position moved forward behind assaulting waves but whole line was unable to make headway owing to	

2449 Wt. W14957/M90 750,000 1/16 J.B.C. & A. Forms/C.2118/12.

• 3 /

Instructions regarding War Diaries and Intelligence Summaries are contained in F. S. Regs., Part II. and the Staff Manual respectively. Title Pages will be prepared in manuscript.

WAR DIARY
~~or~~
~~INTELLIGENCE~~ SUMMARY

(Erase heading not required.)

Army Form C. 2118.

Place	Date	Hour	Summary of Events and Information	Remarks and references to Appendices
August	9. 1916	4.15 PM	Machine gun fire and heavy barrage. Whole line fell back and manned our original front line, Coys hopelessly intermixed with men of other attacking Battalions.	
		12 noon	Orders to withdraw Coys from line and relieve 1/5 Loyal North Lancs in Left Sector in front of TRONES WOOD. Relief completed 5 pm. 5th Kings Own relieved 10th Liverpool Regt. on our right, also during afternoon.	
	10	5pm to Midday	Btn. worked hard clearing trenches and consolidating line.	
	10	4 pm	Relief started by 8th West Kents Regt. 72nd Bde. Relief complete 8 P.M. and Btn. moved back to Bivouacs in F22.	
			Total Casualties from 12 midnight the 8th until 12 midnight the 10th. 8 Officers 130 other ranks.	
	11		Standing by ready to move up and attack again.	
	12	8 PM	Moved off 8 PM to relieve 7th Kings Liverpools in MALTZ HORN Sector.	
		11	arrived Btn. Hqrs 11 P.M. Attack on isolated enemy trench proposed.	
	13	4.35 AM	Attacked with 1 Coy 6th Kings Liverpool Regt. and D Coy 5th South Lancs on isolated enemy trench. Attack driven back by machine gun fire. Attack failed owing to officers and men not knowing ground, and being unable to take advantage of same.	
			Continued relief of 7th Kings Liverpools and completed same 1 pm.	
	13 to 14	1 Pm to 12 midnight	Trenches greatly improved and consolidated and new jumping off trenches dug.	

2449 Wt. W14957/M90 750,000 1/16 J.B.C. & A. Forms/C.2118/12.

4

Instructions regarding War Diaries and Intelligence Summaries are contained in F. S. Regs., Part II. and the Staff Manual respectively. Title Pages will be prepared in manuscript.

WAR DIARY
or
~~INTELLIGENCE SUMMARY~~

(Erase heading not required.)

Army Form C. 2118.

Place	Date 1916	Hour	Summary of Events and Information	Remarks and references to Appendices
August	15		Relieved by 13th Kings Liverpool Regt and 4th Royal Fusiliers, Relief complete 5.30 AM. Returned to Bivouacs F 22 b	
	–	3.40pm	Marched to Billets at MEAULTE	
			Casualties from 8 pm on the 12th to 5.30 Am on the 15th 2 Officers, 80 other ranks	
	17		Transport marched under Brigade Transport Officer to final billets at FRESSENNEVILLE leaving MEAULTE 4 15 pm.	
	19		Btn marched to EDGE HILL and entrained 7pm.	
	20	12.5 Am	Detrained MARTAINVILLE and marched to billets at FRESSENNEVILLE arriving 6 AM.	
	20/28		Training at FRESSENNEVILLE. Small proportion of Btn granted leave to AULTE.	
	28	2.30Pm	Transport moved by road back to MERICOURT	
	29		Moved at 1½ hours notice to fresh billets ERCOURT leaving FRESSENNEVILLE 3 PM. Marched in Thunder storm and arrived very wet.	
	30		Resumed March and entrained PONT REMY 1pm. Detrained MERICOURT 5pm and Bivouaced in open field E 7. Still raining and men very wet.	
	31	1.35Pm	Moved to fresh Bivouacs E 12 a Standing by under short notice to move.	

C. P. James Lt Col
Commanding 1/5 South Lancs Regt

2449 Wt. W14957/M90 750,000 1/16 J.B.C. & A. Forms/C.2118/12.

Vol 4

War Diary

of

1/5th S. Lancs R.

1st September to 30th September 1916

Instructions regarding War Diaries and Intelligence Summaries are contained in F. S. Regs., Part II. and the Staff Manual respectively. Title Pages will be prepared in manuscript.

WAR DIARY 1/5 SOUTH LANCS

or

~~INTELLIGENCE SUMMARY~~

(Erase heading not required.) September 1916

Army Form C. 2118

Place 1916	Date	Hour	Summary of Events and Information	Remarks and references to Appendices
Sep	1		In Bivouac E12a (Sheet 62D N.E) Training resumed.	
	2/4		Standing by, under short notice to move.	
	5		Moved up and relieved 72nd Inf Bde in front of DELVILLE WOOD. Bde dispositions. Front line 1/5 Loyal North Lancs Regt on Right, 1/5 K.O Royal Lancs Regt on Left. 1/5 South Lancs Regt in support in Check Line S.23a. 1/10th Liverpool Regt, in reserve in front of MONTAUBAN. 1/5 South Lancs Regt relieved 8th West Kent Regt. Relief complete 7 P.M.	
	6		Check Line cleaned and improved, and front line visited.	
	7		Bn out at night digging Strong Points 300x in advance of front line trenches held by 1/5 Loyal North Lancs Regt. Four Strong Points dug and communication trench from original front line to Right Strong Point. Casualties 4 officers and 40, O Ranks.	
	8		Strong Points were garrisoned by 1 Offcr and 20 O.R and communication trench held by 2 Offcrs and 60. O.R. About 10 a.m. an enemy 5.9 Battery heavily enfiladed new communication trench and badly damaged it. During the night, Strong Points were completed and connected up, under very accurate sniping fire. In spite of this work was well done, and fully completed. Casualties 4 officers, 45. O.R.	
	9		After completion of digging, Relieved 1/5 Loyal North Lancs Regt. and completed relief by 5 A.M. 164 Bde attacked ALE and HOP ALLEY.	

1875 Wt. W593/826 1,000,000 4/15 J.B.C. & A. A.D.S.S./Forms/C. 2118.

Instructions regarding War Diaries and Intelligence Summaries are contained in F. S. Regs., Part II. and the Staff Manual respectively. Title Pages will be prepared in manuscript.

WAR DIARY

~~or~~

~~INTELLIGENCE SUMMARY~~

(Erase heading not required.)

Army Form C. 2118

Place	Date	Hour	Summary of Events and Information	Remarks and references to Appendices
1916 Septbr	9		on our right at 4.45 PM. Attack failed and enemy pressed our Barricade NE corner of DELVILLE WOOD. "C" Coy sent up from support and barricade held. During the night, Patrols were unable to get touch along E edge of WOOD with 164 Inf Bde, position not clear as enemy were reported to be bombing their way through E side of WOOD.	
	10		Still trying to get touch with 164 Bde but were unable to do so. At night Communication trench was re dug, and Communication trench between Strong Points deepened. Our Right flank was protected at night by Four Posts along E side of WOOD lying in open with trip wire in front of them. Remainder Bde relieved by 123rd Inf Bde, 41st DIVN. We were attached to 164 Inf Bde and held the same line. One Officer and 15 OR captured in front of our Strong Points.	
	11		Bomb attack by 164 Inf Bde on ALE and HOP ALLEY failed. We gained 30x of ALE ALLEY and held same with new barricade. During the night a new line of Strong Points was dug, 150x in advance of the first line of Strong Points, in spite of the severe strain the Bn had gone through, the men dug excellently. A new Strong Point was dug midway between the Right Strong Point and ALE ALLEY	

Instructions regarding War Diaries and Intelligence Summaries are contained in F. S. Regs., Part II. and the Staff Manual respectively. Title Pages will be prepared in manuscript.

WAR DIARY
or
~~INTELLIGENCE~~ SUMMARY
(Erase heading not required.)

Army Form C. 2118

Place 1916	Date	Hour	Summary of Events and Information	Remarks and references to Appendices
Septbr 12			Still trying to get touch with 164 Bde along E edge of wood. During the night 164 Bde established 2 Strong Points in E side of wood, and at last gained touch with us.	
	12/13		Night. Relieved by the 8th Kings Royal Rifles. 14th DIVN. Relief complete 2 AM. Casualties 5th to 12th inclusive 12 officers and 150 O.R.	
	13		Marched back to Transport lines about F8a, arriving 4 AM.	
		11.15am	Marched to rest Camp at D18a.	
	14/15		In Camp resting	
	16		Moved forward to Camp at E9c	
	17		Moved from Camp 2 PM and marched to POMMIER REDOUBT arriving 5 PM. DIVN took over line in front of FLERS and relieved 41st DIVN. Moved forward from POMMIER REDOUBT at 12 midnight, and went into support in SWITCH TRENCH. 165 Bde in front line. 166 Bde in support with 1/5 South Lanc Regt in Switch Trench on Right of FLERS ROAD and 1/10 Liverpool Regt in SWITCH TRENCH on Left of FLERS ROAD. 1/5 K.O. Royal Lancaster Regt. and 1/5 Loyal North Lanc Regt in BROWN and EDGE TRENCHES North edge of DELVILLE WOOD. Very wet weather. trenches in bad condition.	

1875 Wt. W593/826 1,000,000 4/15 J.B.C. & A. A.D.S.S./Forms/C. 2118.

Instructions regarding War Diaries and Intelligence Summaries are contained in F. S. Regs., Part II. and the Staff Manual respectively. Title Pages will be prepared in manuscript.

WAR DIARY
or
~~INTELLIGENCE SUMMARY~~
(Erase heading not required.)

Army Form C. 2118

Place	Date	Hour	Summary of Events and Information	Remarks and references to Appendices
1916 Septbr	18		Rained all day Trenches very poor and no shelter for men. At night 166 Inf Bde relieved 165 Bde. 1/5 K.O. Lancaster Regt. and 1/5 Loyal North Lancs Regt in front line. 1/10th Liverpool Regt. in support just S of FLERS and 1/5 South Lancs Regt. in reserve, and remained in SWITCH TRENCH. with Hqrs and two Coys, on the Right of FLERS ROAD and two Coys on the Left of FLERS ROAD.	
	19		At night had 300 men digging new Communication trench (SOUTH LANCS ALLEY) for 1/5 Loyal North Lancs Regt.	
	20		All Coys out working improving and straightening front lines of 1/5 K.O.R. Lanc. Regt, and 1/5. L. North Lancs Regt. in order that they might be used as jumping off trenches	
	21		At night, 300 men digging jumping off trenches in 1/5 L North Lancs Regt lines.	
	22		300 men digging assembly trench, 50x behind front line held by 1/5. L North Lancs Regt.	
	23		165 Bde relieved 166 Bde. 1/5 S Lancs Regt. relieved by 1/6 Kings Liverpool Regt Relief Complete 12 midnight.	

1875 Wt. W593/826 1,000,000 4/15 J.B.C. & A. A.D.S.S./Forms/C. 2118.

Instructions regarding War Diaries and Intelligence Summaries are contained in F. S. Regs., Part II. and the Staff Manual respectively. Title Pages will be prepared in manuscript.

WAR DIARY

or

~~INTELLIGENCE~~ SUMMARY

(Erase heading not required.)

Army Form C. 2118

Place	Date	Hour	Summary of Events and Information	Remarks and references to Appendices
1916				
Sept 14			Returned to Bivouac 500x S E of POMMIER REDOUBT.	
15			165 Bde attacked successfully, and objective was gained. G O C DIVN thanks 166 Bde for their good digging which greatly helped attacking Bde.	
16/17			Party of 100 men laying light Railway from LONGUEVAL to FLERS	
18			Marched to Billets at RIBEMONT. Left Bivouac 10.50 AM and arrived at Billets 5 PM	
29			Transport of whole Bde moves to area round PONT REMY	
30			Entrained EDGE HILL 3 pm and arrived LONGPRE at 11.30 Pm where we detrained and marched to PONTREMY arriving 4 am Found town occupied by 5th DIVN and had to Bivouac in open field.	

C. P. [illegible] Lieut. Col
1/5 S. L. Regt

1875 Wt. W593/826 1,000,000 4/15 J.B.C. & A. A.D.S.S./Forms/C. 2118.

CONFIDENTIAL

War Diary

of

1/5th S. Lan. Regt.

for the period

1st to 31st October 1916

1/5th South Lancs Regt.

Instructions regarding War Diaries and Intelligence Summaries are contained in F. S. Regs., Part II. and the Staff Manual respectively. Title Pages will be prepared in manuscript.

WAR DIARY
or
~~INTELLIGENCE SUMMARY~~
(Erase heading not required.)

Army Form C. 2118

Place	Date	Hour	Summary of Events and Information	Remarks and references to Appendices
Oct	1st		Remained at PONT REMY.	
	2nd	4.30am	Marched to ABBEVILLE, entrained 7.30am & detrained PROVEN 6.30pm. (Transport on train) marched to J CAMP by International Corner arriving 10.30pm.	
	3rd		Marched to POPERINGHE leaving camp 4.30pm. Entrained 6.30pm, Detrained YPRES 7pm. Relieved INNISKILLING FUSILIERS, 29th Div. in billets in YPRES.	
	4th		Relieved 1st K.O.S.Bs in right sub sector, relief complete 8.30pm Front line B & C Coy support A Coy Reserve D Coy.	
	5th		Enemy machine guns active. Snipers firing into backs of C Coy 1 OR killed. A Coy shelled in support line.	
	6th		Enemy machine guns & snipers very active.	
	7th		Enemy snipers got under by ours snipers & Lewis guns. Enemy machine guns still very active at night	
	9th		D Coy relieved B Coy & A Coy relieved C Coy in front line.	
	10th		3 Enemy snipers accounted for. Officer patrols out every night 1 Officer Killed.	

1875 Wt. W593/826 1,000,000 4/15 J.B.C. & A. A.D.S.S./Forms/C. 2118.

Instructions regarding War Diaries and Intelligence Summaries are contained in F. S. Regs., Part II. and the Staff Manual respectively. Title Pages will be prepared in manuscript.

WAR DIARY
or
INTELLIGENCE SUMMARY
(Erase heading not required.)

Army Form C. 2118

Place	Date	Hour	Summary of Events and Information	Remarks and references to Appendices
Oct	13th		Relieved by 1/5th Kingsown R.L. Regt relief complete 8 30 pm During our stay in trenches much cleaning draining & repairing of trenches was done. Marched back to billets YPRES	
	14th - 21st		In brigade reserve in YPRES. Working parties of 200 daily furnished.	
	22nd		Relieved by 4th Kings Own R.L. Regt, 1 platoon C Coy remained to man the REIGERSBURG DEFENCES & party of 100 men working under 2/2nd W Lancs Field Co. Remainder of Battalion entrained 8 30 pm & moved to O Camp.	
	23rd		In O Camp. Working party of 300 furnished to dig cable trenches H4a central. Working party from YPRES returned	
	24th		Cleaning up & Coy Inspections.	
	25th		Furnished working party of 200 for digging cable trenches. Remainder of battalion training	

1875 Wt. W593/826 1,000,000 4/15 J.B.C. & A. A.D.S.S./Forms/C. 2118.

Army Form C. 2118

Instructions regarding War Diaries and Intelligence Summaries are contained in F. S. Regs., Part II. and the Staff Manual respectively. Title Pages will be prepared in manuscript.

WAR DIARY
or
INTELLIGENCE SUMMARY
(Erase heading not required.)

Place	Date	Hour	Summary of Events and Information	Remarks and references to Appendices
Oct	26th		Working party 200 furnished for cable trenches. Platoon D Coy relieved platoon C Coy in REIGERSBURG DEFENCES. Reconnaissance party of 27 under Lt Draper moved up to YPRES on special duty. Remainder of battalion training.	
	27th		Special party commenced training.	
	28th – 30th		Found 200 men for working party – 30th platoon in REIGERSBURG DEFENCES relieved 1/8th L'pool Regt. Special party & remainder of Battalion training	
	31st		Left O Camp 3.30 pm & entrained for YPRES. Relieved 1/5th Kings Own R.L. Regt. Relief completed 6.30 pm. Working party of 100 OR furnished.	

C. P. James Lt Col
Commanding 1/5th South Lancs Regt

CONFIDENTIAL

Vol XI

War Diary

of

1/5th S Lan. R.

for period

1st November to 30th November 1916

Instructions regarding War Diaries and Intelligence Summaries are contained in F. S. Regs., Part II. and the Staff Manual respectively. Title Pages will be prepared in manuscript.

1/5 South Lancashire Regt

WAR DIARY
or
~~INTELLIGENCE SUMMARY~~

November (Erase heading not required.) 1916

Army Form C. 2118

Place 1916	Date	Hour	Summary of Events and Information	Remarks and references to Appendices
November	1/3		In Billets YPRES. provided working parties 185/200, working under 2/1 West Lancs Field Coy. Town Major. 1/5th K O Royal Lancs Regt. Reconnaissance Party for Raid in Front Line. Patrols out at night. 150 Officers and OR practising raid.	
	4		H.R.H Duke of Connaught with G O C 2nd Army visited the PRISON YPRES. working parties out until noon. Relieved 1/5 K.O Royal Lancaster Regt in the Right Sub. Sector. Relief complete 8 P.M. B and C Coy Front Line. D Coy in X line. A Coy in Congreve Walk. Raiding party numbering 172 left a PRISON.	
	5		Raid on Enemy lines. Left Party very successful, but no enemy encountered. Right Party held up in the Gap by enemy machine guns and Trench Mortars. Result 17th Reserve Division identified. Casualties 2 OR Killed & 4 OR wounded.	
	6		Relieved Coys in front line A Coy relieved B Coy. D Coy relieved C Coy. B Coy in X line C Coy in Congreve Walk. Raiders rejoined their Coys. Period ending 6th inst. work done cleaning and relaying trench boards, opening drains, putting in U framing in front line, general repairs parapet and parados	
	7		Relieved by 1/5 K.O.R Lancs Regt. Moved to Billets YPRES. HQrs Bombers & C Coy PRISON B Coy Town Billets. A and D Coy MAGAZINE. Relief complete 8 Pm	
	8/11		In Billets YPRES. Whole Battalion out in working parties.	
	12		Relieved 1/5 K O R Lancs Regt in Right Sub-sector, relief complete 8.7 P.m. C and B Coy Front line A in X line D in Congreve Walk.	
	15		Coys relieved. Dispositions D and A Coy in Front line C in X line B in Congreve Walk	
	17		Operations by Brigades on our Right and Left. at 1 Pm no shelling in our part.	

1875 Wt. W593/826 1,000,000 4/15 J.B.C. & A. A.D.S.S./Forms/C. 2118.

Instructions regarding War Diaries and Intelligence Summaries are contained in F. S. Regs., Part II. and the Staff Manual respectively. Title Pages will be prepared in manuscript.

WAR DIARY

~~or~~

~~INTELLIGENCE SUMMARY~~

(Erase heading not required.)

November 1916 1/5 South Lancs Regt

Army Form C. 2118

Place 1916	Date	Hour	Summary of Events and Information	Remarks and references to Appendices
November 17			Practice Exercise. Hqrs Left Coy in front line blown in. Casualties 1 OR Killed 4 OR wounded. Period ending 17th inst putting in U frames Front line, General Repairs to Trenches	
18			Relieved by 1/4th K.O. Royal Lancs Regt 164 Bde. Relief complete 8.11 Pm. Entrained for O Camp	
19/25			At O Camp. Inspected by Brig Gen L Green Wilkinson 23rd inst. Time spent cleaning up inspections and training. Many improvements to Camp made. Left Town out of Bde on 25th inst.	
26			Entrained BRANDHOECK 5 Pm and relieved 1/4th K.O Royal Lancaster Regt. YPRES Billets D Coy PRISON A Coy TOWN BILLETS B. C Coy MAGAZINE.	
27			Relieved 1/4th Loyal North Lancs in Right Sub-Sector. relief complete 8.15 Pm.	
29			Raid by 1/10th Liverpool Regt on KAISER BILL 6 prisoners taken	
30			In line	

[illegible] Lt Col.
Commanding 1/5th South Lancashire Regt

1875 Wt. W593/826 1,000,000 4/15 J.B.C. & A. A.D.S.S./Forms/C. 2118.

1/5 S Lancs. Nov 1916.

G.4241

13

Report on a Raid carried out by the 1/5th South Lancashire Regt., 166th Infantry Brigade, 55th Division, on night of 5th/6th November 1916 in accordance with the attached scheme.

---

1. During the 4th and 5th November the 55th Divisional Artillery successfully cut two gaps in the wire, each about 25 yards wide; these gaps were kept open during the night by occasional 18 pdr. and Machine Gun fire.

2. Zero was fixed for 12.30 a.m. on the 6th, at which time a rolling barrage was opened on to the enemy's trenches in the locality selected for the raid and at two other points on the enemy's front. This was the signal for the raiding party to close up as near as possible to the barrage, preparatory to entering the German Trenches. At Zero plus 5 the rolling barrage moved back by lifts of 50 yards per minute to a box barrage enclosing the area to be raided. This Artillery barrage was continued with Heavy Artillery and Field Howitzers firing on selected points in the vicinity and sweeping the Communication trenches and approaches with 60 pdrs.

At Zero plus 5 it was intended that the raiders should enter the German Trenches.

3. The raiding parties left their trenches at 12 midnight 5th, and moved towards the gaps in enemy's wire.

4. The right party were delayed in reaching the gap in wire, the tape men could not get on, as they observed a party of Germans in the gap, and waited till the Germans disappeared.

On arrival at the gap the first group were delayed by concertina wire which had been run out across the gap.

A few of the right party succeeded in entering the

German Trenches, but the opposition there was very strong, bombs, machine guns, trench mortars, and rifle grenades, being used against this party who were unable to penetrate, and returned to our trenches on the signal to return.

However, the left blocking party of the right party got to, and occupied their appointed position in front trench. The Corporal and two men were wounded but number 4099 Rifleman B. CORRIGAN remained at his post though bombed from both sides until signal for withdrawal was given.

The right party withdrew on the signal, carrying their casualties with them.

5. The Left raiding party was more successful. After penetrating the gap in the wire which was 25 yards wide, the first group formed blocks in the enemy's trenches to the right and left of the gap.

The second group went straight through gap in wire, over enemy's first trench, and moved to South side of pond. Between enemy's front line, and EITEL FRITZ FARM buildings, (50 yards from front line) traces of wire were found. A path was found running from farm round S.E. of the pond to the communication trench at point I.5.b.66.46. One of the parties searching the farm were bombed and a machine gun opened fire from a communication trench about I.5.b.66.46. this party also returned at the signal to retire.

6. The party that raided the saphead at I.5.b.31.65. found it blown in and deserted.

7. Parties report generally that the enemy's trenches are 7 to 10 feet deep, very dry and well revetted with brushwood and timber, and trench boarded. Many deep drains were made almost like communication trenches.

8. The Artillery wire-cutting was good and done with a small expenditure of ammunition.

The barrage during the raid was well placed and the shooting good.

9. The raiding parties did not find any German casualties nor did they secure any prisoners, but were rewarded by finding documents in a dugout which definitely established the already suspected presence of the 17th Reserve Division on this front.

Secret

55th Division No. 676 G,

13

G. 4203.

VIII. Corps.

The following reports have been received from 166th Inf. Brigade. Detailed report will be sent later.

Right Party. 1st party failed to locate gap and consequently greatly delayed 2nd Party. 2nd Party got up to gap, found themselves opposed by a party of Germans, and came under Machine-gun fire from the right, and Trench Mortar fire from the front. A few of them succeeded in entering trench, but were driven out with 6 casualties, about the time that the signal for withdrawal went. All casualties were carried back.

Left Party. Found wire at I.5.B.52.54 had been well cut and met with no opposition and proceeded according to programme. No signs of life round EITEL FRITZ FARM. If there are any dugouts there, the entrances are covered up with debris. As party was withdrawing it was fired at from about I.5.B.60.48. No casualties.

Saphead (I.5.B.31.65) This party met with no opposition getting into Saphead, but found some difficulty in getting through the wire which had not been cut. It consisted of high barbed concertina wire. This saphead was much knocked about. Party threw bombs into sap. No reply from sap, but some rifle grenades were fired at them from enemy trench. Party remained in Saphead until left raiding party had withdrawn, and then returned to our trenches.

Our artillery barrage appears to have been excellent. The German Artillery only sent over about 30 shells. Wire in both places was well cut.

Two documents were picked up in a dugout by left raiding party ~~enclosed~~.

[signature] for
Major-General.
Commanding 55th Division.

H.Q., 55th Division.
6/11/16.

CONFIDENTIAL

Vol 12

War Diary

of

1/5th S. Lan. R.

for period

December 1st - 31st 1916

Z19

Army Form C. 2118.

WAR DIARY
or
~~INTELLIGENCE SUMMARY.~~
(Erase heading not required.)

Instructions regarding War Diaries and Intelligence Summaries are contained in F. S. Regs., Part II. and the Staff Manual respectively. Title pages will be prepared in manuscript.

1/5 South Lancashire Regiment December 1916

Place 1916	Date	Hour	Summary of Events and Information.	Remarks and references to Appendices
December			In Right Sub Sector 2 Casualties 1 OR K 1 OR W	
	2		Relieved by 1/5th K O Royal Lancs Regt moved to Billets YPRES. Hqrs Bombers and D Coy PRISON. B and C Coy Magazine Relief complete 7.15 pm A Coy Town Billets	
	3/6		In YPRES. All available men on working parties	
	7		Relieved 1/5 K O Royal Lancaster Regt in Right Sub Sector Disposition "C" Left Sector "D" Coy Right Sector "A" Coy in X Line. B Coy in CONGREVE WALK Relief complete 7.20 pm	
	9		Relieved Coys in front line. Disposition A Coy L Sector B Coy R Sector. D Coy in X Line C Coy in CONGREVE WALK. Coys working on trenches draining and improving	
	12		Relieved by 1/5 K O Royal Lancs Regt, moved to Billets YPRES. Hqrs Bombers C Coy PRISON D Coy Town Billets, A & B Coys Magazine. Relief complete 7.10 pm. All available men on working parties. 1 hours training per day done in addition.	
	17		Relieved by 1/4th Royal North Lancs Regt 164 Brigade. Entrained 7.35 pm for A Camp	
	18		Moved to O Camp. Day spent cleaning up.	
	19/20		Training	
	21		G O C in C visited O Camp. Inspection which should have taken place washed out owing to heavy rain	

1577 Wt. W10791/1773 500,000 1/15 D. D. & L. A.D.S.S./Forms/C. 2118.

Instructions regarding War Diaries and Intelligence Summaries are contained in F. S. Regs., Part II. and the Staff Manual respectively. Title pages will be prepared in manuscript.

WAR DIARY
or
~~INTELLIGENCE~~ SUMMARY.
(Erase heading not required.)

Army Form C. 2118.

1/5th South Lancashire Regiment December 1916

Place 1916	Date	Hour	Summary of Events and Information	Remarks and references to Appendices
December	21/23		Training in O Camp. Working party of 100 for cable burying	
	25		Xmas Day. Holiday "C" Coy won the Brigade Inter Coy Football Competition.	
	26		Training. Inspection of Lewis Guns by Divisional General. Working party for RE's	
	27		Moved to YPRES. relieved the 1/4th Royal North Lancs Regt 164 Brigade. Hqrs Bombers C Coy PRISON. A.B. MAGAZINE D Coy Town Billets	
	28		Relieved the 1/4th K O Royal Lancs Regt in Right Sub sector. Dispositions D Coy L Sector. C Coy R sector. B in X line. A Coy in CONGREVE WALK. Relief complete 7.15 pm	
	30		Coys relieved in front line. Dispositions B Coy L sector A Coy R sector C in X line. D Coy in CONGREVE WALK	
	31		Coys engaged cleaning up draining and improving trenches	

W.N. Pilkington Major
for Lt Col Commanding 1/5 South Lancashire Regt.

1577 Wt. W10791/1773 500,000 1/15 D. D. & L. A.D.S.S./Forms/C. 2118.

220

Vol 13

War Diary

of the

1/5th S. Lan. R

for the period

1/1/17 to 31/1/17.

Instructions regarding War Diaries and Intelligence Summaries are contained in F. S. Regs., Part II. and the Staff Manual respectively. Title Pages will be prepared in manuscript.

WAR DIARY ~~or~~ ~~INTELLIGENCE~~ SUMMARY

(Erase heading not required.)

Army Form C. 2118

1/5 South Lancashire Regiment January 1917

Place 1917	Date	Hour	Summary of Events and Information	Remarks and references to Appendices
January 1			Right Sub-sector. Special Shoot by Gunners 5.30 Pm. 2 Platoons Bombers Lewis Guns withdrawn from Right to X Line. One Platoon from Right placed in MILL COTS.	
2			Relieved by the 1/5th K O Royal Lancaster Regt in Right Sub-sector, moved to billets in YPRES. A Coy. Town Billets. Hqrs. Bombers and B Coy PRISON. C. D Coy MAGAZINE Relief complete 7 Pm.	
3/6			In YPRES. Supplying working parties daily, also Training	
7			Relieved the 1/5th K O Royal Lancaster Regiment in the Right Sub-sector. Dispositions D Coy Right Sector. C Coy Left Sector. A Coy X Line B Coy CONGREVE WALK. Relief Complete 6.30 Pm.	
10			Raid by the 1/5 Royal North Lancs Regt. Portion of our line vacated during preparatory bombardment. Corps Commander visited MILL COTS. Batt Hqrs and CONGREVE WALK Casualties 1 W.	
12			Relieved by the 4/5th Black Watch, 118th Infantry Brigade in the Right Sub-sector. Relief Complete 11.30 Pm. Early in the day wire at C29.7 C29 b cut by German Fire Batteries were informed. 9 Pm in middle of relief Intense Bombardment commenced by Enemy on our front line mainly on the Left and also on front of Battalion on our Left. SOS was sent up from the front line and also given to the Batteries by phone. Our Guns replied in under half a minute. Fire died down about 9.30 Pm After relief Battalion Entrained and moved to "A" Camp. Casualties 4 K 2 W	
13			At "A" Camp. 11 15 Am Transport moved forward to WORMHOUDT	
14			Transport moved forward to MERCKEGHEM. Battalion left "A" Camp and entrained	

1875 Wt. W593/826 1,000,000 4/15 J.B.C. & A. A.D.S.S./Forms/C. 2118.

Army Form C. 2118

Instructions regarding War Diaries and Intelligence Summaries are contained in F. S. Regs., Part II. and the Staff Manual respectively. Title Pages will be prepared in manuscript.

WAR DIARY
or
~~INTELLIGENCE SUMMARY~~

(Erase heading not required.)

1/5 South Lancashire Regiment January 1917

Place	Date	Hour	Summary of Events and Information	Remarks and references to Appendices
1917 January 14			at CHEESEMARKET STN POPERINGHE, detrained at BOLLEZEELE about 5.30 Pm and marched to billets in Training Area at MERCKEGHEM	
15/31			In Training MERCKEGHEM. Cup presented by Brigadier L Green Wilkinson for Football Competition, Battalions in the Brigade won by 1/5 South Lancashire Regt. also Cross Country Race. Teams of 12 open to the Brigade.	

C. P. James Lt Col
Commanding 1/5 South Lancashire Regt.

1875 Wt. W593/826 1,000,000 4/15 J.B.C. & A. A.D.S.S./Forms/C. 2118.

Army Form C. 2118.

Instructions regarding War Diaries and Intelligence Summaries are contained in F. S. Regs., Part II. and the Staff Manual respectively. Title pages will be prepared in manuscript.

WAR DIARY or ~~INTELLIGENCE SUMMARY~~.

1/5 South Lancashire Regt February 1917

(Erase heading not required.)

Place 1917	Date	Hour	Summary of Events and Information	Remarks and references to Appendices
Feby 1/2			At MERCKEGHEM Training	
3			Transport moved forward. Btn Entrained at BOLLEZEELE 8 40 Am detrained CHEESEMARKET Stn POPERINGHE, marched to E Camp and relieved 1/8th Kings Liverpool Regt 164 Inf Bde arrived 6 15 Pm	
4			Transport arrived	
5/8			E Camp Training Working Parties supplied	
9			Moved to MOUTON FARM, ELVERDINGHE, relieved 1/10th Liverpool Scottish	
10/16			AT MOUTON FARM working parties of 10 Officers 405 OR provided. Working on Cable Trench Northern Track Screening Roads. 15th Enemy Aeroplane brought down in flames.	
17			Relieved 4/5th Black Watch (39th Divn) in Brigade Reserve YPRES. Hqrs & C Coy Prison A and D Magazine B Town Billets	
18/20			In Brigade Reserve. Working Parties on Swimming Baths B L R support line on Cambridge T	
21			Relieved 1/5 K O Royal Lancs Regt in Right Sub-sector Dispositions C Coy Left (Platoon Garden of Eden) B Coy Right (Platoon Cambridge Trench) A Coy X Line (Platoon Mill Cotts) D Coy CONGREVE WALK	
24			Changed over. A Coy Right. D Coy Left. C Coy in X Line B Coy CONGREVE WALK	

1577 Wt. W10791/1773 500,000 1/15 D. D. & L. A.D.S.S./Forms/C. 2118.

Army Form C. 2118.

Instructions regarding War Diaries and Intelligence Summaries are contained in F. S. Regs., Part II. and the Staff Manual respectively. Title pages will be prepared in manuscript.

WAR DIARY or ~~INTELLIGENCE SUMMARY.~~

1/5 South Lancashire Regiment February 1917

(Erase heading not required.)

Place 1917	Date	Hour	Summary of Events and Information	Remarks and references to Appendices
Feby 16			Relieved in Right Subsector by 1/4 Loyal North Lancs Regt 164 Infantry Brigade. Relief Complete 11 Pm. Entrained H 17 central (28 NW) detrained BRANDHOECK. marched to O Camp arrived 1 Am.	
17/28			At "O" Camp Training	

J. Dickinson Major
Comdg 1/5 South Lancs Regt.

1577 Wt. W10791/1773 500,000 1/15 D. D. & L. A.D.S.S./Forms/C. 2118.

CONFIDENTIAL

Vol 14

War Diary

of

1/5 S. Lan. R.

for the period

1st to 28th February 1917

Z21

War Diary

of the

1/5th S. Lan. R.

for the period

1st to 3rd March

1917.

From O.C. 1/5 Bn South Lancashire Regt

To Headquarters,
166 Infantry Brigade.

Herewith War Diary for month of March 1917.

B. Humphreys Lieut. & Adjutant
for Lieut Col
3/4/17. Comdg. 1/5th S. F. Bn South Lancs Regt

Instructions regarding War Diaries and Intelligence Summaries are contained in F. S. Regs., Part II. and the Staff Manual respectively. Title Pages will be prepared in manuscript.

WAR DIARY

or

~~INTELLIGENCE SUMMARY~~

(Erase heading not required.)

1/5 South Lancashire Regiment March 1917

Army Form C. 2118

Place 1917	Date	Hour	Summary of Events and Information	Remarks and references to Appendices
March 1/6			Training at "O" Camp	
7			Entrained BRANDHOECK for YPRES 8.50 Pm. Relieved the 1/5 K O Royal Lancs in Brigade Reserve at the ECOLE. Relief complete 11.30 Pm.	
8/11			In Brigade Reserve working Parties 5 Officers 450 O.R.	
12			Relieved the 1/5 K.O Royal Lancs in Right Sub sector (Railway Wood) Relief Complete 3.30 Am. Casualties 6 O.R. wounded.	
13/16			In Right Sub-sector	
17			Relieved by 1/5 Kings Liverpool Regt. 165 Brigade in Right Sub-sector. Relief complete 9.45 Pm. Returned to Billets CANAL BANK.	
18/22			CANAL BANK working Parties 5 Officers 480 O.R.	
23			Relieved 1/5 K.O Royal Lancs in Left Sub sector (WIELTJE) relief complete 11.30 Pm	
24/27			In Left Sub-sector	
28			Relieved by 1/4 K O Royal Lancs Regt. 164 Infantry Brigade. Relief Complete 10.15 Pm. Entrained YPRES detrained BRANDHOECK. To Billets at "O" Camp.	
28/31			Training in "O" Camp	

C. P. [illegible] Lieut Col
Comdg 1/5 South Lancs Regt.

Vol 6

War Diary

of

1/5th S. Lan. R.

for the period

April 1st to 30th, 1917.

Z 23

Instructions regarding War Diaries and Intelligence Summaries are contained in F. S. Regs., Part II. and the Staff Manual respectively. Title pages will be prepared in manuscript.

WAR DIARY

or

~~INTELLIGENCE~~ SUMMARY.

(Erase heading not required.) April 1917

Army Form C. 2118.

Place	Date	Hour	Summary of Events and Information	Remarks and references to Appendices
1917				
April 1/6			In "D" Camp Training.	
7			Relieved the 1/5 K O Royal Lancs Regt. in Brigade Reserve (Right Subsector Railway Wood) in billets at the ECOLE.	
8/11			In Brigade Reserve Supplied working parties R.E's Kings Own 4th South Lancs 171 Tunnelling Coy	
12			Relieved the 1/5 K O Royal Lancs Regt. in the Right Sub. sector Relief Complete 1.30 AM Sergeant T Hallwood and 1 OR Killed	
13/16			In the Right Sub. sector. Casualties 1 OR Killed 5 OR wounded. Night of 15th Intensive bombardment of Enemy Lines Rifle Grenades Stokes Mortars 18 lb Batteries. Retaliation slight	
17			Relieved by the 1/5 Kings Liverpool Regiment. Entrained at YPRES for BRANDHOECK. Marched to Billets at "D" Camp. Relief Complete 2 AM. Large Camouflet blown by Mining Coy at 5.30 AM	
18/26			In D Camp Training. 6 Officers and 200 OR left behind in Billets at YPRES to supply working Parties. Training of Specialists carried on. Lewis Gunners Bombers (Particular attention being paid to Rifle Grenadiers) Snipers Signallers. NCO Classes in Bayonet Fighting under Divisional Instructor. Lewis Gunners receiving special instruction in the Tactical use of Gun	
			Brig-Gen L F Green Wilkinson relinquished Command of the 166 Infantry Brigade (To England) The following letter was addressed by him to the Brigade	
			"On being relieved of the 166th Infantry Brigade, which it has been my constant"	

A7092 Wt. W12839/M1293. 750,000. 1/17. D. D & L., Ltd. Forms/C2118/14.

Army Form C. 2118.

WAR DIARY
or
~~INTELLIGENCE SUMMARY.~~
(Erase heading not required.)

Instructions regarding War Diaries and Intelligence Summaries are contained in F. S. Regs., Part II. and the Staff Manual respectively. Title pages will be prepared in manuscript.

1/5 South Lancs Regt — April 1917

Place	Date	Hour	Summary of Events and Information	Remarks and references to Appendices
1917			" pride to command since its formation. I wish to thank Commanding"	
			" Officers, Officers and Other Ranks for their very loyal cooperation,"	
			" and also to wish them Goodbye, and Good Luck in the future."	
			" It is my very deep regret that we shall no longer serve"	
			" together (sd) L. Green Wilkinson Brigadier General Commanding 166th Infantry Brigade	
			Brigadier General F. G. LEWIS. CB. CMG. assumed Command of the 166th Infantry Brigade.	
April 27			Relieved the 1/5 K O Royal Lancs Regt in the Right Sub-sector Left Section. Front line held Trench I 5.8 (I 5 b 08 40) inclusive to Trench C29.4 (C29 c 7.5. 28 NW 2) inclusive. Dispositions D Coy. 4 Platoons Front line 4 Platoons & Hqrs in CAMBRIDGE T. 'A' Coy 1 Platoon MILL COTTS and GARDEN of EDEN. 3 Platoons ST JAMES T and PRONSE T. B Coy and D Coy. on POTIJZE ROAD. 'B' Coy manning Strong Point	
30			Casualties 1 OR killed and 1 OR wounded.	

C. P. James Lt Col
Comdg 1/5 South Lancs Regt.

A7092 Wt. W12839/M1293. 750,000. 1/17. D. D & L., Ltd. Forms/C2118/14.

CONFIDENTIAL

Vol 17

War Diary

of

1/5th S. Lan. R.

for the period

May 1st - 31st 1917

Z 24

Instructions regarding War Diaries and Intelligence Summaries are contained in F. S. Regs., Part II. and the Staff Manual respectively. Title Pages will be prepared in manuscript.

WAR DIARY ~~or~~ ~~INTELLIGENCE~~ SUMMARY

(*Erase heading not required.*)

Army Form C. 2118

1.

Place	Date	Hour	Summary of Events and Information	Remarks and references to Appendices
			Trench Map ST JULIEN 28 NW 2 Ed 5A " " ZILLEBEKE -do-	
WIELTJE SECTOR	1917 1 May		Battalion holding the Right Sub-sector:- Dispositions: Battalion HQ POTIJZE CHATEAU I.4.a.7.5. A Company (less 2 platoons) FRONT LINE " (2 platoons) CAMBRIDGE TRENCH C " 1 platoon MILL COTS and GARDEN OF EDEN 3 platoons ST JAMES TR and BONSE TRENCH. HQ platoon , POTIJZE DEFENCES from I.4.a.70.45 – I.4.b.2.3. B + D Coys – 2 Companies BRIGADE RESERVE – POTIJZE RD.	
		8am	The Brigadier General visited the sub-sector and made a tour of trenches. Working parties – (provided daily)	
		8am	1 Officer 50 other ranks working on dug outs (Potijze Rd) under 422 Field Coy R.E.	
		9pm	1 NCO + 15 men on drainage under [illegible] South Lancs R.	
		9.30pm	1 Officer 50 other ranks on CAMBRIDGE RD under 419 Field Coy R.E.	
			In addition the following parties are working within the Battalion daily:-	
		8am	1 NCO 16 men on front line under Bn Pioneer	
		9pm	" " 32 " —do— "	
		9.30pm	2 parties each 1 NCO + 5 – Wiring	
	2 May	7.30/9.30pm	Enemy artillery shelled junction of POTIJZE and MENIN RDS with about 99 – 10.5cm and 15cm shells. 2 other ranks D Company wounded.	
	3 "		Our 4.5 howitzers active against enemy's rear positions during the day.	

1875 Wt. W593/826 1,000,000 4/15 J.B.C. & A. A.D.S.S./Forms/C. 2118.

Instructions regarding War Diaries and Intelligence Summaries are contained in F. S. Regs., Part II. and the Staff Manual respectively. Title Pages will be prepared in manuscript.

WAR DIARY
or
~~INTELLIGENCE SUMMARY~~
(Erase heading not required.)

Army Form C. 2118

2.

Place	Date	Hour	Summary of Events and Information	Remarks and references to Appendices
	3rd May Contd		Aeroplanes of both sides up all day.	
		4 pm	A fight between six machines took place over WIELTJE without apparent results.	
		5 pm	Hostile artillery fired 90-10cm [illegible] shells on the STRAND [illegible]. As soon as they [illegible] knocked [illegible] shelling ceased, no damage done.	
			YPRES was shelled all day with [illegible] [illegible] round [illegible] [illegible]	
		11 am	Hostile balloon N.E. of WIELTJE [illegible] [illegible] [illegible].	
	4th May	3.30 am	Two of our Snipers lay out in NO MANS LAND at C.29.d.00.44, to observe and report on enemy front line. They returned to our line at 9.15 pm	
			B Company relieved A Company in the Front Line and Cambridge Trench. A Company returned to "B" Days [illegible] on POTIJZE ROAD. Relief complete 11.5 pm	
			In the afternoon 12, 77mm shrapnel burst over POTIJZE WOOD, 6 on C.29.1 and 4 on HAYMARKET. YPRES was heavily shelled during the day.	
			Both sides had aeroplanes up all day, many German machines coming over our line.	
		8.45 pm	A fire lasting to 9.15 pm seen towards ST JULIEN.	
	5 May.	11 am	Front line was lightly shelled about C.29.3, I.5.9. with 77mm shells. Our 18 pounders replied effectively.	
		am	In early morning working party on front line trench when shell dropped - 2 killed, 1 died of wounds 2 wounded	
		9 am	2 hostile aeroplanes crossed over our lines, but returned in the direction of PASSCHENDALE	
		5 pm	and again over RAILWAY WOOD at 5 pm. They were attacked by our planes, and one fell in flames in our line near HOOGE.	
		8 pm	Another hostile plane appeared over our front line, flying very low, being driven back at 8.45 pm. Our aeroplanes were very active all day. Enemy again shelled [illegible]	
		10.30 pm	[illegible] observed behind enemy line at bearing of 122° true from C.29.3. Suggesting an ammunition dump	

1875 Wt. W593/826 1,000,000 4/15 J.B.C. & A. A.D.S.S./Forms/C. 2118.

Instructions regarding War Diaries and Intelligence Summaries are contained in F. S. Regs., Part II. and the Staff Manual respectively. Title pages will be prepared in manuscript.

WAR DIARY
or
~~INTELLIGENCE SUMMARY.~~
(*Erase heading not required.*)

Army Form C. 2118.

3.

Place	Date	Hour	Summary of Events and Information	Remarks and references to Appendices
	6 May		Received G.O.C. 55 Divn's remarks on report of snipers who lay out in NO MANS LAND from 3.30am to 9.15 pm on 4th May. "A very useful report, shows what can be done by plucky energetic action, in the way of getting intelligence."	
		9.30 am	Hostile plane flying low over his lines at 9.30 am & was driven back over ZONNEBEKE by anti-aircraft.	
		5.30 pm 8.30	Hostile planes flew over this sub-sector. Our aeroplanes active all day.	
			YPRES was heavily shelled and ST JEAN at intervals during the day.	
		11 pm	"D" Company relieved "C" Company in support LINE (1 platoon MILL COTS and GARDEN OF EDEN) 3 platoons ST JAMES TRENCH AND PROWSE TR). "C" Company returned to "D" Coys billets in BRIGADE RESERVE	
		7am	2Lt F. SMETHURST and 5 other ranks proceeded with the first party to the SECOND ARMY Rest Camps at AMBLETEUSE near BOULOGNE, for 14 days.	
	7 May	11am	Our artillery put up a creeping barrage on hostile front from I12.a.01.61 to J5.6.42.83 with 18 pounders, and 4.5 Howitzers 6" [illegible]. Enemy mildly retaliated with a few 4.2s & 77mm shells on CAMBRIDGE TR and HAYMARKET – no damage was done.	
		8.45 pm and 11 pm	A heavy bombardment for five minutes was carried out along the whole SECOND ARMY FRONT, against the enemy's communications and dumps. In retaliation enemy barraged round front line, but not very heavily	
	8 May	11am	Hostile artillery shelled POTIJZE CHATEAU and POTIJZE WOOD with about 20 – 8" shells. No damage was done. 1 other rank wounded.	
		9.30 pm	We blew a mine at I12.c.28.91. which was seized and consolidated by the Right Brigade.	

A7092 Wt. W128.9/M1293. 750,000. 1/17. D. D & L., Ltd. Forms/C2118/14.

Instructions regarding War Diaries and Intelligence Summaries are contained in F. S. Regs., Part II. and the Staff Manual respectively. Title Pages will be prepared in manuscript.

WAR DIARY

~~or~~

~~INTELLIGENCE~~ SUMMARY

(Erase heading not required.)

Army Form C. 2118

4

Place	Date	Hour	Summary of Events and Information	Remarks and references to Appendices
	9 May	am 1.25	Battalion relieved in the Right sub-sector by 1/4th Bn (Kings Own) Royal Lancaster Regiment 164 Infantry Brigade, during a very quiet night. Marched to Ypres and entrained at the ASYLUM 2.25 am. Detrained POPERINGHE 3.5 am. Marched to "L" Camp L.3.d.2.6 arriving 4.40 am. Got down in billets (huts and tents) until 11 am.	
		7.30 am 2.30 pm 5.5 pm	The G.O.C. Division visited the camp inspecting cookhouses and billets. Day spent in cleaning up and Company inspections.	
L CAMP.	10 May	5 am	Reveille. Battalion in Training.	
		7.30 am	German aeroplane passed over camp and was fired on by anti-aircraft guns.	
		5 pm	The Major General gave a lecture to all officers on Platoon Training at the Reinforcement Camp.	
	11 May	9.30 am	Inspection by Brig. Genl Commanding.	
	12 May	8 am	Route march "L" Camp – CROSS RDS L2A – CROSS ROADS L1C – FORK RDS L4C – CROSS ROADS L10a – L Camp.	
		11 am	Captain Mills, Machine Gun School lectured on (a) Employment of machine guns with advanced guards (b) machine gun barrages to all officers at the REINFORCEMENT CAMP.	
	13 May		Brigade CHURCH PARADE (C of E) – Drums played by our band.	
	14/16 May		Proceeded with Training	

1875 Wt. W593/826 1,000,000 4/15 J.B.C. & A. A.D.S.S./Forms/C. 2118.

Instructions regarding War Diaries and Intelligence Summaries are contained in F. S. Regs., Part II. and the Staff Manual respectively. Title Pages will be prepared in manuscript.

WAR DIARY
or
INTELLIGENCE SUMMARY
(Erase heading not required.)

Army Form C. 2118

5.

Place	Date	Hour	Summary of Events and Information	Remarks and references to Appendices
L. Camp	18th May	pm 3.30	Relieved in Divisional Reserve by 6th Bn Welsh Regt and marched to the Hop Store, Poperinghe, where teas were served.	
		7.45	Entrained for Ypres. detrained ASYLUM, and marched to the ECOLE (BRIGADE RESERVE). A B & D Coys in the ECOLE – C Coy less 2 platoons in HALF MOON TRENCH, on MENIN RD	
YPRES: Ref. Trench map ZILLEBEKE 10,000	19/24		Providing working parties averaging 450 – 500 daily. Ypres shelled each day with H.E. shells especially in neighbourhood of ASYLUM, the STATION RAMPARTS and MENIN DUMP.	
			On the night 23rd/24th the Divisional north boundary, Brigade and Battalion boundaries were changed.	
			166 Brigade (5th Kings Own R.L.) handed over to [illegible] Brigade ([illegible] Kings Own R.L.) from I.5.8 to I.5.5 inclusive.	
			2 Platoons C Coy in HALF MOON TR. relieved by [illegible] R.L.R. and rejoined Company on RD.	
	25/26	2.15 am	Relieved 5th Kings Own Royal Lancaster Regt, and [illegible] Company [illegible] Bn Kings Liverpool Regt in RAILWAY WOOD and became GARRISON BATTALION.	
			Dispositions	
			Headquarters MINE I.11.b.4.2.	
			Right Front Company – D – 1 platoon front line 2 platoons MINE DUGOUTS 1 platoon [illegible]	
			Centre Company – A – 1 " " " 2 " " " 1 "	
			Left Company – C – 2 platoons FRONT LINE 2 platoons CAMBRIDGE RD. [illegible]	
			Reserve Company – B – BEEK TRENCH	
			[illegible] Lt. [illegible] wounded – later died of W.	

1875 Wt. W593/826 1,000,000 4/15 J.B.C. & A. A.D.S.S./Forms/C. 2118.

Instructions regarding War Diaries and Intelligence Summaries are contained in F. S. Regs., Part II. and the Staff Manual respectively. Title Pages will be prepared in manuscript.

WAR DIARY
~~INTELLIGENCE~~ SUMMARY

(Erase heading not required.)

Army Form C. 2118

(6)

Place	Date	Hour	Summary of Events and Information	Remarks and references to Appendices
RAILWAY WOOD	26 May		Our artillery active on enemy lines all day, firing on IDENTITY TRENCH, and [illegible] IDIOT AVENUE etc with field guns and [illegible] with results.	
			50 - 10.5cm fired by enemy on WEST LANE near junction with BEEK TRENCH at intervals during the day. 80 - 77mm and 12 - 10.5cm on CAMBRIDGE TR [illegible] and RIFLE FARM between 5 and 7pm in retaliation of our Trench Mortar fire, Stokes Mortars having fired on the BARRICADE. [illegible] other ranks wounded.	
		11.30pm - 2.30am	3 Patrols out on Battalion front reconnoitring [illegible], GORDON, Nos 3, 4 and 5 Craters, but no sign of the enemy was found.	
			During the morning enemy shelled YARES [illegible] 280 [illegible] shells fell upon the RAMPARTS, and [illegible] between [illegible] am and 7.30am the [illegible] [illegible] 2/Lt [illegible] and [illegible] [illegible] [illegible]	
	27 May	11am to 12.30pm	Our heavy artillery fired [illegible] [illegible] [illegible] [illegible] on enemy front line and supports. [illegible] [illegible] [illegible] [illegible] the [illegible] LANE and IGUANA AVENUE [illegible] which [illegible] [illegible] [illegible] in many places and left [illegible] of [illegible] STATION BUILDINGS. There was no retaliation. Enemy retaliated [illegible] on CAMBRIDGE TRENCH [illegible] 16 - 4.2 shells.	
		7am	5 enemy aeroplanes flying low crossed over our lines and were fired on by [illegible] [illegible] [illegible] [illegible]. [illegible] killed. 1 OR wounded. Patrols again out on our front, but no enemy encountered.	
	28 May	6.35am	Enemy plane [illegible] brought down by anti-aircraft M.G. [illegible] [illegible] enemy lines.	
	28 May	6am - 8am	Hostile aeroplanes flew over RAILWAY WOOD [illegible] for half an hour and [illegible] for an hour [illegible] [illegible] small arms fire. Hostile balloon behind BELLEWAARDE RIDGE was hauled down on approach of our aeroplanes.	

1875 Wt. W593/826 1,000,000 4/15 J.B.C. & A. A.D.S.S./Forms/C. 2118.

Instructions regarding War Diaries and Intelligence Summaries are contained in F. S. Regs., Part II, and the Staff Manual respectively. Title pages will be prepared in manuscript.

WAR DIARY

~~or~~

~~INTELLIGENCE~~ SUMMARY.

(*Erase heading not required.*)

Army Form C. 2118.

Place	Date	Hour	Summary of Events and Information	Remarks and references to Appendices
RLY WOOD	28 May		Our field guns again active, cutting gaps in enemy wire, also Trench Mortars. Enemy appears to be tired [of] mending his front line, and is concentrating on his rear lines of defence. New wire 8 yards deep on two foot six inch stakes has been put up running from CAMEROON AVENUE C.30.c.64.99 in front of GREY RUIN and joining up with main wire round FREZENBERG line.	
		6 pm	Our heavy artillery fired on IDLE SAP from 6 – 7.30 pm and trenches on and behind the BELLEWAARDE RIDGE.	
		10 pm	We blew a camouflet under No 12 CRATER which did not break the surface. Part of CRATER SAP TRENCH and bombing post fell in. We fired rifle bombs and Lewis guns at COTTER CRATER. No action by enemy.	
	29.		Our guns and batteries active all day. At 5 pm we fired 50 – 18 pounder shrapnel on IDENTITY TRENCH	
		6 pm	Enemy retaliated on [illegible] TRENCH and WEST LANE with salvos of 77 mm and 10.5 cm.	
		8 pm	Hostile plane flew over our line, and fired a WHITE flare followed by one bursting into two red and green stars. Enemy searchlights were in use behind	

H.Q. [illegible] 11.20 pm.

A6945 Wt. W11422/M1160 350,000 12/16 D. D. & L. Forms/C./2118/14.

Instructions regarding War Diaries and Intelligence Summaries are contained in F. S. Regs., Part II. and the Staff Manual respectively. Title pages will be prepared in manuscript.

WAR DIARY
or
INTELLIGENCE SUMMARY.
(*Erase heading not required.*)

Army Form C. 2118.

Place	Date	Hour	Summary of Events and Information	Remarks and references to Appendices
	29 May	10·30 pm	We blew a large mine about 60 x 80 yards just SOUTH of 2A CRATER. There was no action by enemy except a little sniping. We consolidated and wired the near lip of the CRATER. 2 men wounded. The enemy made no attempt to hinder our party or to seize his own lip. The crater formed obliterates COTTER, NEW COTTER and NO 12 CRATERS. A communication trench was pushed out from the front line connecting up the SOUTHERN extremity and the trench on the lip. An existing trench was cleared making a second communication trench from the northern extremity. Our lip is very high giving a good command of enemys lines and a view of BELLEWAARDE LAKE. The Brigade Major was at Bn HQ during operations. Patrols report enemy very quiet and no signs of any work or attempts to mend his wire.	
	30 May		Message received from Brig General F. G. Lewis as follows. "I congratulate you on the excellence of your arrangements last night." Our field guns [illegible] with wire cutting. 6 of our aeroplanes crossed enemy lines about 6 a.m.	
		4·30 pm	The G.O.C. Division visited the trenches, and expressed himself highly pleased with the previous nights work and congratulated the C.O.	

A6945 Wt. W11422/M1160 350,000 12/16 D. D. & L. Forms/C./2118/14.

Instructions regarding War Diaries and Intelligence Summaries are contained in F. S. Regs., Part II, and the Staff Manual respectively. Title pages will be prepared in manuscript.

WAR DIARY
or
~~INTELLIGENCE SUMMARY.~~
(Erase heading not required.)

Army Form C. 2118.

9.

Place	Date	Hour	Summary of Events and Information	Remarks and references to Appendices
RAILWAY WOOD	30 May	4.30 pm	Neighbourhood of BECK TR and WEST LANE shelled with about 6 x 5.9s.	
		6pm	The left GROUP took part in a practice barrage in conjunction with machine guns on left of RLY WOOD SECTOR.	
			Our artillery continued their programme of harassing the enemy's approaches and communications during the night. 2 other ranks wounded.	
	31 May	9am	Our 18 pounders fired on BELLEWAARDE RIDGE intermittently from 9am	
		10.30	to 10.30am. Hostile 5.9 battery fired about 40 rounds in the	
			neighbourhood of SOUTH LANE and WEST LANE. Our aeroplanes brought	
			down one hostile balloon in flames on our right flank. Our heavies	
			again bombarded enemy support and rear positions all day and	
			their shelling was [illegible] with. 3 other ranks wounded.	

C.P. James Lieut-Colonel
Comdg 1/5 Bn South Lancashire Regt.

A6945 Wt. W11422/M1160 350,000 12/16 D. D. & L. Forms/C./2118/14.

CONFIDENTIAL

Vol 18

War Diary

of

1/5th S. Lan. R.

for the period

June 1st to June 30th, 1917

Z25

Army Form C. 2118.

Instructions regarding War Diaries and Intelligence Summaries are contained in F. S. Regs., Part II. and the Staff Manual respectively. Title pages will be prepared in manuscript.

WAR DIARY
~~or~~ ~~INTELLIGENCE~~ SUMMARY.

(Erase heading not required.)

1/5 South Lancashire Regt

Place	Date	Hour	Summary of Events and Information	Remarks and references to Appendices
			Ref: Trench Map. ZILLEBEEKE 28 N.W. 1/10,000	
RAILWAY WOOD	1 June		Forming GARRISON BATTALION, holding line from I.5.1 to I.11.1 inclusive	
		3 am	Under cover of machine gun and Artillery fire, 500 gas bombs were discharged from projectors upon the area approximately enclosed by the YPRES – ROULERS RAILWAY and ICE LANE. Double green flares were sent up by the enemy	
		3.15 am	Hostile artillery barraged the front line CAMBRIDGE TRENCH and EAST LANE for 45 minutes. 1 7 Other Ranks D Coy wounded	
			During the day our heavy artillery continued the bombardment of enemy support and reserve trenches. Our 60 lb T.M's fired on IDEA TR and enemy wire at intervals. Hostile 4.2's fired in retaliation on our FRONT LINE, CAMBRIDGE TRENCH, BEEK TR, and WEST LANE. 2 Other Ranks B Coy wounded.	
		8.10 pm	Hostile plane flying low over sector was driven off by A.A.	
		3.30 pm	A practice barrage took place from YPRES – ROULERS RAILWAY to the SOUTH.	
	2 June	3 am	60 gas bombs discharged from projectors on enemy trench, action followed as on 1st inst, but artillery was not so active.	
		3.20 am	Enemy blew a camouflet about 30 feet the north of BLISS CRATER, this did not ~~[illegible]~~ break the surface.	

A6945 Wt. W11422/M1160 350,000 12/16 D. D. & L. Forms/C./2118/14.

Army Form C. 2118.

Instructions regarding War Diaries and Intelligence Summaries are contained in F. S. Regs., Part II. and the Staff Manual respectively. Title pages will be prepared in manuscript.

WAR DIARY 2.
or
~~INTELLIGENCE~~ SUMMARY.

(*Erase heading not required.*)

Place	Date	Hour	Summary of Events and Information	Remarks and references to Appendices
	2 June	9.30 am	One of our planes brought down in flames behind enemy lines by Anti-aircraft fire and another was forced down in our lines at 9.30 am. A hostile machine low over RLY WOOD at 8 am was fired on by LEWIS and MACHINE GUNS. Our Heavies continued daily bombardment BELLEWAARDE RIDGE etc being considerably knocked about. During the day enemy shelled FRONT LINE CAMBRIDGE TRENCH, JUNCTION TRENCH, and WEST LANE were shelled with salvos of 77 mm and 10.5 cm shells.	
	3 June	4 am	The enemy blew a mine at I.12.a.2.2. no action followed. There are two craters one at I.12.a.12.20 - 15 yds dia and one at I.12.a.22.16, 20 yds in dia.	
		3 pm	to 3.30 pm Corps Heavy Artillery bombarded selected points and a barrage was put by the Divisional Artillery on the front from CAMEL TRENCH to CAMBRAI TRENCH at barrage on enemy's lines on the left of Divl front. We discharged Smoke on our front from MUD LANE to C.29.17. Retaliation slight on our front. Enemy artillery active on WEST LANE, and trench mortars active. Lieut [illegible] and 7 other ranks wounded (2 died following day).	
	4 June		— Comparatively quiet day — 4 O.R. wounded.	
	5 June	12.30	A fighting patrol under Lieut Vincent Maudsley entered the enemy's trenches at	

A6945 Wt. W11422/M1160 350,000 12/16 D. D. & L. Forms/C./2118/14.

Instructions regarding War Diaries and Intelligence Summaries are contained in F. S. Regs., Part II, and the Staff Manual respectively. Title pages will be prepared in manuscript.

WAR DIARY

or

~~INTELLIGENCE SUMMARY.~~ 3

(*Erase heading not required.*)

Army Form C. 2118.

Place	Date	Hour	Summary of Events and Information	Remarks and references to Appendices
	5 June		I 12.a.05.94 and blew up the O.P. at that point. The enemy sent up double red flares after the explosion, and put down a barrage on our front line, supports and communication trenches about the YPRES – ROULERS RAILWAY, six minutes later. The Observation Post destroyed was about 6 feet by 4 feet composed of concrete and steel girders with timber on the top. No entrance from the outside was discovered. The enemy trench about here is badly smashed and is 4 ft deep revetted with brushwood. Lieut V. Maudsley wounded and 1 ORank killed. During the day our front and Support trenches were shelled with 10.5 cm and 7.7 cm shells. Our artillery carried out its programme of wire cutting and destructive fire.	
	6 June		Generally quiet day, but slight shelling during the day with 10.5 cm and 7.7 cm. 75 rounds of STOKES MORTARS and 100 rounds of 2" mortars were fired on enemy trenches East of MOMBER CRATER and at JAMES CRATER. 2 ORanks wounded.	
		1 pm	Menin Rd and all traffic roads from YPRES were bombarded with Lachrymatory and Gas Shells. This continued all night.	
	7 June	3.10 am	Attack launched on the Right by II ANZAC and X Corps against the MESSINES and WYSCHAETE RIDGE. Explosion of the mines could be clearly seen. At the same time enemy sent up S.O.S on our front and at 3.15 a barrage	

A6945 Wt. W11422/M1160 350,000 12/16 D. D. & L. Forms/C./2118/14.

Instructions regarding War Diaries and Intelligence Summaries are contained in F. S. Regs., Part II. and the Staff Manual respectively. Title pages will be prepared in manuscript.

WAR DIARY

~~INTELLIGENCE~~ SUMMARY. 4.

(*Erase heading not required.*)

Army Form C. 2118.

Place	Date	Hour	Summary of Events and Information	Remarks and references to Appendices
	7 June		of all calibres was put on our line SOUTH of the YPRES – ROULERS RAILWAY	
		5.30 am	One of our planes brought down by hostile aircraft near HELL FIRE C.P. Hostile balloon broke away at 6.30am enemy had 3 up but these were frequently pulled down on approach of our machines.	
		10 am	Enemy shelled neighbourhood of WEST LANE with 30 – 77mm shells and at	
		3.30pm	dropped 40 · 10.5cm round CAMBRIDGE Rd and PICCADILLY.	
			Our heavy artillery bombarded enemy trenches & field guns his front systems. Very	
	8 June		Quiet day – except for light shelling of WEST LANE at 4.30 am enemy inactive. 2/Lt Worthington (killed)	
	9 June	12.30 am	A fighting patrol under 2/Lt W.N. WILLIAMS left our lines to destroy a concrete dug-out or emplacement about I 12 c 48.73. Had difficulty in negotiating the very broken ground owing to the darkness. Enemy was very alert and opened fire with machine guns. The enterprise was intended to be a surprise one it was not carried through.	
		2am	We blew a camouflet about 30 yards N. of BLISS CRATER	
		6.45am	An Unter-Offizier of the [?]th Infantry Regiment came into our lines at I.12.[illegible] This prisoner left his trenches N of the YPRES – ROULERS RLY and said he had lost his way. His Division 233rd[?] relieved a Naval Division about 3 weeks ago	

Instructions regarding War Diaries and Intelligence Summaries are contained in F. S. Regs., Part II. and the Staff Manual respectively. Title pages will be prepared in manuscript.

WAR DIARY

~~or~~

~~INTELLIGENCE SUMMARY.~~

5.

(*Erase heading not required.*)

Army Form C. 2118.

Place	Date	Hour	Summary of Events and Information	Remarks and references to Appendices
RAILWAY WOOD			He states that the order of battle of his division is - from North to South 484th Inf Regt, 449th Inf Regt 456th Inf Regt.	
			The remainder of day activity on both sides was normal. 1. OR B Coy wounded.	
	10 June		Quiet generally but enemy shelled neighbourhood of BEEK TR with 9.2's and lightly shelled WEST LANE and SOUTH LANE at intervals throughout the day 1. OR "C" Coy wounded. Lieut T.W.S. Arnold returned to duty.	
	11 June		Some heavy shells were fired on front, support & Reserve trenches and YPRES was intermittently shelled throughout the day, and quite heavily from	
		4:30	pm and through the night, gas shells being employed. 1, OR A Coy wounded.	
	11/12th		Relieved by 10th (Scottish) Bn Kings (Liverpool) Regt and moved into Reserve with HQ at H.1.A.50.70 (Sheet 28 NW BELGIUM) together with A Coy and 2 platoons of D. C B and 2 platoons of D at MACHINE GUN FARM and L.8 at (H.5.C.90.90). The latter 2½ Coys providing working parties in forward area. 1 O Rank killed and 3 OR wounded (B Coy)	
	13		Batting, cleaning up, and Coy inspections. The G.O.C DIVN visited the Camp At night A Company & 2 platoons of D changed over, C Coy and remaining platoons of D ~~relieving~~ taking over camp at H.1A 50.70.	

Instructions regarding War Diaries and Intelligence Summaries are contained in F. S. Regs., Part II. and the Staff Manual respectively. Title pages will be prepared in manuscript.

WAR DIARY

~~INTELLIGENCE SUMMARY~~

(Erase heading not required.)

Army Form C. 2118.

Place	Date	Hour	Summary of Events and Information	Remarks and references to Appendices
	14 June		Proceeded with cleaning, completing kit, bathing &c.	
	15 June		In the evening 'C' Coy moved to MACHINE GUN FARM and A and D Companys relieved 1/5th (Kings Own) Royal Lancaster Regt in Brigade Reserve at MENIN RD and DIXMUDE ST. with HQ about I.9.c.90.50 (ZILLEBEKE) B, C, Coys and HQ details at L.8 and M.G. FARM. Major W.H. Pickington DSO i/c of Detachment. Companies moving into YPRES came under heavy shell fire. Working parties provided by Coys in YPRES and M.G. FM. 4 other ranks A Coy wounded.	
	15/16		Detachment at M G Fm came under H.E. shell fire from 11.30pm until about 3am – casualties nil.	
	16		YPRES again heavily shelled, gas shells also being employed, nine hostile aeroplanes over YPRES. 2 other ranks C Coy wounded (1 died) ~~2 Coy wounded~~	
	17		1 Enemy aeroplane brought down in flames in their lines. MENIN RD, GATE and RAMPARTS shelled also ECOLE in the afternoon. Enemy employed gas shells at night. 1 O Rank C Coy wounded.	
	18	7.8am	Enemy planes patrolled our lines, one brought down in flames on right of Divisional front. Unceasing bombardment on MENIN RD all day.	

A6945 Wt. W11422/M1160 350,000 12/16 D. D. & L. Forms/C./2118/14.

Instructions regarding War Diaries and Intelligence Summaries are contained in F. S. Regs., Part II. and the Staff Manual respectively. Title pages will be prepared in manuscript.

WAR DIARY

~~INTELLIGENCE~~ SUMMARY.

(Erase heading not required.)

Army Form C. 2118.

Place	Date	Hour	Summary of Events and Information	Remarks and references to Appendices
	18 June		and YPRES generally. 1 O.Rank 'C' Coy and 1 O.Rank D Coy wounded	
	19 "		Shelling of YPRES continued and neighborhood of MACHINE GUN FARM and HIGH ST. shelled by night. 1 OR wounded D Coy.	
	20 "	7.27	Lieut W.H. Foster and 6 O.Ranks proceeded to ZAEGERS CAPPEL billeting for Battalion; and Detachment at M.G. FARM followed by 4.15 pm train from POPERINGHE. Whilst entraining the station was lightly shelled. Arrived ESQUELBECQ 7.20 pm sheltered from heavy showers and at 7.35 marched to ZAEGERS CAPPEL where they stayed the night.	
	20/21st		HQ and A + D Coys relieved in YPRES by 7/8th Kings Own Scottish Borderers and marched to MERSEY CAMP. YPRES and roads leading into it were continually shelled during relief. 2, O.Ranks A Coy killed, 8 wounded (2 Died of Wds)	
		10am	Detachment at ZAEGERS CAPPEL proceeded by omnibus to QUELMES AREA and took over billets for Battalion at villages of LEULINE, AUDENTHUN and ETREHEM with Headquarters at LEULINE.	
	22.	9.30am	Remainder of Battalion entrained POPERINGHE for ST.OMER arriving	
		3 pm	at Rest Area.	

A6945. Wt. W11422/M1160. 350,000. 12/16 D. D. & L. Forms/C./2118/14.

Instructions regarding War Diaries and Intelligence Summaries are contained in F. S. Regs., Part II. and the Staff Manual respectively. Title pages will be prepared in manuscript.

WAR DIARY
~~or~~
~~INTELLIGENCE SUMMARY~~.
(*Erase heading not required.*)

Army Form C. 2118.

8

Place	Date	Hour	Summary of Events and Information	Remarks and references to Appendices
	23 June		Day devoted to cleaning up clothing and equipment and Coy inspections. 70 rank reinforcements joined.	
	24 "		C.O. inspected Companies on parade. Lieut [illegible] Price joined for duty.	
	25 "		Capt [illegible] L. Morris proceeded to HQ. Third Army in connection with PRISONER OF WAR [illegible]	(A.G. [illegible])
	26		In Rest Area. Training Preparing Practice Trenches	
	27		do	
	28		do	
	29		Advance party under 2Lt Hargreaves left for new billets at ESQUERDES	
	30		Battalion and Transport moved to new billets at ESQUERDES arriving 8.15 Am	
			Congratulatory messages received during month	App 1, 2, 3, 4
			C.P. James Lt Col Comdg 1/5 South Lancashire Regt	

A6945 Wt. W11422/M1160 350,000 12/16 D. D. & L. Forms/C./2118/14.

1.

55th Division No. 656 I.G.

Divisional Artillery.
164th Infantry Brigade.
165th Infantry Brigade.
166th Infantry Brigade.

There has lately been great improvement in the daily patrol reports received at Divisional Headquarters. They, in common with the intelligence and observers' reports, have reached a very satisfactory standard, and furnish daily a mass of very useful information. Reports on special operations have also been clear and concise.

Great credit is due to the Officers, N.C.Os and men responsible for rendering such reports, not only for the form and contents of them, but also in many cases for the enterprise and determination shown in obtaining the information recorded.

Such information, whether from patrols, observers, F.O.Os, Snipers, Sentries, Intelligence Officers, or any other Officers, N.C.Os or men, when clearly and accurately set down, and promptly sent in, is of great use to Brigade and Divisional Headquarters even during comparatively quiet periods of trench warfare. But during more active fighting it is simply invaluable, and may often have a direct influence on the success of operations in hand.

I hope and believe that when it comes to the turn of this Division to attack the enemy, what has been learnt and practised during the past months will not be forgotten, but that the high standard now reached will be maintained.

Enterprise and watchfulness in obtaining information, care and accuracy in recording it, promptness in sending it forward are what is required. I feel sure that I can trust all ranks, who are doing such good work now, to remember this, and that these requirements will be met.

H. S. Jeudwine

55th Division H.Q., Major General.

6th June 1917. Commanding 55th Division.

2.

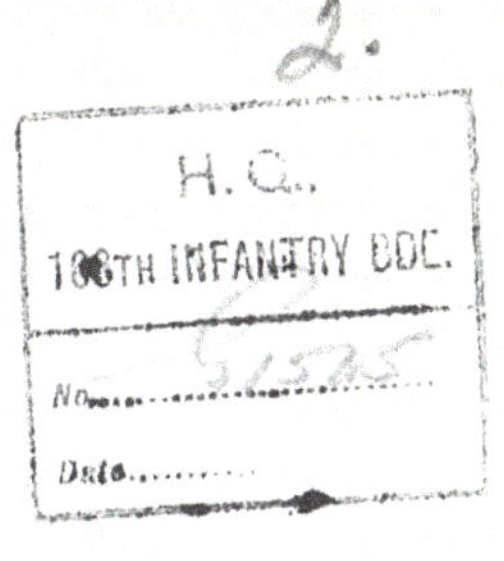

55th Division No 690 G.
****

164th Inf. Bde. Divl. Engineers.
166th Inf. Bde. 1/4th S.Lancs R.
Divl. Artillery. "Q"

The Major General Commanding has been informed that the Commander of the 19th Corps has expressed great satisfaction at the good work done recently in the line by the Divisional Artillery, Divisional Engineers and Pioneers and the 164th and 166th Infantry Brigades.

The Major General was sure that all ranks would respond as they have done to any call made on them, and this appreciation has given him great pleasure as confirming the opinion of the work which he had already formed himself.

Care has been taken in organisation and superintendence, and industry and determination shewn in performance of tasks. The spirit in which the work has been tackled by Brigadiers, Commanding Officers, Officers entrusted with special tasks, and all N. C. O's and men under them is most creditable, and an earnest of success in other tasks which may fall to the lot of the 55th Division in the future.

T. Rose Price.
Lieut-Colonel.,
General Staff, 55th Division.

55th Division H.Q.
9th June 1917.

CONFIDENTIAL. 55th Division AQC.594.

C.R.A.	166th Brigade.	Camp Adjutant.	Belgian Mission.
C.R.E.	Div.Train.	196th M.G.Coy.	Canteen Officer.
Signals.	A.D.M.S.	'G'	Theatre Officer.
Camp Commdt.	D.A.D.O.S.	O.C.Reinft.Camp.	Baths Officer,
164th Brigade.	A.P.M.	Div.School,	Div.Gas Officer.
165th Brigade.	A.D.V.S.	French Mission.	Senior Chaplain(C.ofE)
			Senior Chaplain (Non C. of E.)

The following message was received by the Major General Commanding from General Sir Herbert Plumer on the transfer of the 55th Division from the 2nd to the 5th Army :-

"To-morrow the 55th Division will be transferred, for a time at any rate, from the 2nd Army.

I am indeed sorry to lose them.

You have done such first rate work since you have all been up here, and the Division is one I should always wish to have under me.

Will you tell your Division that I am quite sure they will do anything they are asked successfully, and will you wish them all from me the very best of luck."

9/6/17.

Lieut.Colonel,
A. A. & Q. M.G. 55th Division.

11/6/1917.

4

MESSAGE.

FROM:-
Lieut-General Sir Aylmer Hunter-Weston, K.C.B., D.S.O., M.P.

TO:-
The Officers, Warrant Officers, Non-Commissioned Officers and Men of the 55th (West Lancashire) Division.

To my great regret, the development of the military situation necessitates your leaving my command.

During the time that the Division has been in my Corps, all ranks from General to Private have done splendid service to the State. You have, for these many months, held one of the most important and difficult sections of the Line, and during that period have greatly improved both the defences of the Sector and your own efficiency.

It has been a privilege and a pleasure to me to have the 55th (West Lancashire) Division under my command. You have done splendidly, and your many successful raids show that you realise the importance of care and thoroughness in preparation, and of boldness, courage and determination in action.

It is by Discipline, Thoroughness, Determination, Devotion to Duty and Self-sacrifice, on the part of each and all of us, that our victory in this great war for Justice, Right and Liberty will be attained. I much hope that it may be my good fortune to serve with you again.

AYLMER HUNTER-WESTON.

June, 1917.

LIEUT-GENERAL.

166
55 / 2.26

WO 95/2919

C O N F I D E N T I A L.

+++++++++++++++++++++++++

W A R   D I A R Y

O F

1/5th BATTALION   S O U T H   L A N C A S H I R E   REGIMENT.

FROM: -   1st   J U L Y,   1917

TO :-   31st   J U L Y,   1917.

==================

(VOLUME 30.)

Instructions regarding War Diaries and Intelligence Summaries are contained in F. S. Regs., Part II. and the Staff Manual respectively. Title pages will be prepared in manuscript.

WAR DIARY
1/5th South Lancashire Regt.
~~INTELLIGENCE SUMMARY~~
(Erase heading not required.)

Army Form C. 2118.

Place	Date	Hour	Summary of Events and Information	Remarks and references to Appendices
ESQUERDES.	1 July		Battalion settled down in new rest billets on SOUTH side of RIVER.	
		10am	Brigade Church Parade (C of E) at SETQUES	
		11am	R.C. parade at PARISH CHURCH ESQUERDES.	
	2nd / 7 July		TRAINING. — Tactical exercises, co-operation with aircraft. Brigade Schemes. Practising the attack in relation to forthcoming operations with tanks, aircraft, machine guns and Trench Mortars.	
	8 July	10am	Church Parade – C of E at SETQUES, R.C. at ESQUERDES at 11am	
	9th "		"INSTRUCTIONS for OPERATIONS" received from BRIGADE (G125/68)	
	10/14		TRAINING (Battalion and Brigade) with Special schemes and practice attack (semi-open warfare) carried out daily on BRIGADE TRAINING AREA.	
	14 "		"BATTALION SCHEME for OPERATIONS" issued to O.C. Companies, Flank Battalions and Brigade	APPENDIX. I
	15 "		Attended Brigade Church Parade near SETQUES, had dinner then marched to QUELMES to attend BRIGADE SPORTS at 2.30pm. Fine day and good attendance. We carried off a good share of the events and won the Brigade trophy (bronze statue) presented to the Colonel by Brigadier Genl. J.G. Lewis.	
	16/19 July		Proceeded with general and special training. Capt J. Shufflebotham accidentally wounded by bomb 17/7/17	

Instructions regarding War Diaries and Intelligence Summaries are contained in F. S. Regs., Part II. and the Staff Manual respectively. Title pages will be prepared in manuscript.

WAR DIARY
or
INTELLIGENCE SUMMARY.
(Erase heading not required.)

Army Form C. 2118.

Place	Date	Hour	Summary of Events and Information	Remarks and references to Appendices
	20 July	7.30am	Marched to ST-OMER entraining 10am.	
		2pm	Arrived POPERINGHE and proceeded to B camp where tea was served.	
		5/30pm	Companies moved to forward Area by platoons. A and C Coys to YPRES B and D Coys and HQ at L.4 and GOLDFISH CHATEAU. Working parties to be provided daily and Brigade carrying party to work under Lieut Plowman on dumps. Our bombardment by heavies proceeded on back areas, also wire cutting and destruction of strong points and trenches; and a harassing fire kept up on enemy's communications. DEAD END was heavily shelled before midnight	
	21st		A and C Companies moved to billets in L.4. 1 Other rank wounded. Our Bombardment continues. Enemy sent gas shells into and heavily shelled YPRES. VLAMERTINGHE also was shelled.	
	22nd		Usual activity. 2 O.R. wounded.	
	23rd		YPRES – particularly the RAMPARTS heavily shelled with gas shells. Lieut W.K. Williams and 5 O.Ranks wounded (afterwards died).	
	24th		"A" and "C" Coys moved to YPRES relieving 2 Companies of 1/4th (Pioneer) Bn South Lancs Regt. about I.7c.70.60 (Sheet 28 NW) for work under C.R.E.	

A6945 Wt. W1142/M1160 350,000 12/16 D. D. & L. Forms/C./2118/14.

Instructions regarding War Diaries and Intelligence Summaries are contained in F. S. Regs., Part II. and the Staff Manual respectively. Title pages will be prepared in manuscript.

WAR DIARY
or
~~INTELLIGENCE SUMMARY.~~
(Erase heading not required.)

Army Form C. 2118.

Place	Date	Hour	Summary of Events and Information	Remarks and references to Appendices
	24 July		Enemy active in counter battery work. RAMPARTS and DEAD END were shelled with 15 cm shells. 2 O.Ranks wounded.	
			OPERATION ORDERS and ORDERS for MOVE TO ASSEMBLY POSITIONS received from Brigade	App. II and
	25 "	2 pm to 4 pm	(Practice barrages were carried out in conjunction with Right Divl Artillery. Wire cutting registration and harassing fire were continued. Other Rank wounded.	
	26 July		Situation normal.	
	27 July		In the afternoon enemy guns active in counter battery work 5 OR. wounded (1 died later)	
	28 "		Completed equipping and arrangements for the assault. H and Coys returned from	App 13&14
	29th 30 July		16 OR wounded (2 killed). In the evening Companies moved into assembly positions Headquarters having moved to WIELTJE dugout in the afternoon. The Colonel on Brigade instructions returned to Transport Lines as one of the Two Battalion Commanders in Reserve. Major S. R. Pilkington DSO accompanying the Battalion into action as C.O. Capt D. Hibbert MC as Second in Command and Adjutant. Capt KP Aubrey, Lt S. de Pennington, Capt L Roughley and Capt H.G. Whitaker Commanding A, B, C, D Companies respectively	

36945 Wt. W11422/M1160 350,000 12/16 D. D. & L. Forms/C./2118/14.

Instructions regarding War Diaries and Intelligence Summaries are contained in F. S. Regs., Part II. and the Staff Manual respectively. Title pages will be prepared in manuscript.

WAR DIARY

~~or INTELLIGENCE~~ SUMMARY.

(*Erase heading not required.*)

Army Form C. 2118.

Place	Date	Hour	Summary of Events and Information	Remarks and references to Appendices
WIELTJE	31 July	am 3.50	Attack launched. Battalion was on the Right of the Brigade front with the LIVERPOOL SCOTTISH on its left. Objective The BLACK LINE. When the men formed up, in Artillery formation, outside it was very dark and difficult to get the proper direction. This was made much more difficult by the fact that the Battalion on the Right advanced half right across our front. There was very little hostile shell fire to interfere with the advance. After crossing the BLUE LINE and getting extended the Sections got somewhat mixed but leaders down to Section Commanders showed bravery and skill and reorganised Sections as they advanced. After leaving the BLUE LINE Machine Gun fire became more and more severe. The enemy had marked spots on which to concentrate such as crossing the STEENBEEK and gaps in hedges which were everywhere well wired. The advance was made from shell hole to shell hole by Sectional Rushes. Support fire was given by Rifles and Lewis Guns until within about 200 yards of the objective when Machine Gun fire from SPREE FARM.	

WAR DIARY

~~INTELLIGENCE~~ ~~SUMMARY~~.

(*Erase heading not required.*)

Army Form C. 2118.

Instructions regarding War Diaries and Intelligence Summaries are contained in F. S. Regs., Part II. and the Staff Manual respectively. Title pages will be prepared in manuscript.

Place	Date	Hour	Summary of Events and Information	Remarks and references to Appendices
			and CAPRICORN TRENCH to NORTH of SPREE FARM held our men up. We had the help of two tanks, one of which crushed down the wire in front of CAPRICORN and then dealt with the Trench itself, and the other went past SPREE FARM and up to POND FARM, silenced the M.G. and enabled the men to reach and take the Trench which by that time was empty except for men who were taken in dugouts.	
			Consolidation was immediately begun but owing to enemy aircraft flying low over trench giving the position away, it was impossible to carry out the Strong Point where intended. Lewis Guns were sent forward into CAPRICORN SUPPORT on either side of the road, and touch was established on both flanks.	
			Casualties – 2/Lieut S.H. FIELD was killed whilst leading his platoon, 2/Lieutenants H.R. SWEENEY, H.F. FALLON, S.H. LORD, R.G. ALLEN & W.B. BAMBER were wounded during the attack. 2/Lieut J.H. Beach is missing and believed to be killed. At midnight our casualties were 1 Officer 27 OR killed, 5 Officers 133 ORs wounded 1 Officer 11 ORs missing. But the day had gone well all objectives secured.	

A6945/ Wt. W11422/M1160 350,000 12/16 D. D. & L. Forms/C./2118/14.

E.P. [illegible] Lieut Colonel
Cmdg 1/5 South Lancashire Regt.

APP I

Secret

O./1.

S C H E M E F O R O P E R A T I O N S.

B Y

Lieut. Colonel C.P. James, D.S.O., Commanding
1/5th Bn. SOUTH LANCASHIRE REGIMENT.

C O N T E N T S.

ACKNOWLEDGE.

D Nisbett ....Captain

14th July, 1917. Adjutant 1/5th SOUTH LANCASHIRE REGIMENT.

COPIES TO :-

Nº 1. 166 Infantry Brigade.
2. Battalion on Right.
3. Battalion on Left.
4. Commanding Officer.
5. Second in Command.
6. Adjutant.
7. O.C. "A" Company.
8. " "B" "
9. " "C" "
10. " "D" "
11. Assistant Adjutant.
12. Transport Officer.
13. Medical Officer.
14. Intelligence Officer.
15. Signalling Officer.
16. Quartermaster.
17. Brigade Liaison Officer.
18. Brigade Carrying Officer.
19.)
20.) WAR DIARY.

COPY Nº : ......

INSTRUCTIONS FOR OPERATIONS.

1. The Fifth Army will attack on a wide front on a day to be known as "Z" day. II Corps on Right, XVIII Corps on Left of XIX Corps. 15th Division on Right, 39th Division on Left of 55th Division. Artillery will work under Corps scheme.

2. 55th Division will attack with 165 Brigade on Right, Left Blue Line Battalion , Left Black Line Battalion , 166 Brigade on Left. These 2 Brigades will each secure Blue and Black Lines. 164 Brigade will pass through them and secure Green and Purple Lines. 116 Brigade will be on Left of 166 Brigade. 166 Brigade will attack with 1/5th Bn. Kings Own R.L.R. on Right, 1/5th Bn. Loyal North Lancs. Regt., on Left, and secure Blue Line. 1/5th Bn. South Lancs. Regt., will pass through 1/5th Kings Own R.L.R., and 1/10th Liverpool Scottish will pass through 1/5th Loyal N. Lancs., and secure Black Line.

3. Zero and time of Synchronisation at Battalion Headquarters, will be notified later.

4. For a period of 3 to 4 days on returning to the Line, the Battalion will be at (L.4.) GOLD FISH CHATEAU, with 10th Liverpool Scottish holding the WIELTJE SECTOR, and two remaining Battalions in Camp, West of YPRES.
During this period all Companies will:-
(1) Complete their preparations.
(2) Reconnoitre assembly positions and tracks.
(3) Study enemy front.
(4) Take compass bearings to definite landmarks.

5. Two to three days before Zero, 1/10th Liverpool Scottish, and 1/5th South Lancs. Regt., will be relieved by 1/5th Kings Own R.L.R. and 1/5th Loyal North Lancs. Regt., and will go back to camps West of YPRES, where issue of all extra articles to be carried by the men will be completed.

6. On night X/Y, Battalion will return to (L.4.) GOLD FISH CHATEAU.

7. On "Y" day, movement of all kinds must be restricted to an absolute minimum. All ranks will be told of the imperative necessity for complying with this order.

8. On night Y/Z Battalion moves into Assembly Trenches in accordance with Map Nº 1.

ATTACK.

9. Brigade and Battalion's 2 Company Boundaries as well as Objectives are shewn on Map 2.

10. Brigade will move forward to assault in two lines of two Battalions.
(a) 1st Line will move out at Zero from the British Trenches and take first objective, viz :-

CALIFORNIA, CALL, CAMBRIA TRENCHES.
" " " SUPPORT.
" " " RESERVE.

and consolidate on Blue Line.

(b) 2nd Line will move forward and pass through Blue Line at Zero + 71 minutes and take Second Objective.

CAPRICORN TRENCH,
" SUPPORT,

and consolidate on Black Line.

If they have not already done so, 1/10th Liverpool Scottish will push forward from Black Line at Zero + 200 minutes and occupy CANVAS and CAPITAL trenches and consolidate on green dotted line to conform to action of Left Division.

11. Battalion will attack on two Company Frontage
10 Yards between Lines of Waves
40 Yards between Waves and Companies.
Men extended to 8 yards.
From Right to Left Companies will be as follows :-

1st Line	B.	D.
2nd Line	C	A.

Battalion Headquarters will move behind last wave and establish 1st Forward Command Post at C.23.d.45.60. When Black Line is consolidated Battalion Headquarters will again move forward and establish 2nd Forward Command Post at C.24.a.40.55.

12. Mopping Up.

2nd Line Companies will each provide 1 platoon of Moppers Up under an officer to follow the Leading Wave and mop up CAPRICORN TRENCH.

2nd Line Companies will each drop one platoon under an officer to follow the Battalion and deal with any buildings or Strong Points where the enemy may still be active.

One Stokes Mortar will be attached to each of these platoons.

13. Two Machine Guns will follow behind the Centre of the last Wave; These guns are available to assist in demobilising any German Artillery as well as to repel Counter-Attacks.

14. Companies will re-organise and consolidate at the earliest moment and will be prepared to move forward from the Black Line. To this end every opportunity of studying the ground must be taken and bearings of all prominent landmarks obtained.

15. Strong Points will be constructed at :-

Sub Right Sector.	C. 18. d. 45.00. C. 24. b. 50.80.
Sub Left Sector.	C. 18. d. 30.25. C. 18. d. 15.55.

R. E. under Divisional orders will construct a Strong Point, at C. 24. d. 90.60. On completion this will be garrisoned by 1/5th Bn. Kings Own R. L. Regt.

16. Posts will be pushed well forward towards CAPRICORN KEEP and the high ground South of POND FARM.

17. **Protection.** Officers and N.C.O's are reminded of the importance of safeguarding their flanks. Every effort must be made to maintain touch with troops on Right and Left, but should connection be lost, patrols or picquets must be at once pushed out; this applies to sections, platoons etc. quite as much as to Battalions. In a similar fashion steps must be taken to keep ground in front of positions occupied, under observation.

18. The possibility of the enemy having guns between Blue and Black Lines, and between Black and Green should be realised. Patrols, preferably with Lewis Guns, should be pushed out to prevent the guns being served (see para. 14) in addition to the usual posts with Lewis Guns.

19. Details of Artillery Barrage are not yet available. Probably it will open at ZERO on Front Line and move forward at plus 6 at a rate of 100 yards in 4 minutes.

20. Machine Gun Barrage will be placed on area between Blue and Black Lines, and, after capture of former on Black Line till advance from Blue Line begins, and so on.

21. Battalion Dumps will be pushed forward and direction boards fixed.

22. Each Battalion will draw name boards for hostile trenches and will affix them.

23. All Officers will carry

(a) A new edition of the 1/10.000 Trench Map (Portions of ST. JULIEN and ZONNEBEKE sheets combined). These will be issued later.
(b) 1/10.000 Barrage Map. (To be issued later).
(c) A message form with map on back will also be issued and carried by Officers and N.C.O's.

24. Contact Aeroplanes will fly over at hours to be notified.

25. S.O.S. Signal will be notified later.

Thislett .... Captain

Adjutant 1/5th Bn. SOUTH LANCASHIRE REGIMENT.

14th July, 1917.

APPENDIX I.

ADMINISTRATIVE DETAILS.

1. DRESS AND EQUIPMENT.

Will be as laid down in S.S. 135 Section XXXI with the following exceptions :-

(a) Entrenching tool and carrier will not be carried by men who go into action with heavy pick or shovel.

(b) Pack instead of haversack on the back.

(c) S. A. A. 120 rounds instead of 170. S.A.A. to be carried in bandoliers inside pouches and when used slung across body.

(d) Rations and Water. Two days Iron Rations and a second waterbottle (filled with weakly made tea without milk or sugar) will be carried in the pack.

(e) Picks and Shovels. 75 per cent of strength will carry big tools in proportion of 3 Shovels to 1 pick.

(f) Extra pair socks.

(g) Wire cutters, Large, 10 - 1st wave D Company.
10 - 1st wave B Company.

(h) Very Pistols 1" and cartridge will be used for S.O.S. Signals.

(i) Surplus kits will be stored in sandbags; greatcoats being tied in bundles.

(j) Arrangements are being made for new Divisional Store in POPERINGHE to take surplus kits. Location will be issued later.

2. DRINKING WATER SUPPLY.

(a) In addition to reserves of water at Dumps, 4 - 200 gallons reservoirs are available on Line LIVERPOOL TRENCH - CONGREVE WALK.

(b) A supply of water will be brought up for consumption during Y/Z night so that waterbottles need not be used.

(c) Men will be given some hot tea and rum shortly before ZERO.

(d) The Medical Officer is responsible for testing all sources of drinking water, which must be labelled (a) DRINKABLE or (b) POISONOUS.

(e) Companies must endeavour to send back to Dumps all empty water-tins as the supply of these is limited.

3. CARRYING PARTIES.

Battalion Carrying Parties will be supplied as under :-

(a) Brigade, 1 Officer and 2 Sections.
(Total of not less than 20 men.)

(b) M. G. C. 8 men.

(c) T. M. B. 10 men.

(d) Battalion 20 men under Sergeant Potter.

(a) (1). Brigade Carrying party to be organised in 4 squads, each consisting of personnel supplied by one Battalion. (It will work under the Staff Captain).

(2) Parties to assemble in corridor between WIELTJES dugouts and the AID POST on Y/Z night at an hour to be notified later. Parties from rear Battalions entering corridor through the AID POST, parties from front Battalions through No 6 entrance.

(3) At ZERO all parties will come out as rapidly as possible into Junction with ADMIRALS TRENCH and MONMOUTH TRENCH and await orders; Officers reporting to the Staff Captain.

(4) Parties will probably be used for replenishing the Battalion Dumps, each squad carrying to its own Battalion Dump; later it will be used for establishing Advanced Battalion Dumps.

(5) Parties to know all routes to and from the Brigade Dumps to each Battalion Dump, and will reconnâitre forward routes to Advanced Battalion Dumps.

(6) Parties will be rationed by Brigade H.Q. after X/Y night.

(b) and (c). These parties will work entirely under the M. G. C. and T. M. B.

(d) This party will move behind last wave carrying wire which will be dumped at Battalion Advanced Dump, junction of CAPTAIN AVENUE and CAPRICORN TRENCH. They will then return for further loads of Ammunition and Stores.
Companies will draw from Battalion Advanced Dump.

YUKON PACKS will be allotted as follows:-

Brigade Carrying Party:	5th R. Lanc. R.	3
	10th L'Pool. R.	2
	5th S. Lan. R.	2
	5th N. Lan. R.	3
		10.
Battalions each		8
M. G. C.		8
T. M. B.		10.

4. TRANSPORT.

(a) Transport Lines will be located near VLAMERTINGHE. Transport will probably move to these lines about "X" or "Y" day.

(b) Staff Captain will inform Brigade Transport Officer where stores are to be sent.

In the event of the above information not reaching Brigade Transport Officer by 6 p.m., he will bring up Pack Sections to ST. JEAN where he will receive orders as to guides and dumps.

(c) Battalion Pack Sections on returning will report to Brigade Bombing Officer at Brigade Dump, Junction LONE STREET with CONGREVE WALK and will load ammunition, R.E. Stores etc, for a second journey to Battalion or Advanced Brigade Dumps.

(d) Spare men must accompany drivers to load and unload, and to replace casualties.

5. ENEMY RUSES. Attention is drawn to S.S. 163 and S.S. 135 para. XXVIII with reference to Booby Traps, Landmines, Bombs etc.

6. PRISONERS. Attention is drawn to S.S. 135 para. XXVI.

7. NOTICE BOARDS. IN and OUT trenches are being marked with notice boards. Notice boards with names of trenches etc., in German lines will be sent to Battalion Dumps. They are to be fixed as early as possible. Notice Boards marked "BOMBS", COY. H.Q." etc., will be sent to Battalion Dumps.

8. LOCATION OF BATTLE DUMPS.

DUMPS.	GRENADES S.A.A. etc.	R.E. MATERIAL.	REMARKS.
Brigade Dumps.	Nr. junction LONE Street with CONGREVE WALK.	—	—
Battalion Dumps:-			
5th S. Lan. R.	C.28.b.6.1.	C.28.b.6.4.	Junction of WARWICK TRENCH with LONE TRENCH.
5th R. Lanc. R.	C.28.b.7.3.	C.28.b.7.5.	

(a) All Grenades in Brigade and Battalion Dumps will be detonated.
(b) No written orders or demands for Stores from Brigade Dumps will be required.

9. STORES TO BE MAINTAINED AT BRIGADE AND EACH BATTALION DUMP.

	Brigade Dump.	Battalion Dump.
Grenades.		
Nº 5 Mills.	6000	2000
"P" Grenades.	200	100
Rifle Grenades.		
Nº 23 Mills or Nº 20.	2000	1:000
Very Lights.		
1"	800	200
1 1/2 inch.	200	50
Trench Mortar Ammunition.		
3"	2000	—
S.O.S. Signal.	50	25.
Pistol Webley.	2000	500
S. A. A.	100000	50:000
Flares.	2000	500
Miscellaneous.		
Petrol tins, 2 gallon.	200	100
Barbed wire.	500 coils.	100 coils
	(40 - 60 yards each).	
Concertina barbed wire	250 coils.	50 coils.
Plain wire.	20 "	5 "
Screw Iron Pickets 5'	500	150
" " " 3'	1000	250
Mauls.	10	2
Sandbags	20000	5:000
Tracing Tapes	10 (50 yds) rolls)	

9. STORES. (Continued).

	Brigade Dump.	
Staples, boxes.	2	
Baby Elephants.	4	
Rolled Steel joists.	25	
Corrugated Iron Sheets.	50.	
Shovels.	400	
Picks.	200	
Wire Cutters.	50	
Hedging Gloves.	50	
Hammers.	6	
Hand saws.	5.	
Notice boards marked with names of German trenches, Coy.H.Q., S.A.A., Bomb Stores etc.	---	Battn Dump.
Bridges	22	(16 allotted L.S. (6 " S.L.

Reserve of Bridges in Brigade Dump.

APPENDIX XI.

SIGNAL COMMUNICATIONS.

The following will be the arrangements for Signal communications during the forthcoming operations.

The various methods to be employed are set out in diagrams Nos 1, 2, 3, and 4, attached.

The principles laid down in S.S. 148 will be adhered to as closely as possible.

COMMUNICATION BETWEEN BRIGADE AND BATTALIONS.

Prior to ZERO.

(i) Battalions in WIELTJE
FULLERPHONE and
ORDERLY.

(ii) Other Battalions in Brigade area by
FULLERPHONE
VISUAL and
RUNNER.

(iii) Battalions when outside Brigade area by
D.R.L.S. THROUGH DIVISION and
CYCLIST ORDERLY from BRIGADE.

ZERO onwards.

(i) Battalions in WIELTJE by
TELEPHONE and
ORDERLY.

(ii) Battalion Forward Command Posts through Brigade Forward Stations by
TELEPHONE
FULLERPHONE
POWER BUZZER and AMPLIFIER
VISUAL
RUNNERS and
PIGEONS.

(iii). Battalion Forward Command Posts to Brigade H.Q. by Contact Aeroplane shutter during Aeroplane flights. This means is only to be resorted to when all other means of communication have failed.

COMMUNICATION BETWEEN BATTALIONS AND COMPANIES.

By VISUAL and RUNNER.

LOCATION OF BRIGADE FORWARD STATIONS.

(i) Blue line Brigade Forward Station C.23.c.5.6.
(ii) Black " " " " Near RAT FARM. C.[illegible].b.

LOCATION OF BATTALION FORWARD STATIONS.

(i) Blue Line Forward Station C.23.d.45.60.
(ii) Black Line Forward Station C.24.a.40.55

MARKING OF SIGNAL STATIONS.

Every Signal Station will be marked with a triangular Blue and White board placed in a conspicuous position.

Direction boards will also be used in the vicinity of Signal Stations to indicate the way to these points.

2/Lt. Price will draw these from Battalion H.Q. at a date and time to be notified later.

LINES TO BE LAID.

The lines each unit will lay are indicated in Diagram Nº 1. No two wires are to follow the same route. Those laid by Battalions should follow roughley the centre of the Battalion advance.

Each Battalion will be provided with a minimum of 6 one man drums of cable for this purpose.

AEROPLANE CONTACT PATROL.

(i) An Aeroplane will be in position to observe from ZERO onwards.

(ii) Battalion Aeroplane Contact personnel and apparatus will go over with Battalions Forward Command Posts.

(iii) Brigade Aeroplane Contact Station will open at WIELTJE immediately after ZERO.

RUNNERS.

(i) Brigade H.Q. runners will wear two red runner bands on left fore-arm.

(ii) Runner routes to Forward Stations will be marked every 50 yards by Blue and White stakes as soon as the advance commences.

(iii) Special attention is directed to S.S. 148 page 27 (c) re "carrying of messages in right hand breast pocket".

PIGEONS.

One pigeoneer with small supply of birds will be attached from Brigade H.Q. to each Battalion. Economy in expenditure of this service is essential. These men should be attached to Battalion Forward Command Posts.

ATTACHMENT TO DIVISIONAL SIGNAL COMPANY.

Three runners will be detailed by each Battalion to report to O.C. Signals, Divisional H.Q. at a date and time to be notified later. These men are for duty at Divisional Runner posts.

ATTACHMENT TO BRIGADE SIGNAL SECTION.

Each Battalion will send personnel as under to report to Brigade Signal Officer at WIELTJE.

3 SIGNALLERS.
4 RUNNERS.

Date and time to be notified later.

REPRESENTATIVE OF BRIGADE COMMANDER AT BRIGADE FORWARD STATION.

Lieut. D.S. HAMILTON, 1/5th Loyal North Lancs Regt.

This Officer will be responsible for the proper performance of the necessary coding cyphering of messages and will decide the question of priority in any case of pressure of traffic.

REPRESENTATIVE OF BRIGADE SIGNAL OFFICER AT BRIGADE FORWARD STATION.

Sergeant S.H. BEWICKE, R.E.

CODE NAMES ETC.

New code names, calls etc., are being prepared and will be communicated later.

SIGNAL CONTACT WITH 164 INF. BDE. WHEN ADVANCING.

All Signal Stations of 166 Infantry Brigade will be prepared where possible to receive and pass on messages from 164 Infantry Brigade or any of its units.

Blue Line Brigade Forward Station will keep Signal Contact with 164 Infantry Brigade Advanced H.Q. on Black Line.

Black Line Brigade Forward Station will keep Signal Contact with 164 Infantry Brigade Forward Station on Green Line.

APPENDIX 2.

DIAGRAM No 1
LINES

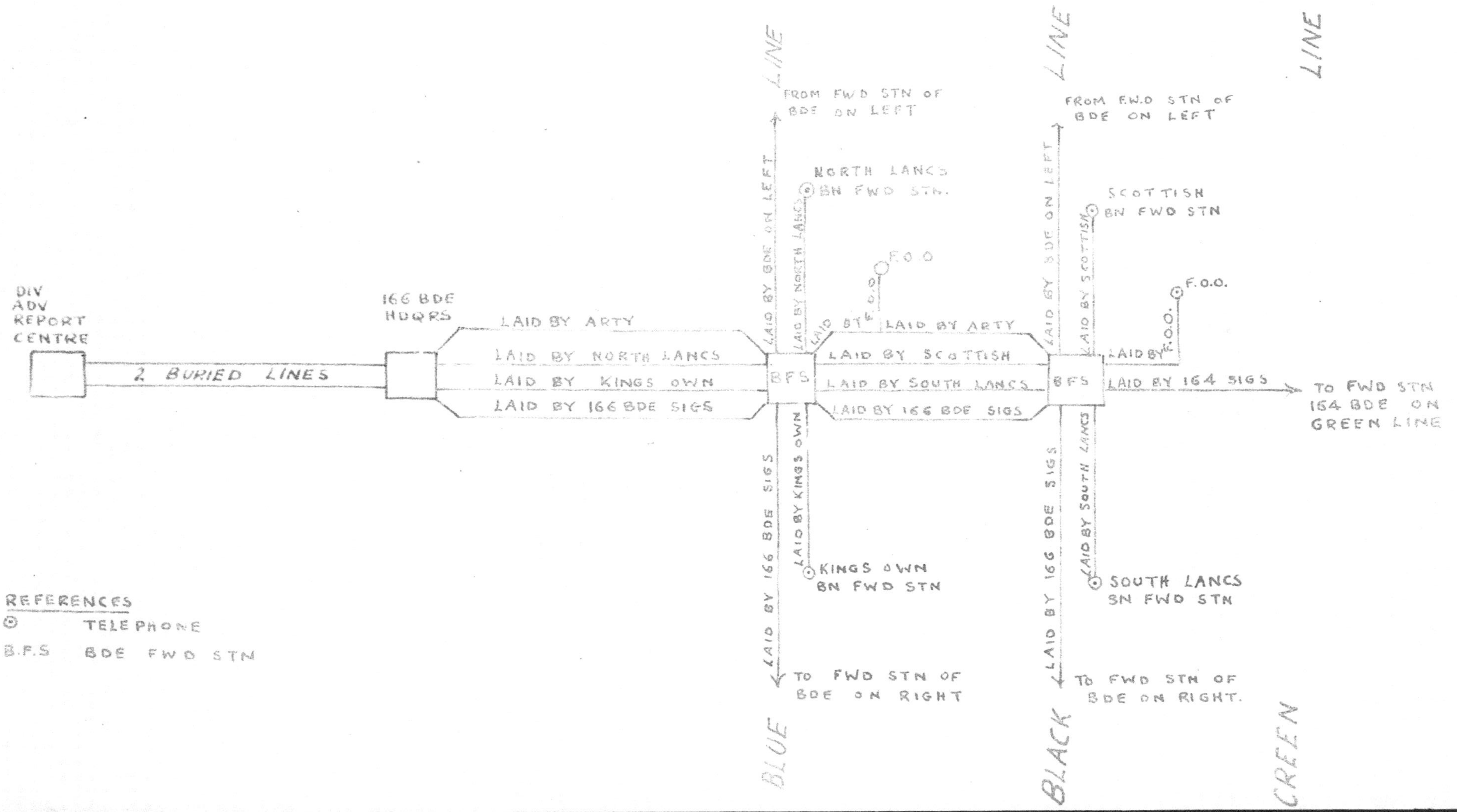

DIV ADV REPORT CENTRE

2 BURIED LINES

166 BDE HDQRS

LAID BY ARTY

LAID BY NORTH LANCS

LAID BY KINGS OWN

LAID BY 166 BDE SIGS

BFS

LAID BY BDE ON LEFT

FROM FWD STN OF BDE ON LEFT

LAID BY NORTH LANCS

NORTH LANCS BN FWD STN.

LAID BY F.O.O

F.O.O

LAID BY 166 BDE SIGS

TO FWD STN OF BDE ON RIGHT

LAID BY KINGS OWN

KINGS OWN BN FWD STN

BLUE LINE

LAID BY ARTY

LAID BY SCOTTISH

LAID BY SOUTH LANCS

LAID BY 166 BDE SIGS

BFS

LAID BY BDE ON LEFT

FROM FWD STN OF BDE ON LEFT

LAID BY SCOTTISH

SCOTTISH BN FWD STN

LAID BY F.O.O.

F.O.O.

LAID BY 166 BDE SIGS

TO FWD STN OF BDE ON RIGHT.

LAID BY SOUTH LANCS

SOUTH LANCS BN FWD STN

BLACK LINE

LAID BY 164 SIGS

TO FWD STN 164 BDE ON GREEN LINE

GREEN LINE

REFERENCES

⊙ TELEPHONE

B.F.S BDE FWD STN

APPENDIX 2

DIAGRAM No 2
WIRELESS

REFERENCES
W — WIRELESS STN
A — AMPLIFER
⊕ — POWER BUZZER
B.F.S — BDGE. FWD STN

BLUE LINE
BLACK LINE
GREEN LINE

NORTH LANCS BN FWD STN
SCOTTISH BN FWD STN
KINGS OWN BN FWD STN
SOUTH LANCS BN FWD STN

DIV ADV REPORT CENTRE W

W ⊕ A POTIJZE

166 BDE H.Q. ⊕ A

⊕ A 165 BDE. H.Q.

B.F.S ⊕ A

B.F.S ⊕ A

164 B.F.S. ⊕ A

APPENDIX 2

DIAGRAM Nº 3
VISUAL

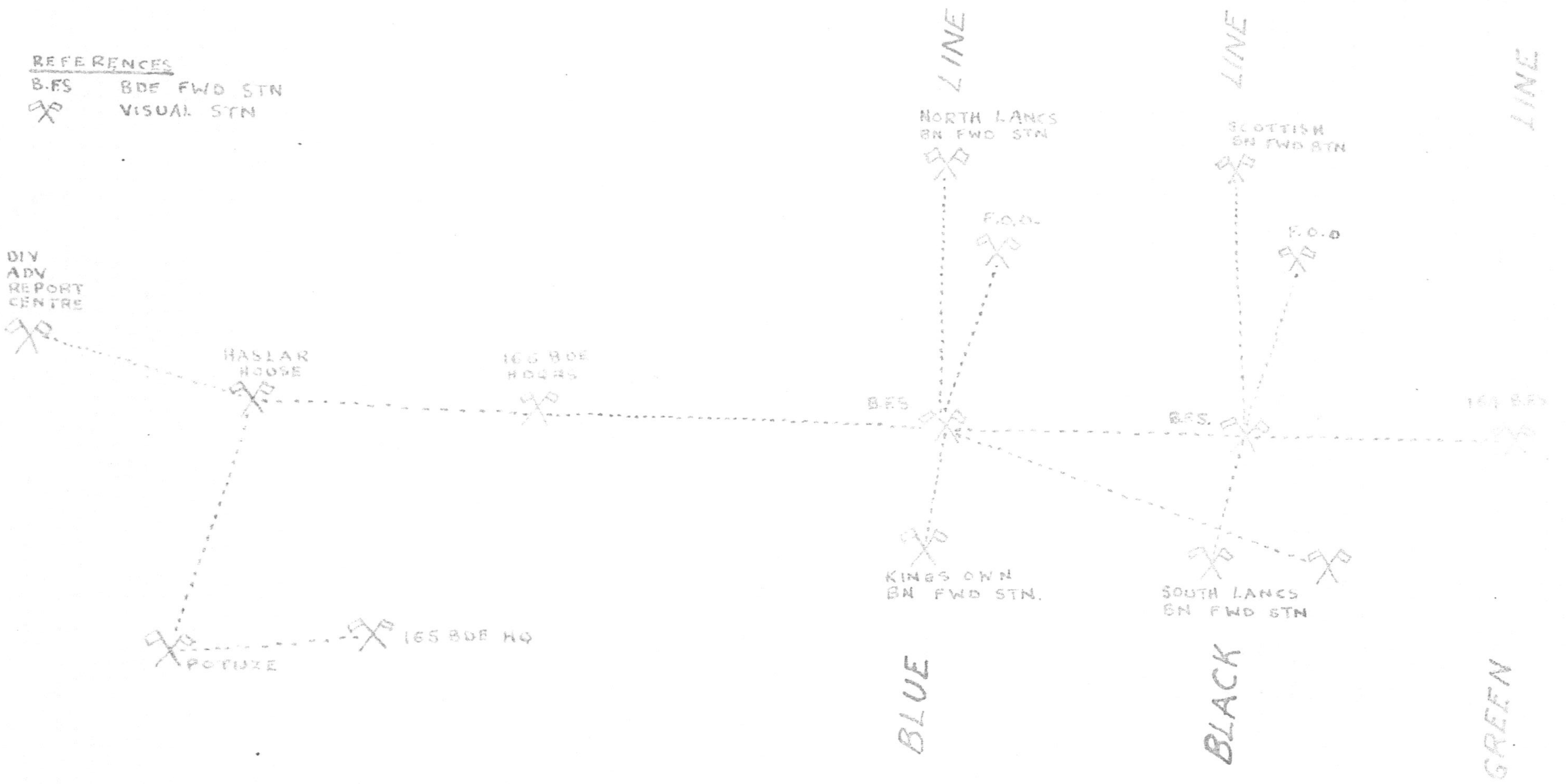

REFERENCES
B.F.S BDE FWD STN
VISUAL STN

DIV ADV REPORT CENTRE
HASLAR HOUSE
165 BDE HQRS
POTIJZE
165 BDE HQ
B.F.S
NORTH LANCS BN FWD STN
F.O.O.
KINGS OWN BN FWD STN.
B.F.S.
SCOTTISH BN FWD STN
F.O.O
SOUTH LANCS BN FWD STN
BLUE LINE
BLACK LINE
GREEN LINE

APPENDIX 2

DIAGRAM No 4
— RUNNERS —

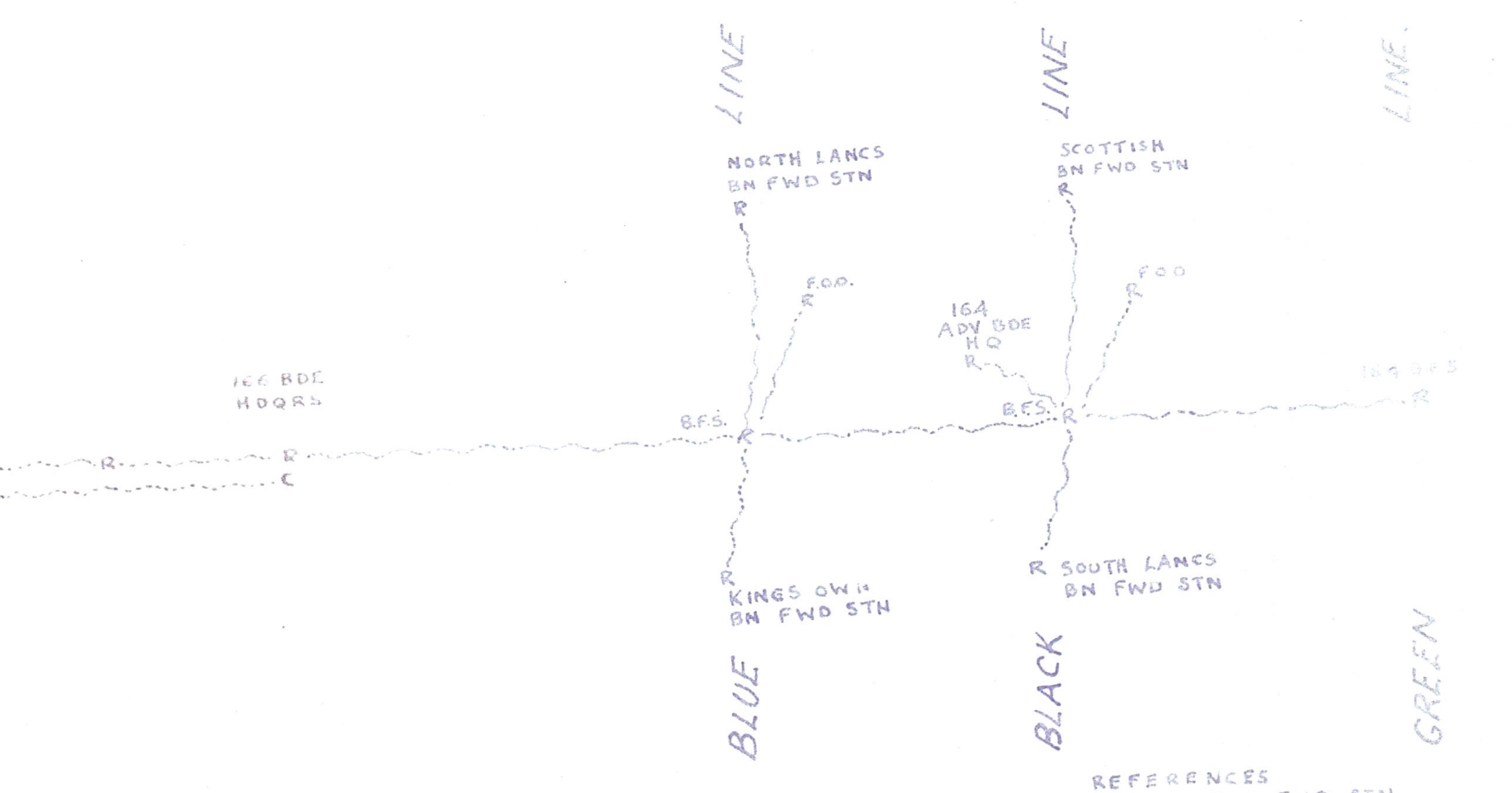

APPENDIX III.

TRAFFIC CONTROL WIELTJE.

As from 9 p.m. Y/Z night to ZERO the following traffic rules will apply to all persons using WIELTJE DUGOUTS – East of Nº 7 dugout.

ENTRANCE.

1. A. "IN" Traffic for:-

166 Brigade H.Q.	2, 7.
166 M. G. C. "	2.
166 T. M. B.	9.
5th N. Lan. R.	1.
10th L'Pool R.	1
5th S. Lan. R.	1.
5th R. Lanc. R.	1.
Artillery.	1.
164 Bde. dugout Nº	26. C.28.8.
" " " "	24, "G" shaft.

NOTE. Machine Gun team of C.28.6. will use Nº 7 as an IN and OUT way to the emplacement.

B. "OUT" Traffic.

Remaining exits will be used, Nº 5 in case of emergency only.

2. ALL Traffic will move in an Easterly Direction.

3. With the exception of the passage to "G" shaft allotted to 166 T.M.B. passages are not to be blocked.

4. Forward traffic personnel of Divisional H.Q., Divisional Artillery and 164 Infantry Bde., proceeding to dugouts Nº s. 28, 33, and 26 will have the right of way through the galleries but must observe the above rules.

5. Sentries will be posted at the following pointsto ensure that the above rules are observed :-

Post.	Found by.
Entrance to Nº 12 dugout.	5th R. Lanc. R.
Bifurcation of galleries by Nº 21 dugout.	5 th N. Lan. R.

6. After 9 p.m. Y/Z night sentries on entrances and exits will be found as follows :-

5th R. Lanc. R.	10, "F" "G".
10th L'pool. R.	3. 7.
5th S. Lan. R,	1, 2, 8.
5th N. Lan. R.	C.28.8., 11, 12.
166 T. M. B.	9.

These sentries will be found from men not going forward in the attack and will remain at their posts until they receive further orders from Brigade H.Q.

Besides carrying out the duties in the Standing Orders for their posts, these sentries will ensure that the rules in paras. 1 and 2 are observed.

7. In case of urgent necessity Commanding Officers may issue written passes to enable individuals to contravene these orders. (Passes must bear an Office stamp).

APPENDIX III (Continued).

8. 5th N. Lan. R. will be responsible for the defence of WIELTJE until the above instructions come into effect; the allottemnt of Machine Guns and Trench Mortars will be as usual.

APPENDIX IV.

FORWARD MOVEMENT BY TRACKS ON Y/Z NIGHT.

1. 1/5th South Lancashire Regiment.

Blue Track to Bridge 1B - thence Blue Track LA BRIQUE and LIVERPOOL TRENCH - and across country to LONE STREET.

Map of Tracks may be seen at Battalion Headquarters.

APPENDIX V.

MEDICAL.

1. REGIMENTAL AID POSTS.

(a) Y/Z NIGHT.
Location of Regimental Aid Posts for 4 Attacking Battalions C.28.a.8.3. (BILGE TRENCH).

(b) "Z" DAY.
Advanced Regimental Aid Posts will be established by M.O near 1st Battalion Command Post to commence with, and later at 2nd Battalion Command Post.

(c) ZERO plus 6 hrs. 20 mins.
The evacuating Field Ambulance will open Forward Advanced Dressing Station at Regimental Aid Post at C.28.a.8.3. (BILGE TRENCH) relieving M.O's 1/5th R. Lanc. R., 1/5th N. Lan. R., who move to Advanced Regimental Aid Posts, relieving M.O's 1/5th S. Lan. R. & 1/10th L'Pool R. who will establish Regimental Aid Posts in rear of BLACK Line.

(d) Location of new Regimental Aid Posts to be notified to Brigade H.Q. at once by R.A.M.C. runner attached for communication purposes.

2. COLLECTING POSTS.

(a) Location C.27.d.3.1. (JUNCTION ROAD), 1 Sergeant 8 O/R. R.A.M.C. with supply of wheeled stretchers, carrying stretchers field dressings etc.

(b) ADVANCED DRESSING STATION.
Location I.1.b.9.3. (CANAL BANK) accomodation 50 stretcher cases.

(c) MAIN DRESSING STATION.
RED FARM (G.5.d.8.3.)

(d) CORPS COLLECTING STATION FOR WALKING WOUNDED.
MILL - VLAMERTINGHE (H.8.a.9.8.)

(e) CORPS REST STATION FOR SICK AND SLIGHTLY WOUNDED.
HILLHOEK (Present Divisional Rest Station).

3. COLLECTION AND EVACUATION OF WOUNDED.

(a) Forward area to Regimental Aid Posts by Regimental S.B's, and Field Ambulance Stretcher Bearers to Regimental Aid Post.

(b) Regimental Aid Posts to Collecting Posts by Field Ambulance bearers via NEW JOHN STREET - GARDEN STREET.

(c) Collecting Posts to Advanced Dressing Station. Stretcher cases by light railway which passes Advanced Dressing Station, serious cases requiring redressing will be off loaded.

(d) As advance continues, evacuation will be by wheeled stretchers from Forward Advanced Dressing Station to light railway or motor ambulance.

4. WALKING WOUNDED.

(i) Will be directed via GARDEN STREET to Collecting Post ~~at~~ ST. Jean. Thence ST. JEAN ROAD - Infantry Track No 5 to I.3.a.2.5. (old drying-room) where a tea kitchen is established. Equipment (less box respirators) will be dumped here.

(ii) Route to VLAMERTINGHE will be clearly marked by notice boards.

(iii) Horsed ambulances and charabancs will mott wounded as far as forward as possible.

5. Field Ambulance Stretcher Bearers.

(i) Zero plus 30 minutes - 1 Officer 80 bearers will arrive at present Brigade front to assist Regimental stretcher bearers and in clearing Regimental Aid Posts.

(ii) Zero plus 6 hours 50 minutes - 1 Officer 80 bearers will arrive at BLACK line to assist 164 Brigade.

(iii) All bearers moving Eastward must carry a stretcher.

(iv) Any stretchers salved or not required will be dumped at the nearest Collecting Post.

6. COMMUNICATION.

At each Regimental Aid Post will be stationed 1 N.C.O. and 4 men of the Field Ambulance. They will be used primarily as runners between Regimental Aid Posts and Advanced Dressing Station. They may also be used as bearers but not in front of Regimental Aid Posts.

APPENDIX VI.

STRAGGLER POSTS.

1. Brigade Straggler Posts will be found as follows:-

1/5th S. Lan. R. - Head of LONE STREET - C.28.c.15.32.
1/10th L'Pool R. - " " GARDEN " - C.27.d.55.75.

Each post will consist of 3 Regimental Police.

2. DUTIES OF POSTS.

(a) To collect all armed or unarmed stragglers seen moving through the Brigade Line. One policeman to conduct them in formed bodies of 10 to Divisional Stragglers Post on CANAL I.1.b.6.4., where they will be handed over to Sergeant M.M.P.

(b) To know Posts on Right and Left.
" " nearest R.A.M.C. Collecting Post.
" " position of Advanced Prisoners of War Cage.
" direct wounded men and prisoner escorts.

3. DIVISIONAL STRAGGLER POSTS to be found as follows :-

Nº of Post.	Position.	O.R.	Remarks.
1.	CANAL BRIDGE (I.1.b.3.4.)	3.	1/5th N. Lan. R. from Regimental Police.

Report to A.P.M. at Divisional H.Q. noon "X" day, and will remain attached during period Division is engaged.

4. DIVISIONAL STRAGGLERS COLLECTING STATION.

(a) In row of small cottages at H.8.a.2.9. on the VLAMERTINGHE - POPERINGHE Main Road.

(b) Stragglers will be equipped as fully as possible, given a hot meal, and returned under escort to their 1st Line Transport, and receipt obtained.

APPENDIX VII.

LIAISON OFFICERS ETC.

The following officers have been selected for Liaison Officers and Understudies :-

	Divisional Liaison Officer.	-	Captain DICKINSON, 5th S. Lan. R.
+	Brigade on Right	-	2/Lt. E.W.W. ARNOLD. 5th S. Lan. R.
+	Brigade on Left	-	Lt. R.E. AINSWORTH, 10th L'pool R.
+	Liaison Officers for Brigade.	-	2/Lt. MAC DONALD, 5th R. Lanc. R. 2/Lt. FERGUSON, 10th L'Pool R. 2/Lt. (?) (To be notified later). 5th S. Lan. R. 2/Lt. JONES, 5th N. Lan. R.
+	Brigade Forward Station Officer	-	2/Lt. A.S. HAMILTON, 5th N. Lan. R.
	Understudy to Brigade Major.	-	Lt. AIMLE, 10th L'Pool. R.
	Understudy to Staff Captain	-	Lt. DAVEY, 10th L'Pool. R.
	Understudy to Brigade Bombing Officer	-	Lt. BOYDSTONES, 5th R. Lanc. R.
	Understudy to Brigade Signal Officer	-	Lt. HARGREAVES, 5th S. Lan. R.
	Understudy to Brigade Intelligence Officer	-	2/Lt. Ingham, 5th S. Lan. R.

\+ Report to Brigade Headquarters concerned at ZERO minus 120.

APPENDIX VII (Continued)

LIAISON POINTS.

BRIGADE ON RIGHT - 165th Infantry Brigade.

1. C.29.a.4.7. (where boundary crosses German front Line.)
2. Brigade boundary on Reserve Line. (C.23.c.99.00.)
3. C.23.d.60.30.
4. C.24.a.60.05.
5. BANK FARM (C.24.b.35.55.)

INTER BATTALION.

10. Inter Battalion boundary CALL SUPPORT.
11. " " " CALL RESERVE.
12. " " " BLUE Line.
13. Where German wire crosses Track at C.23.b.85.85.
14. South end of Pond C.18.c.7.3.

Battalions will detail special parties to get into touch at those liaison points as under:-

1.)
2.) 1/5th R. Lanc. R.
3.

4.) 1/5th S. Lan R.
5.)

10, 11, 12, 13, 14 - Blue and Black Line Battalions concerned.

MAP No 1.

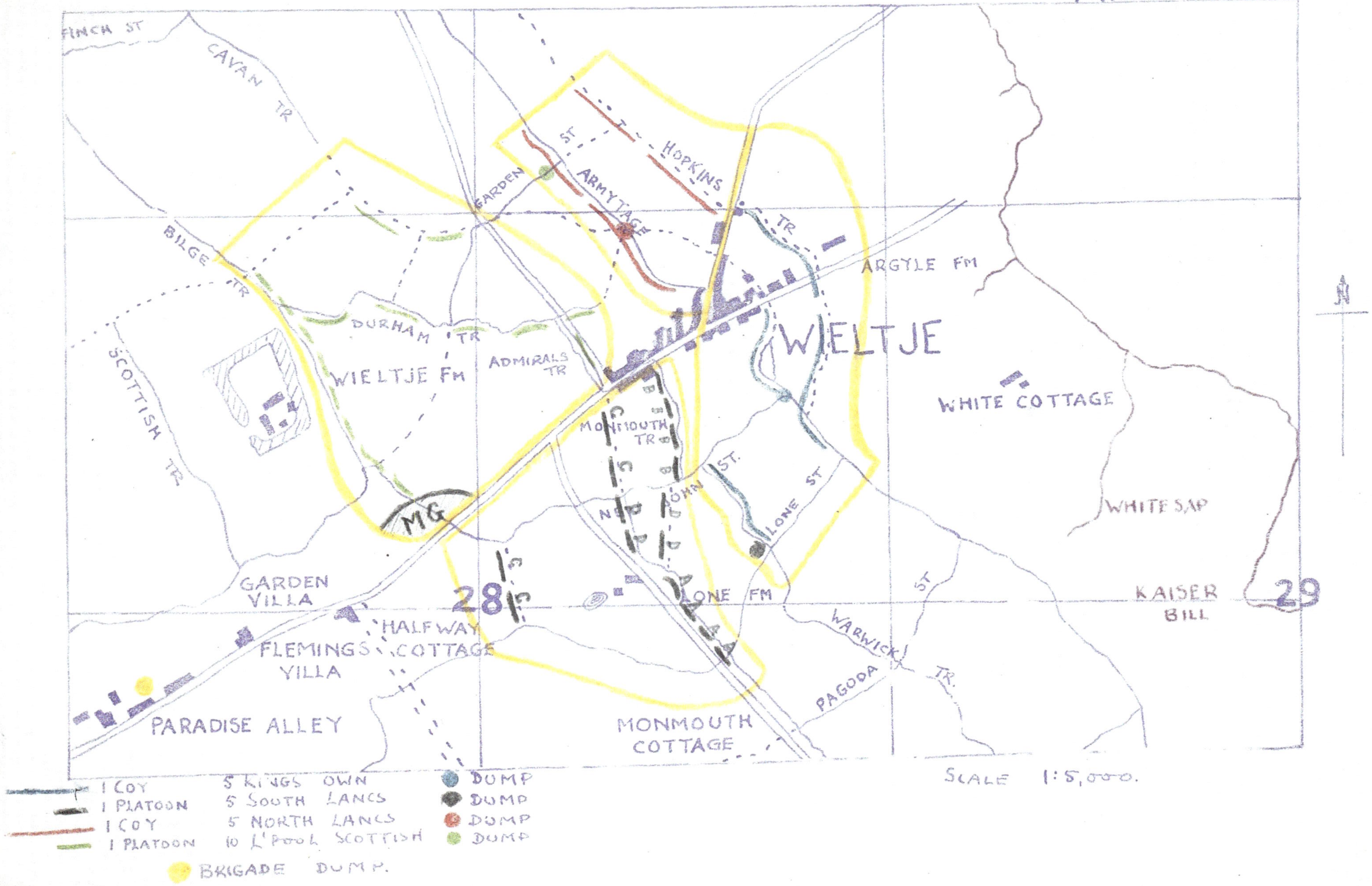

N

FINCH ST
CAVAN TR
BILGE TR
SCOTTISH TR
GARDEN ST
ARMYTAGE
HOPKINS TR
DURHAM TR
ADMIRALS TR
WIELTJE FM
WIELTJE
ARGYLE FM
WHITE COTTAGE
WHITE SAP
MONMOUTH TR
JOHN ST.
LONE ST
LONE FM
MG
GARDEN VILLA
HALFWAY COTTAGE
FLEMINGS VILLA
PARADISE ALLEY
MONMOUTH COTTAGE
PAGODA
WARWICK TR.
ST
KAISER BILL
28
29

SCALE 1:5,000.

1 COY	5 KINGS OWN	DUMP
1 PLATOON	5 SOUTH LANCS	DUMP
1 COY	5 NORTH LANCS	DUMP
1 PLATOON	10 L'POOL SCOTTISH	DUMP

BRIGADE DUMP.

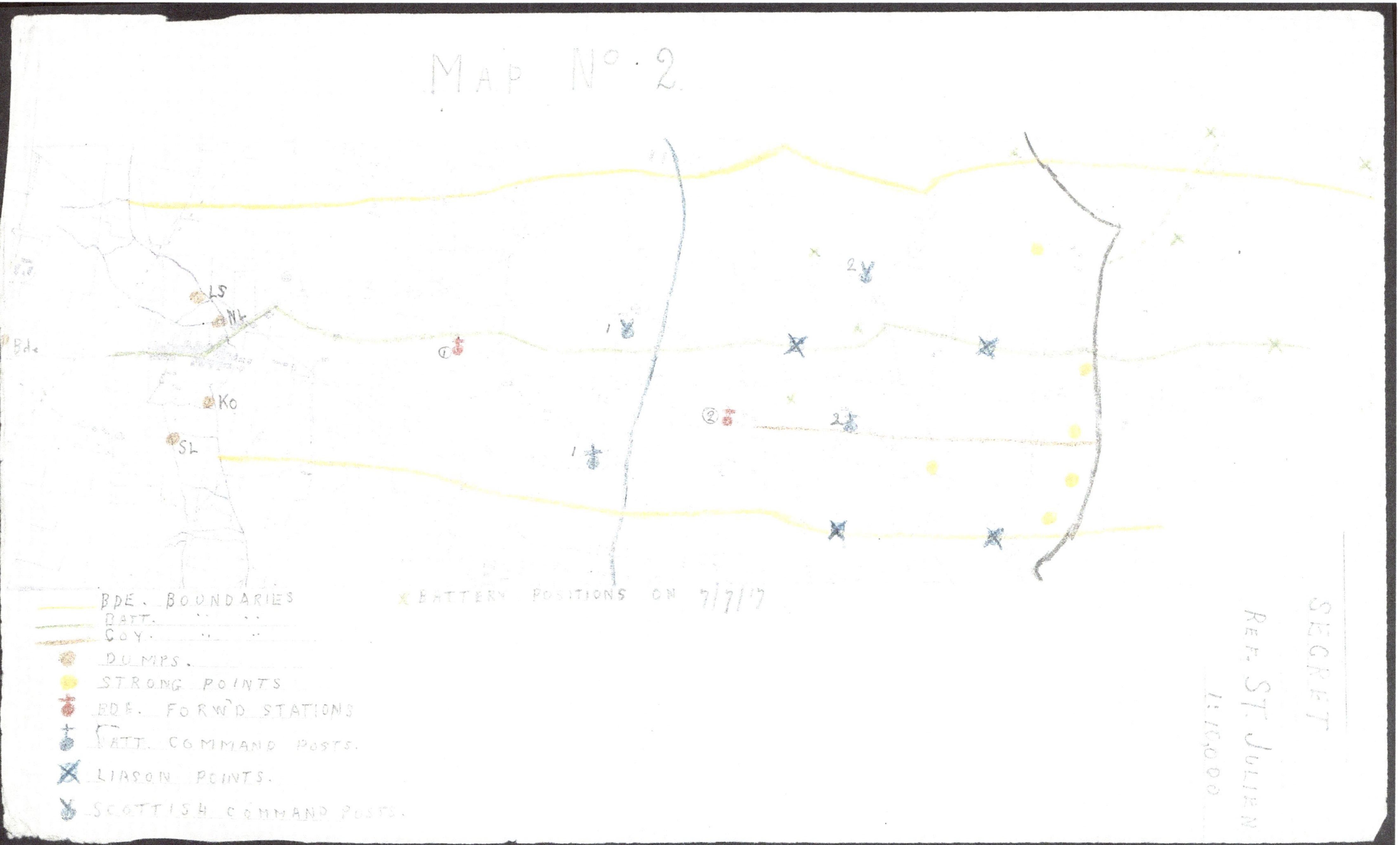

MAP No. 2

SECRET

REF. ST. JULIEN 1:10,000

LS

NL

Bde

KO

SL

1

2

× BATTERY POSITIONS ON 7/7/17

BDE. BOUNDARIES

BATT. " "

COY. " "

DUMPS.

STRONG POINTS

BDE. FORW'D STATIONS

BATT. COMMAND POSTS.

LIASON POINTS.

SCOTTISH COMMAND POSTS.

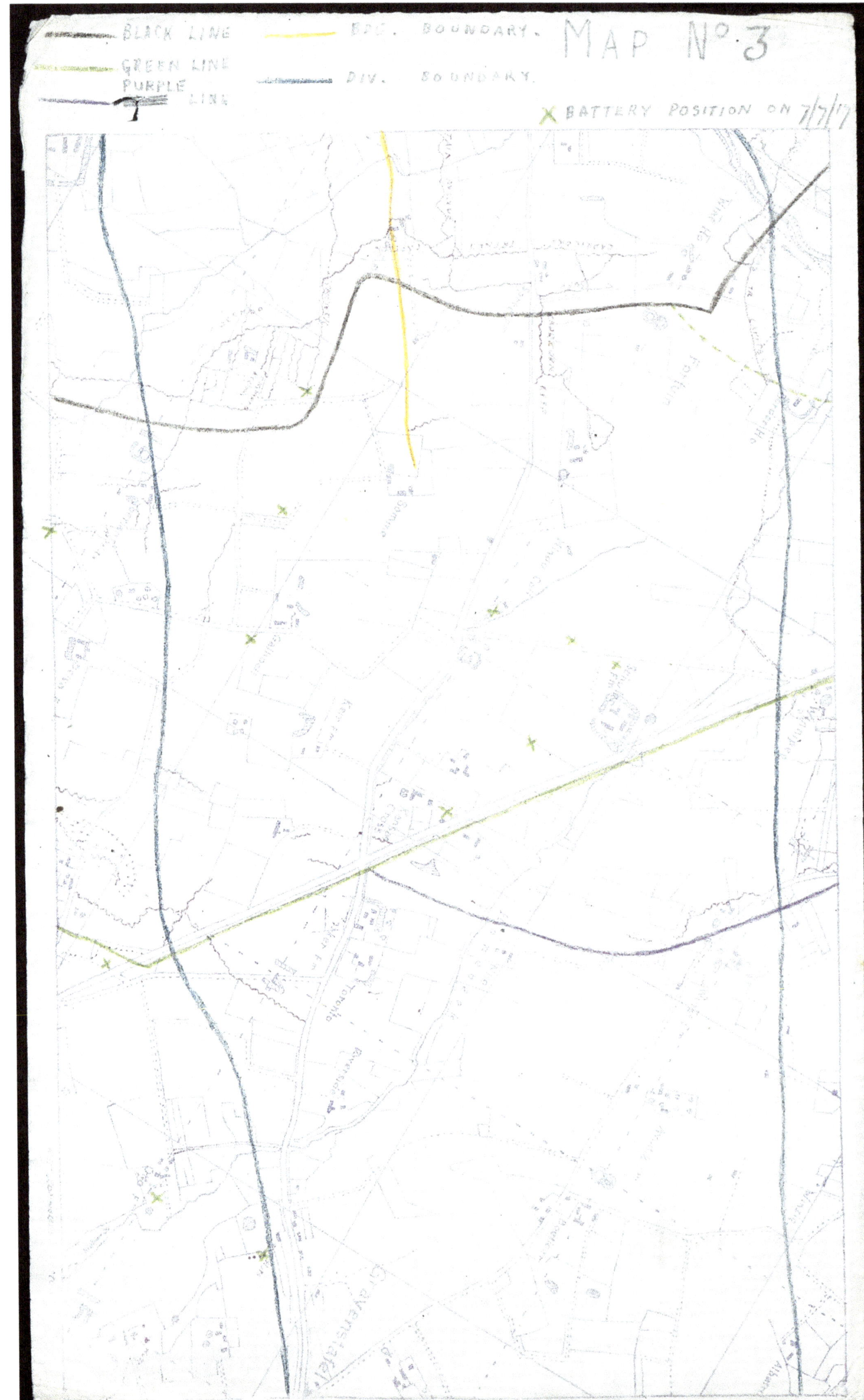
MAP No. 3
BLACK LINE
GREEN LINE
PURPLE LINE
BDE. BOUNDARY.
DIV. BOUNDARY.
X BATTERY POSITION ON 7/7/17

X/Y NIGHT.

Serial No.	Unit.	Location.	Destination.	Route.	Distance.	Remarks.
1.	5th N.Lan.R. (less 1 Coy)	Left sub-sector WIELTJE Section.	Assembly trenches. Map "A".			LIVERPOOL TRENCH to be clear by 10.30.pm.
2.	5th R.Lanc.R. (less 1 Coy)	Right sub-sector. WIELTJE Section.	- do -			CONGREVE WALK to be clear by 10.30.pm.
3.	1 Company 5th R.Lanc.R.	DERBY CAMP.	- do -	No.1 Track -H.12.b.4.7. - thence Road junction I.1.c.25.25.-SALVATION CORNER- I.1.b.15.05. - CANAL Track - No. 1 Bridge - No.6 Track - LIVERPOOL TRENCH.	8900^x	By platoons at 200^x distance, leading plat. to leave DERBY CAMP at 7.p.m.
4.	1 Company 5th N.Lan.R.	- do -	- do -	- do -	-do-	By plats. at 200^x distance following rear plat. of 5th R. Lanc.R.
5.	10th L'pool R. (less 2 Coys).	- do -	- do -	- do -	-do-	As above. Following rear plat. of 5th N.Lan.R.
6.	1 Company 10th L'pool R.	"P.1."	KAAIE DEFENCES.	Direct to No.1 Track thence by No.1 Track to H.12.b.4.7. thence Road junction I.1.c.25.25. - SALVATION CORNER - I.1.b.15.05 - CANAL Track - No. 1 Bridge.	5700^x	Not to move on to No. 1 Track until last platoon of 2 Companies 10th L'pool R. from DERBY CAMP have passed.
7.	1 Company 10th L'pool R.	"P.1."	DIXMUDE ST (billets occupied recently by Pioneers).	No.1 Track - I.1.c.1.1. thence by No.4 Track to DIXMUDE ST.		Follows above Coy. by platoons at 200^x distance.

X/Y NIGHT (continued).

Serial No.	Unit.	Location.	Destination.	Route.	Distance.	Remarks.
8.	166 M.G.C.	CANAL BANK.	LA BRIQUE.	No.6 Track.		To move in small parties at 300x distance, clearing CANAL BANK by 5.am. "Y" day. Subsection of S By. at present employed on harassing fire, will rejoin S Bty. under orders from O.C. 166 M.G.C.

Y/Z NIGHT.

Serial No.	Unit.	Location.	Destination.	Route.	Distance.	Remarks.
9.	5th N.Lan.R.	Assembly Tr. Map "A".	Assembly Trs. Map C plus ADMIRALS TR. "N" of Bn. boundary and DURHAM TR. "X" of junction of NEW GARDEN ST.			To clear BILGE TRENCH by 8.45.pm.
10.	5th R.Lanc.R.	Assembly Trs. Map "A".	Assembly Trs. Map "C".			To be "E" of OXFORD ROAD by 10.30.pm.
11.	10th L'pool R. (less 2 Coys).	CONGREVE WALK and LIVERPOOL TRENCH.	Assembly Trs "Map C" plus SCOTTISH TR. and less trenches alotted to 5th N. Lan. R.			To be East of LIVERPOOL TRENCH by 11.pm.
12.	1 Company 10th L'pool R.	KAAIE DEFENCES.	- do -	No.6 Track.	2000x	In parties of not more than 12 at 5 minutes interval between 8 and 9.pm.

Y/Z NIGHT (continued).

Serial No.	Unit.	Location.	Destination.	Route.	Distance.	Remarks.
13.	1 Company 10th L'pool R.	DIXMUDE STREET.	Assembly trenches Map "C" plus SCOTTISH TR. and less Trenches allotted to 5th N. Lan.R.	No. 5 Track to CONGREVE WALK.	2300ˣ	In small parties between 8 & 9.pm.
14.	5th S.Lan.R.	"L.4."	Assembly trenches Map "C".	Road junction I.1.c.25.30. thence SALVATION CORNER - I.1.b.15.05. - CANAL Track - Bridge No.1 - No. 6 Track.	4500ˣ	Move by p lats. at 200 yds interval. Leading plat. to move at 8.15.pm. (not crossing the CANAL before 9.pm)
15.	166 M.G.C. (H.Q).	LA BRIQUE.	Assembly positions Map "C".		To move in small parties to assembly positions between 8 & 9.pm. Subsections allotted to Bns. will get in touch with Bns. and any guns that require to be moved will do so between 12.m.n. and 1.am. "Z" day. M.G. positions C.23.2. & C.28.6. will be taken over by Lewis guns of 5th S.Lan.R. by 10.p.m.	
16.	166 T.M.B.	LA BRIQUE.	Assembly positions Appendix "D".		To move in small parties to assembly positions in rear of No. 15.	

Y/Z

Y/Z NIGHT (continued).

Serial No.	Unit.	Location.	Destination.	Route.	Distance.	Remarks.
17.	Bde. Carrying Party.					
	5th N.Lan.R. Section.	Forward Trenches.	BILGE Corridor.			Enter By No.1 entrance at 8.15.pm. "Y" day.
	5th R.Lanc.R. "	- do -	- do -			- do - 8.p.m. "Y" day.
	5th S.Lan.R. "	"L.4"	- do -			Enter via R.A.M.C. Dressing Station on BILGE TRENCH on arrival of Bn.
	10th L'pool R. " is cancelled.					

18. Carrying Party for Trench Mortar Battery.
From 5th N. Lan. R., 5th R. Lanc. R. and 10th L'pool R. report to O.C. 166 T.M.B. in "G" shaft corridor between dugout 34 and main corridor by 9.p.m. "Y" day.
From 5th S. Lan. R. on arrival of Battalion. All parties enter by No. 1 entrance during daylight.

S E C R E T.   Copy No....3....

166 INFANTRY BRIGADE ORDER No. 88.

Reference Maps ST JULIEN and ZILLEBEKE 1/10,000. Sheet 28.N.W. and 27.N.E. 1/20,000.

23rd July 1917.

1. Brigade will move to its assembly positions in accordance with attached tables.

2. Officers will carefully reconnoitre their routes beforehand.

3. Battalion Headquarters and boundaries between Battalions on X/Y night /"Y" day and Y/Z night are shown on map already issued.

4. The necessity for quiet and absence of unusual lights on Y/Z night is again impressed on all ranks.

5. Completion of all moves will be reported to Brigade H.Q.

B. Wilkinson

CAPTAIN.
Brigade Major, 166 Infantry Brigade.

Issued to Signals..7/45pm

Copy No. 1. 5th R. Lanc. R.
2. 10th L'pool R.
3. 5th S. Lan. R.
4. 5th N. Lan. R.
5. 166 M. G. C.
6. 166 T. M. B.
7. 55th Division.
8. 164 Infy. Bde.
9. 165 " "
10. 116 " "
11. 196 M. G. C.
12. 98 Coy. A.S.C.
13. 17 Coy. "F" Bn. H.B. M.G.C.
14. B. G. C.
15. Brigade Major.
16. Staff Captain.
17. Bde. Signal Officer.
18. Bde. Transport Officer.
19. War Diary.
20. File

APP III

S E C R E T. Copy No....7....

166 INFANTRY BRIGADE ORDER No. 29.

Reference 1/10,000 Maps
ST JULIEN, ZONNEBEKE
and ZILLEBEKE.

24th July 1917.

1. The Fifth and Second Armies and First French Army will attack one a day to be known as "Z" day -
IInd Corps on Right.
XIXth Corps in the Centre.
XVIIIth Corps on Left.
15th Division on Right.
55th Division in Centre.
39th Division on Left.

2. 55th Division will attack BLUE and BLACK lines with 165 Infantry Brigade on Right, 166 Infantry Brigade on Left. 164 Infantry Brigade will pass through and secure the GREEN line and push out outposts to the pencil line. The 116 Infantry Brigade will be on Left of 166 Infantry Brigade.

3. Divisional, Brigade and Battalion boundaries and objectives are shown on "Z" Map.

4. ZERO will be notified later.

5. Units will send a representative to Brigade H.Q. to synchronise between 11.p.m. and 12 midnight Y/Z night.

6. 449 I.R. is holding the Sector in front of the Brigade.
One Battalion in front system, ~~one~~
One Battalion STUZZ PUNKT line.
One Battalion GHELUVELT - LANGEMARCK line.

7. Intention is -
(a) With the object of preparing for a further advance to capture and occupy as a line of resistance the enemy's G.L.x line and to throw out strong outposts to obtain a footing on the GRAVENSTAFEL SPUR and occupy enemy works as far as about line TORONTO - AVIATIK FARM.
(b) Should enemy evacuate GRAVENSTAFEL SWITCH and ZONNEBEKE - STADEN line to push forward line of resistance in touch with Division on our Right to the GRAVENSTAFEL SPUR with same object as (a).
It is not intended to attack any position in which enemy shows resistance beyond objectives laid down in (a).

8. Troops will be in their ZERO positions by 2.a.m. "Z" day.

9. Brigade will attack in two lines -

1st line	1/5th R. Lanc. R.	on Right
	1/5th N. Lan. R.	on Left
2nd line	1/5th S. Lan. R.	on Right
	1/10th L'pool R.	on Left.

x GHELUVELT-LANGEMARCK

10. Boundary between Battalions will be ;-
Road HASLAR HOUSE to LYTHAM COT, thence to hedge north of L.R.B. COTTAGE (inclusive to right) and thence C.T. to second E of PICKELHAUBE (inclusive to right) thence an imaginary line to Pond in C.23.b. (inclusive to right) to hedge C.18.c.2.1. to C.18.c.55.25. (inclusive to right) to C.T. running from second C of CAPRICORN trench to first P of CAPRICORN SUPPORT (inclusive to right) to O of POND farm by ~~should~~ SOUTH end of POND at C.18.c.7.3.

11. First line will capture and consolidate the enemy front system of trenches up to and including the BLUE LINE -
(a). Each Battalion moves on a two company frontage. Each platoon with two lines will form one wave - distance 10 yards. Distance between waves and companies 25 yards.
(b). Companies will "Leapfrog" leading wave to go as far as GERMAN Support line ('moppers up' follow and deal with German front line). Second wave passing through ~~the~~ German reserve line - subsequent waves pass through to BLUE LINE.
(c). At zero 5th R. Lanc. R. and 5th North Lan. R. will move out getting close to barrage ready to advance the instant it lifts at zero plus 6.
(d). 5th R. Lanc. R. will push forward posts into CARNATION TRENCH and CAMBRAI AVENUE.

12. Second line will capture and consolidate enemy second line system (STUTZPUNKT LINE) up to and including BLACK LINE passing through BLUE LINE at zero plus 75.
(a). Battalions will move forward as for first attack - distance between companies may be increased to 60 yards.
(b). 16 bridges are available for 10th Liverpool R. and 6 for 5th South Lancs. R. for use in case the STEENBEEK is swollen; they will be drawn by units concerned from BRIGADE DUMP forthwith. ~~ON~~
(c) 5th S. Lan. R. will push posts well along towards CAPRICORN KEEP towards the high ground South of POND FARM.
(d) 10th L'pool R. will get a footing on the triangular knoll South of "FORTUIN" and immediately push on posts into CANVAS and CAPITAL TRENCHES.
(e) If they have not already done so 10th L'pool R. will push forward from BLACK line at ZERO plus 233 and capture CANVAS and CAPITAL TRENCHES up to BORDER HOUSE, consolidating on GREEN dotted lines so as to conform to Left Division whose Left will begin to advance at ZERO plus 200.

13. Two Stokes guns and two Machine guns are placed at disposal of each Battalion from ZERO for its assault.

14. 164 Infantry Brigade will ;-
(a) At ZERO plus 330 pass through the BLACK line to capture and consolidate G.L. line up to and including GREEN line and will push forward posts to about the line TORONTO - AVIATIK FARM.
(b) At ZERO plus 500 if enemy evacuate GRAVENSTAFEL SWITCH and ZONNEBEKE - STADEN Line establish a line of resistance along GRAVENSTAFEL SPUR in touch with Flank Divisions about GRAVENSTAFEL and on GREEN line respectively. For service of reconnaissance 1 Troop North Irish Horse (Lieut. GRIGG) is at disposal of this Brigade.

22. The IN and OUT trenches (Map "B") will be used as such from ZERO - 30. 10th L'pool R. and 5th S. Lan. R. respectively will be responsible for controlling traffic from that time till leading Battalions of 164 Infantry Brigade pass through.

15. Each Battalion will be prepared at short notice to move in any direction as soon as the line in front of it is secured either to that line or beyond it to support, to relieve or to push on (as in 14 (b)). To this end reorganisation will be carried out absolutely as early as possible.

16. As soon as GREEN line is captured 1/5th K.Lanc.R. and 1/5th N. Lan. R. will be closed to about 300 yards West of BLACK line in readiness to support or relieve 164 Infantry Brigade.

17. All possible assistance will be given to 164 Infantry Brigade by provision or carriage of stores, communications etc.

18. (a) 36th and 55th Divisional Artillery, 108th and 150th A.F.A. Brigades will cover the Divisional front assisted by Corps Heavy Artillery (34 Batteries).
(b) In addition to the creeping barrages (see special map) other barrages will be placed on enemy but so timed as to keep ahead of troops following closely on creeping barrage.
(c) After capture of BLACK line 3 Brigade R.F.A. move to advanced positions for attack on GREEN line: remaining 3 Brigades move to near BLUE line as soon as Infantry advance from BLACK line.

19. Machine gun arrangements have been notified but no variation of barrage programme can be made except with Divisional approval.

20. Tank arrangements have been notified, Map T8 is attached showing their routes. If Tanks are late in arriving at BLUE line they will follow up Infantry as soon as possible proceeding to their ~~alternate~~ ultimate objectives "mopping up" on route.

21. Contact Aeroplanes will if attack proceeds as ~~akm~~ arranged only call for flares at times when BLUE, BLACK and GREEN lines have been reached but Infantry can light flares should it be considered necessary to make known the position of their front line at other times.

22. Orders have been issued separately as to:-
1. Moves to and location of assembly positions and cutting wire
2. Method of consolidation and dumps.
3. Construction and garrisoning of strong and supporting points.
4. Moves of Battalion Headquarters.
5. Employment of Stokes and Machine guns.
6. Move of BLUE Battalions to near BLACK line.
7. Machine gun barrage.
8. Tank and Aeroplane arrangements.
9. Signal arrangements.
10. ~~WIELTJE~~ traffic control and allotment.
11. Use of tracks.
12. Carrying parties.
13. S.O.S. Signals.
14. Liaison.
15. Employment of R.E.
16. Supplies, Stores, Water.
17. Casualties, Medical and Veterinary arrangements.
18. Police, Prisoners of War and Stragglers.
19. Transport and Pack animals.
20. Equipment.
21. Maps.

24. The following maps have been issued :-

"A" and "C" Assembly positions.
"B" IN and OUT trenches.
"F" Visibility maps.
"G" Forward Tracks and Supporting Points.
"Y" WIELTJE dugout system.
"Z" Boundaries and objectives.
"R" Barrage Map.
"T.2" Tank routes.
"T" Tracks.

25. Brigade Headquarters will be at WIELTJE in first instance. Advanced Reports Centres are fixed provisionally at (a) C.23.c.5.6. and (b) near RAT FARM C.23.b.

B. Wilkinson
CAPTAIN.
Brigade Major, 164 Infantry Brigade.

Issued to Signals. 8/7 pm

Left Group

Copy No.			
1. 55th DIVISION.		11. ~~276 Bde.~~ R.F.A.	
2. 164 Infy Bde.		12. 17th Coy."F" Bn.H.B. M.G.C.	
3. 165 Infy Bde.		13. B. G. C.	
4. 116 Infy Bde.		14. Brigade Major.	
5. 5th R.Lanc.R.		15. Staff Captain.	
6. 10th L'pool R.		16. Bde. Signal Officer.	
7. 5th S. Lan. R.		17. Bde. Transport Officer.	
8. 5th N. Lan. R.		18. War Diary.	
9. 166 M. G. C.		19. File.	
10. 166 T. M. B.			

Secret

A.G. 38. G125/227

All recipients 166 Infantry Brigade Order No. 89.

Addendum 1.

Para 7(b) Delete and substitute :-

"(b) Should enemy evacuate GRAVENSTAFEL SWITCH and ZONNEBEKE - STADEN Line, to push forward line of resistance in touch with the Division on our Right to the GRAVENSTAFEL SPUR with same object as (a). The line of resistance will not however be advanced to the line of the GRAVENSTAFEL SPUR until it has been ascertained that the line of resistance of the 44th Infantry Brigade is being advanced to the SEINE ~~SANE~~ - BEECHAM - ABRAHAM HEIGHTS. Line.

[signature] Lt/Col

CAPTAIN.

27/7/1917. Brigade Major, 166 Infantry Brigade.

G/125/231

App. II

SECRET.

All recipients 166 Infantry Brigade Order No. 88.

The attached serial numbers of Movement Table issued with 166 Infantry Brigade Order No. 88 are issued in substitution of those already in possession.

Trench maps to be amended accordingly :-

X/Y NIGHT.

Serial No.	Unit.	Location.	Destination.	Route.	Distance.	Remarks.
3.	1 Company 5th R.Lanc.R.	DERBY CAMP.	Assembly trenches. Map "A"	No.1 Track - H.12.b.4.7. - thence road junction I.1.c.25.30. - thence Wooden Road to I.1.c.99.60. - Brigge I.1.d.40.60. - thence by Northern Bank of CANAL to No. 1 Bridge - No. 6 Track - LIVERPOOL TRENCH.	8900^{x}	By platoons at 200^{x} distance, leading plat to leave DERBY CAMP at 7.p.m.
4.	1 Company 5th N.Lan.R.	- do -	- do -	- do -	- do -	By plats at 200^{x} distance following rear plat. of 5th R.Lanc.R.
5.	10th L'pool R. (less 2 Coys.)	- do -	- do -	- do -	- do -	As above. Following rear plat. of 5th N. Lan. R.
6.	1 Company 10th L'pool R.	- do -	KAAIE DEFENCES.	Direct to No.1 Track - thence by No.1 Track to H.12.b.4.7. - thence road junction I.1.c.25.30. - thence Wooden Road to I.1.c.99.60. - Bridge I.1.d.40.60. - thence by Northern Bank of CANAL to No. 1 Bridge.	5700^{x}	As above following rear plat. of 10th L'pool R. (less 2 Companies).

X/Y NIGHT (Continued)

Serial No.	Unit.	Location.	Destination.	Route.	Distance.	Remarks.
7.	1 Company 10th L'pool R.	"P1"	DIXMUDE ST (billets occupied recently by Pioneers).	No.1 Track - I.1.c.1.1. thence by No. 4 Track to DIXMUDE STREET.		Not to move on to No. 1 Track until last platoon of Coys. of 10th L'pool R. from DERBY CAMP have passed - then follows by platoons at 200^x distance.

Y/Z NIGHT.

Serial No.	Unit.	Location.	Destination.	Route.	Distance.	Remarks.
14.	5th S.Lan.R.	"L4"	Assembly trenches Map "O".	Road junction I.1.c.25.30 thence Wooden Road to I.1.c.99.60. thence Bridge I.1.d.40.60. - thence by Northern Bank of CANAL to Bridge No. 1 - No. 6 Track.	4500^x	Move by plats. at 200^x interval. Leading plat to move at 8.15.pm. (not crossing the CANAL before 9.pm.)

28/7/1917.

D. Wilkin [signature]

CAPTAIN.
Brigade Major, 166 Infantry Brigade.

1:10 000 SHEET 28
R.2.
TRENCHES CORRECTED TO 18-7-17.
T.B.31
LEGEND
WIRE, TRENCHES OR BUILDINGS PARTIALLY DESTROYED
NEW WORK
AREA PHOTOGRAPHED TO-DAY WITHIN PURPLE LINES
DELIVERED TO CORPS SIGNALS 5.30 AM
27-7-17
GRAVENSTAFEL SWITCH
Gravenstafel
Abraham Heights
Winchester Fm
Wellington
Albatross Fm
Aviatik Fm
Boetleer
Calgary Grange
Berlin
Van Meulen
Boethoek
Bourdeaux Fm
Springfield
Van Isackere
Dochy Fm
Toronto
Riverside
Fokker Fm
Keir Fm
Gallipoli
Delva Fm
Schuler Fm
Hanebeek
Kansas Cross
Waterloo
Otto Fm
Hamburg
Scale 1:10,000.
YARDS 500 400 300 200 100 0 500 1,000 1,500 2,000 YARDS

1:10 000
R.I.
Wieltje
Frezenberg
Verlorenhoek
Hanebeek
Fortuin
Scale 1:10,000.
5TH FIELD SURVEY COY, R.E. (1196)
10-7-17.
No. 2 Advanced Section, A.P.&S.S.
YARDS 500 400 300 200 100 0 500 1,000 1,500 2,000 YARDS

C O N F I D E N T I A L.

W A R   D I A R Y

O F

1/5th BATTALION

SOUTH LANCASHIRE REGIMENT

FROM: 1st AUGUST, 1917

TO: 31st AUGUST, 1917.

(V O L U M E: 31.)

Instructions regarding War Diaries and Intelligence Summaries are contained in F. S. Regs., Part II. and the Staff Manual respectively. Title pages will be prepared in manuscript.

WAR DIARY
15th South Lancashire Regt.
or ~~INTELLIGENCE SUMMARY.~~
(*Erase heading not required.*)

Army Form C. 2118.

Place	Date	Hour	Summary of Events and Information	Remarks and references to Appendices
CAPRICORN TRENCH (MOUSSE ST JULIEN)	1 Aug	Night 31/1st	A Barrage was put down on the enemy line as movement had been seen behind POND FARM, but no enemy came through. Rain fell heavily throughout the night. Standing Patrols were out about 150 yards from CAPRICORN SUPPORT. Our working party was periodically swept by M.G. FIRE. Enemy sniper was active from direction of DONT TRENCH but did little damage. Enemy fired at regular intervals with High explosives on concrete dug out in CAPRICORN TRENCH. Salvos were regularly placed on Road behind SPREE FARM. A constant barrage was placed about 100 yards behind CAP TRENCH. Warning had come through prisoners statements that a counter attack was expected that afternoon. Our artillery put down a barrage and no counter attack materialized. At Dark enemy bombarded our system chiefly CAP SUPT and ground in between. 2 wounded prisoners were found in dugout in CAP SUPT. When bombardment died down patrols were sent out 300 yds from CAP SPT on right. There was no trace of enemy. Our left patrol saw 2 or 3 large patrols moving between POND FARM and FORT HILL. Rain still fell heavily.	
			Casualties O Ranks 3 Killed 29 Wounded 3 died of wounds	

A6945 Wt. W11422/M1160 350,000 12/16 D. D. & L. Forms/C.2118/14.

Instructions regarding War Diaries and Intelligence Summaries are contained in F. S. Regs., Part II, and the Staff Manual respectively. Title pages will be prepared in manuscript.

~~WAR~~ DIARY
or
~~INTELLIGENCE SUMMARY~~.
(*Erase heading not required.*)

Army Form C. 2118.

Place	Date	Hour	Summary of Events and Information	Remarks and references to Appendices
	2 Aug		The morning was fairly quiet with intermittent shelling. In the evening about "STAND TO" our artillery opened out on left in front of ST JULIEN. Enemy sent up a large number of S.O.S signals, and his barrage fell all along the line. While this was still on we were relieved by the ROYAL IRISH RIFLES. This was carried out without many casualties and BATTALION moved into Brigade RESERVE in WIELTJE with HQrs in	
WIELTJE			WIELTJE DUGOUTS. Lieut [illegible] was wounded. 1 OR killed 9 wounded.	
			The Medical Officer (Capt [illegible]) remained in charge of the DRESSING STN at RAT FARM (a concrete emplacement) although that was subject to continuous shelling all the time of occupation, and many direct hits were made.	
	3 Aug		Comparatively quiet day. Relieved 10/30 pm by the 11th Inniskilling Fusiliers entrained YPRES pm for VLAMERTINGHE and bivouacked for the night, after being issued with rum and hot tea.	
	4 Aug	[illegible]	Entrained for POPERINGHE and marched to camp at L.15.b.9.1 arriving . . In tents all ground pretty wet.	
	5 Aug		CHURCH PARADE in Camp. later Roll Call. The Brig Genl addressed the men congratulating them on their work. Changed underclothing and cleaned up generally.	

Instructions regarding War Diaries and Intelligence Summaries are contained in F. S. Regs., Part II. and the Staff Manual respectively. Title pages will be prepared in manuscript.

WAR DIARY
~~or~~
~~INTELLIGENCE~~ SUMMARY.
(*Erase heading not required.*)

Army Form C. 2118.

Place	Date	Hour	Summary of Events and Information	Remarks and references to Appendices
NR POPERINGHE	5 Aug	8am	Billetting party of 1 Officer (Lieut C.O.L. LEIGH CLARE) and 5 other ranks entrained ABEELE STN for AUDRUICQ at 9.30 am	
	5/6 Aug		Resting until —	
	6 Aug	7pm	when we marched to ABEELE STN where we entrained at 8 pm.	
	7 Aug	3.15am	Detrained at AUDRUICQ proceeded by motor lorries for TOURNEHEM arriving 4am. Bedded down. Breakfast 11 am	
		11.30am	Bathing. Coys & HQ.	
			In the evening drafts - total 165 other ranks joined from No 6 Infantry Base and 33rd DIVL Reinforcement Camp.	
	8 Aug	11am	Inspection by G.O.C. DIVISION at J.33a.8.8 (Sheet 27 A. NE). Congratulated the Brigade in on its share of the advance.	
	9 Aug		Draft of 92 other ranks joined from Reinforcement Camp. Company route marches and training	
	10/22		Clothing and re-equipping. Platoon, company and Battalion training. Route marches. Recreational training and field firing	

A6945 Wt. W11422/M1160 350,000 12/16 D. D. & L. Forms/C./2118/14.

Instructions regarding War Diaries and Intelligence Summaries are contained in F. S. Regs., Part II. and the Staff Manual respectively. Title pages will be prepared in manuscript.

WAR DIARY
or 4
~~INTELLIGENCE~~ SUMMARY.
(Erase heading not required.)

Army Form C. 2118.

Place	Date	Hour	Summary of Events and Information	Remarks and references to Appendices
TOURNEHEM	23 Aug		Company training in the morning In the afternoon played the RAMC in DIVL FOOTBALL TOURNAMENT final. Good game. In last ten minutes RAMC scored 1st goal result 1. Nil –. After the match Major Genl H S Jeudwine CB (Divl Comdr) presented the CROSS COUNTRY RACE CUP won by the BATTALION previously also the medals (bronze) for the match.	
	24/25		Battalion and Company training. [illegible]	
	26		Battalion SPORTS at GUEMY. Capt J Shufflebotham rejoined from hospital	
	27/31		Brigade and Battalion Training.	
			During August men who had been in the recent fighting proceeded in parties of 50 daily to CALAIS and officers for 48 hours – The following officers reinforcements reported for duty on 22nd. 2nd Lieut A. J. Little, A R. Stallworthy, W Young, H. Francis, G. Johncock, K. Mackenzie, A. Dandridge, A W Pavey, L Dinnis all of "The Buffs" and 2nd Lieut R. Marrow – South Lancs R.	

[illegible] Lt Colonel
Cmdg 1/5th South Lanc R

A6945 Wt. W11422/M1160 350,000 12/16 D. D. & L. Forms/C./2118/14.

55th (WEST LANCASHIRE) DIVISION,

SPECIAL ORDER OF THE DAY,

3rd August, 1917.

To All Ranks of the 55th (West Lancashire) Division.

Before you went into action on the 31st July, I told you how confident I was that the Division would do its duty, and maintain its reputation and the reputation of the grand Regiments to which you belong.

You have done more than that.

The attack you made on the 31st is worthy to rank with the great deeds of the British Army in the past, and has added fresh glory to the record of that Army.

The courage, determination, and self sacrifice shewn by Officers, Warrant Officers, Non-Commissioned Officers and men is beyond praise. It is a fine exhibition of true discipline, which comes from the mutual confidence of all ranks in themselves, their comrades, their leaders, and those under them. This in its turn is the product of hard training. Your doings on the 31st show how well you have turned this training to account.

You captured every inch of the objectives allotted to you. It was not your fault that you could not hold all you took. You have broken and now hold in spite of weather and counter attacks a line that the enemy has strengthened and consolidated at his leisure for more than two years.

This will I believe be the beginning of the end. When your turn comes to go forward again you will know your own strength, - and the enemy will know it too.

I am proud of what you have done, and am confident that with such troops ultimate victory is certain.

H. S. Jeudwine

Major General,

Commanding 55th (West Lancashire) Division.

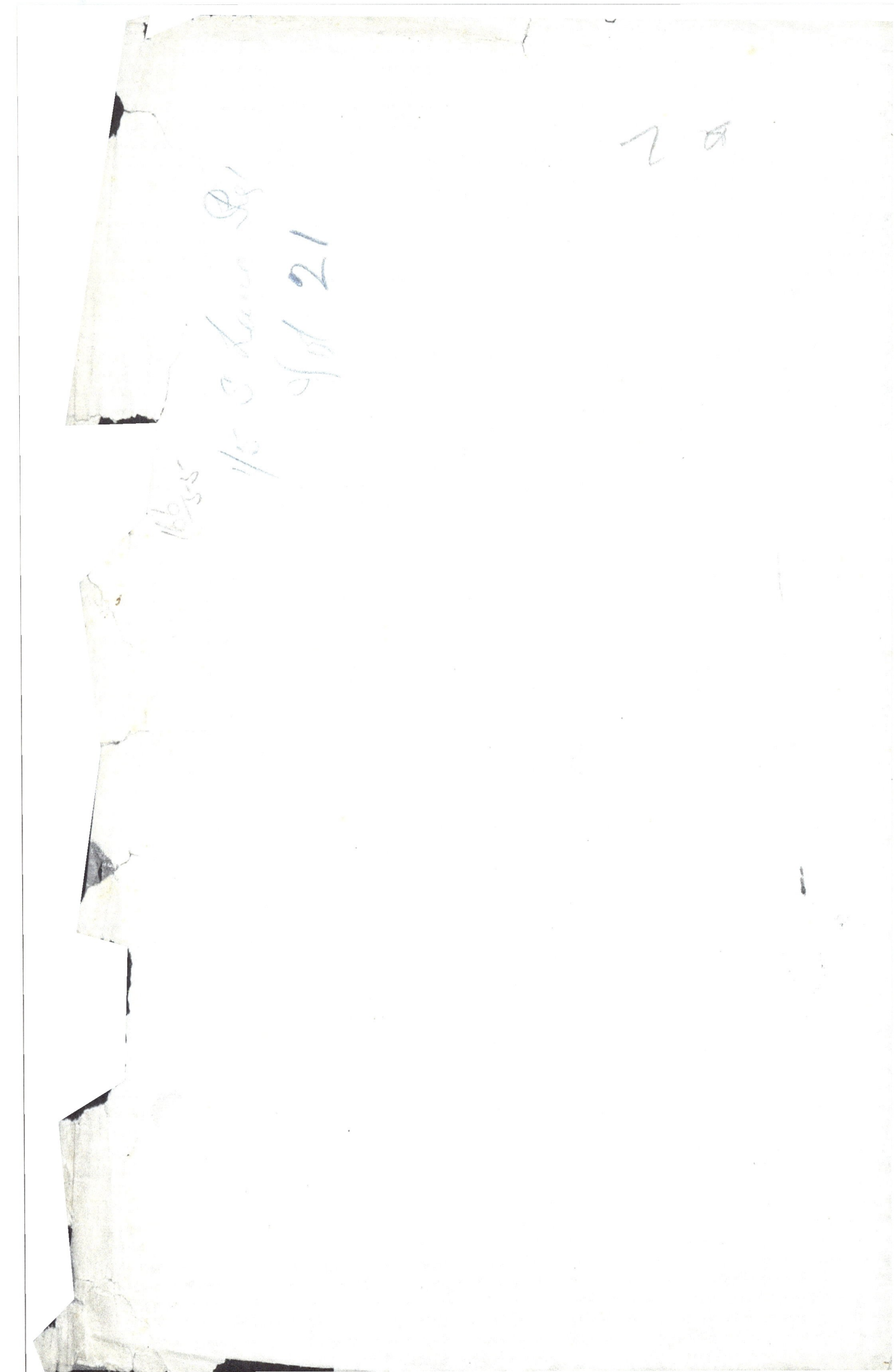

C O N F I D E N T I A L.

W A R   D I A R Y.

O F

1/5th Battalion

SOUTH LANCASHIRE REGIMENT.

FROM: 1st SEPTEMBER, 1917.

TO: 31st SEPTEMBER, 1917.

V O L U M E: 37.

Army Form C. 2118.

Instructions regarding War Diaries and Intelligence Summaries are contained in F. S. Regs., Part II, and the Staff Manual respectively. Title pages will be prepared in manuscript.

WAR DIARY
or
~~INTELLIGENCE SUMMARY.~~
(*Erase heading not required.*)

5th Bn South Lancashire Regt

Place	Date	Hour	Summary of Events and Information	Remarks and references to Appendices
TOURNEHEM	1 Sept		Morning – Training. Afternoon – Recreational Training	
	2 "		Brigade Church Parade (C of E) at 3 Range and distribution of Ribands awarded in recent operations. [Capt C. R. McLeod – 10th L.R's joined 5th; Lt L. B. Taylor – 6th Somerset " 2nd; " [illegible] Kitchen " 2th; " [illegible] Wellington " 2th; " [illegible] Pemberton 3rd / 3/5 S.L.R.; " [illegible] Ashcroft; " [illegible] [illegible] 1/5th]	
		2.30pm	Afterwards Brigade Rifle competition	
	3 Sept to 9th		Platoon, Company, Battalion and Brigade Training. 8 Sept – Major L. Henderson to 5th Loyal N. Lancs as 2nd in Comd.	
	9th	11am	Brigade Church Parade	
	10		DIVISIONAL EXERCISE. 164/165 Brigades in the attack. South Lancs as Skeleton Enemy. The Commander in Chief (Sir DOUGLAS HAIG) was present at the exercise and expressed himself as "much pleased with the appearance of the DIVISION and especially with the alertness and keenness shown by the younger officers" when in conversation with the G.O.C. DIVISION.	
	11		Received Warning order for move on 12/13th.	
	12	7am	Transport marched from TOURNEHEM under orders of B.T.O to VLAMERTINGHE AREA, halting for 1 night at WORMHOUDT AREA.	
	13	6am	Breakfasts. Advance party (2/Lt Dandridge + 4 OR) left Nordausques by motor lorry at 6 am	
		6.30am	Battalion marched to Nordausques to AUDRUICQ arriving 9 am	

A6945 Wt. W11422/M1160 350,000 12/16 D. D. & L. Forms/C./2118/14.

Army Form C. 2118.

Instructions regarding War Diaries and Intelligence Summaries are contained in F. S. Regs., Part II. and the Staff Manual respectively. Title pages will be prepared in manuscript.

WAR DIARY
~~INTELLIGENCE~~ SUMMARY.

(*Erase heading not required.*)

Place	Date	Hour	Summary of Events and Information	Remarks and references to Appendices
AUDRUICQ.	13 Sept		Entrained 10.45am for YPRES NORTH AREA.	
		4.30	Arrived and detrained at VLAMERTINGHE.	
YPRES, N. AREA			Headquarters at and Battalion billeted in vicinity of GOLDFISH CHATEAU	
WIELTJE FORWARD AREA	14/15		Relieved 1/5th Gloucestershire Regt in RIGHT SUBSECTOR of Left Section of V Corps front with Headquarters at BANK FARM.	
			DISPOSITIONS – front line system from the GRAVENSTAFEL ROAD to a point approximately C.19.c. 80.75 "C" Coy on the Right (POMMERN CASTLE) "D" Coy on the left (SOMME).	
			A and B Coys in support under MAJOR PILKINGTON DSO in the OLD GERMAN FRONT LINE SYSTEM between CAMBRAI AVENUE and CAMEROON AVENUE. 1 OR wounded	
	15	4am	Gas bombs discharged by 6" Trench Mortars at IBERIAN.	
			Sentry groups pushed forward, and patrols sent out on Company fronts for the purpose of gathering any information regarding the enemy, location of advanced posts, positions of machine guns	
		9.15am	Our artillery put up barrage on line running roughly from D.20.c.35 to D.[illegible] 88. and H.E. + Shrapnel barrage put up at	
		4.25pm	on same line for half an hour. Enemy generally quiet	

A6945 Wt. W11422/M1160 350,000 12/16 D. D. & L. Forms/C./2118/14.

Army Form C. 2118.

Instructions regarding War Diaries and Intelligence Summaries are contained in F. S. Regs., Part II, and the Staff Manual respectively. Title pages will be prepared in manuscript.

WAR DIARY

~~INTELLIGENCE~~ SUMMARY.

(Erase heading not required.)

Place	Date	Hour	Summary of Events and Information	Remarks and references to Appendices
	15 Sept		Received warning order from BRIGADE for night 15/16 to extend to the SOUTH and take over portion of the front now held by 8th LANCS FUS (135 Inf Bde) from present RIGHT DIVL boundary to ZONNEBEKE STREAM.	
			Two platoons of 3 Company were accordingly ordered up from SUPPORT and moved into LINE at 8.30 pm.	
			Enemy machine guns active during the night, seen to fire from [illegible] at HILL 35 and direction of [illegible] [illegible] artillery [illegible] shelled [illegible] 5 TRACK near of [illegible] FARM.	
	16		Situation during night fairly quiet.	
		5/30 6/30 am	Enemy aeroplanes very busy over our lines and firing their machine guns, dropped 2 white flares near ZONNEBEKE [illegible] and green and white flares on our right.	
		10am	Practice barrage by DIVISION on right was put down to which the enemy replied by heavy bursts of fire mainly on the FREZENBERG RIDGE with all calibres up to 15 cm.	
		7pm	Instructed by Brigade to work on preparation of forward Assembly	

Instructions regarding War Diaries and Intelligence Summaries are contained in F. S. Regs., Part II. and the Staff Manual respectively. Title pages will be prepared in manuscript.

WAR DIARY
or INTELLIGENCE SUMMARY.
(*Erase heading not required.*)

Army Form C. 2118.

Place	Date	Hour	Summary of Events and Information	Remarks and references to Appendices
	16		Area for Battalions other than improvements on Batn H.Qrs. This was	
			communicated to Companies and work was commenced improving	
			existing cover and linking up shell holes	
			Divisional Artillery kept up harassing fire on strong points, roads	
			and approaches paying special attention to old battery positions	
			Lt. 2/Lt. Lees-Coke attached for duty to 166 Trench Mortar Bty and	
			2nd Lt. L.J. BAYLEY to R.F.C. as observer	
	17		Generally quiet night.	
			In early morning our artillery shelled vicinity of Hill 35 with 4.5in	
			and 18 pounders.	
		6am	Our artillery opened out well on the right. Enemy dropped a	
			few gas shells around POMMERN CASTLE and put down a light	
			barrage on Front line and BANK FARM – POMMERN CASTLE line	
			Party of 100 other ranks who had returned to Transport Lines	
			previous night i/c CAPT E.R. McLEOD reported to O.C. RED FARM	
			R.A. for duty as stretcher bearers in forthcoming operations	

A6945 Wt. W11422/M1160 350,000 12/16 D. D. & L. Forms/C./2118/14.

Instructions regarding War Diaries and Intelligence Summaries are contained in F. S. Regs., Part II. and the Staff Manual respectively. Title pages will be prepared in manuscript.

WAR DIARY

or

~~INTELLIGENCE~~ SUMMARY.

(*Erase heading not required.*)

Army Form C. 2118.

Place	Date	Hour	Summary of Events and Information	Remarks and references to Appendices
	17	10 am	Artillery cut wire in front of AISNE HOUSE. [Heavy [illegible] on right [illegible] during this period and again [illegible] 9 am to 10.30 [illegible] enemy [illegible] [illegible] [illegible] his BANKEN – POMMERN CASTLE [illegible]]	
			Casualties for 17th 2Lt H.P. WOLSTENCROFT wounded, 6 OR Killed 12 OR wounded	
			A Company, 2 platoons B Coy and HQ details from [illegible] and OLD GERMAN FRONT LINE SYSTEM under MAJOR PILKINGTON were relieved by 7th KINGS LIVERPOOL REGT and moved into DIVISIONAL RESERVE in YPRES NORTH AREA	
	18	5 am	200 gas projectors discharged by N Special Coy RE on 5 CROSS ROADS D13 b 55.30 from position at C18d 7.5.	
		6 am / 10 am	Trial artillery barrages on the BRIGADE FRONT in co-operation with DIVISION on our right	
			Our artillery kept up a harassing fire on enemy positions, and our aircraft active over enemy lines.	
	Night 18/19		Battalion relieved by 9th KLR and moved into DIVISIONAL RESERVE (OO. [illegible])	App. I.
YPRES NORTH AREA.	19		Day devoted to drawing reserve rations re-equipping and completing deficiencies. All great coats and spare kits dumped.	
			Operation Orders issued to all concerned in accordance with 166 Bde O/I dated 19/9/17. Add [illegible] to OO. 97 and OO. 96.	App. II & III

A6945 Wt. W11422/M1160 350,000 12/16 D. D. & L. Forms/C./2118/14.

Instructions regarding War Diaries and Intelligence Summaries are contained in F. S. Regs., Part II. and the Staff Manual respectively. Title pages will be prepared in manuscript.

WAR DIARY

~~INTELLIGENCE~~ SUMMARY.

(Erase heading not required.)

Army Form C. 2118.

Place	Date	Hour	Summary of Events and Information	Remarks and references to Appendices
WIELTJE	19		Remaining in DIVISIONAL RESERVE, moved to OLD BRITISH LINE at WIELTJE with Headquarters at WARWICK FARM.	
	20	am 5.40	Attack launched by II and V ARMIES.	
		12 noon	Received instructions from Lt Col DREW (representing 165 Bde ADVANCED HQ) to reinforce 1/9th KINGS LIVERPOOL REGT by 2 companies.	
			Orders were issued and B & C Companies moved up with CAPT J. DICKINSON MC.	
		1.30pm	Remaining Companies moved to shell holes round POMMERN CASTLE, together with BN HQ.	
		4pm	HILL 37 and GALLIPOLI COPSE captured by B and C Companies and were reinforced by A & D Coys under CAPT A G WHITAKER at 4/30 pm.	
			Details of attack and subsequent counter attacks given in BATTN NARRATIVE	APP I
	21		Remained in possession all during day and withstood counter attack	
		6.30	pm, broken by artillery barrage, and onwards until night of	
	22/23		when Battalion was relieved by 2/6th SOUTH STAFFS REGT.	
			Casualties from 19th up to relief 2 Ofrs 19 Ranks Killed, 5 Died of Wounds	
			143 Wounded, 11 missing. These figures include officers.	

A6945 Wt. W11422/M1160 350,000 12/16 D. D. & L. Forms/C./2118/14.

Instructions regarding War Diaries and Intelligence Summaries are contained in F. S. Regs., Part II. and the Staff Manual respectively. Title pages will be prepared in manuscript.

WAR DIARY

or

~~INTELLIGENCE~~ ~~SUMMARY~~.

(Erase heading not required.)

Army Form C. 2118.

Place	Date	Hour	Summary of Events and Information	Remarks and references to Appendices
			Casualties – 2/Lt P.W. ELINN, 2/Lt A.J. LITTLE killed, CAPTAIN S. DICKINSON	
			MC, 2/Lts A. MORROW, N PEMBERTON, F FAIRHURST, [illegible] PH YOUNG wounded.	
			Many congratulatory messages received as a result of our success	App II
	22/23		moved into huts in YPRES NORTH AREA, where hot meals, tea and	
			rum was served.	
YPRES N AREA	23	10.30 am	Moved by busses from OUDERDOM – VLAMERTINGHE ROAD to	
			WATOU No 2 AREA, L.8d and L.8c (Sheet 27 NE)	
WATOU No 2 AREA			After dinner was served Battalion rested for the day. [illegible]	
	24	9am	Brigadier General [illegible] addressed the Battalion, thanking	
			them and expressing his pleasure for the work accomplished.	
			CAPT [illegible] rejoined with party from [illegible] also [illegible]	
			with party attached [illegible] COY R.E. [illegible] at DIV [illegible]	
	25		Kit inspections and re-equipping changing of clothing	
	25/26	12.30	marched to PROVEN where we entrained at	
	26	4.40 am	with transport and proceeded to MIRAUMONT arriving at	
		2.50	detrained and ~~marched~~ to the BARASTRE AREA arriving in camp	
		8pm	and taking over billets	

A6945 Wt. W11422/M1160 350,000 12/16 D. D. & L. Forms/C./2118/14.

Instructions regarding War Diaries and Intelligence Summaries are contained in F. S. Regs., Part II, and the Staff Manual respectively. Title pages will be prepared in manuscript.

WAR DIARY

~~or INTELLIGENCE SUMMARY.~~

(*Erase heading not required.*)

Army Form C. 2118.

Place	Date	Hour	Summary of Events and Information	Remarks and references to Appendices
near BAPAUME	27th and 28th		Resting, men allowed out of camp	
	29th	8am 40	Marched with Transport Brigaded to AIZECOURT LE BAS where battalion was accomodated in huts	
	30th	4pm	Marched via AIZECOURT LE BAS, LONGAVESNES, and VILLERS FAUCON to EPEHY into BRIGADE RESERVE. Dispositions:—	
EPÉHY (Sheet 62c France Ed I)			Headqrs & B Coy — VAUGHANS BANK } in relief of 15th Sherwood Foresters 105 INF BDE	
			A Coy. MEATH and LIMERICK POSTS	
			C " in WILLOWS	App II
			D " KILDARE POST.	

Lieut Colonel Cmdg, 1/5th South Lancs Regt

A6945 Wt. W11422/M1160 350,000 12/16 D. D. & L. Forms/C./2118/14.

SECRET.

R.A.
C.R.E.
Signals.
164th Brigade.
165th Brigade.
166th Brigade.
1/4th S. Lan. R.
196 M.G.Company.
Camp Commandant.
Divl. Train.
S.S.O.
A.D.M.S.
D.A.D.V.S.
Officer i/c Div. Bomb Store.
Officer i/c Emergency Div. Bomb Store.
"G".
V. Corps "Q".
59th Division.

H.Q. ... INFANTRY ... A/81/21 17/9/17.

55th DIVISION INSTRUCTION NO. 5.

FORMATION OF DUMPS AND SUPPLY ARRANGEMENTS.

1. FORMATION OF DUMPS.

Dumps of S.A.A., Grenades and R.E. Material will be as follows :-

Divisional Main Grenade Dump - H.8.a.4.9. (500 yards W. of VLAMERTINGHE.)

Divisional Emergency Grenade Dump - ST. JEAN.

Divisional R.E. Main Dump - H.8.a.5.9.

Divisional R.E. Emergency Dump - ST. JEAN - WIELTJE Rd. (600 yards W. of WIELTJE).

RIGHT BRIGADE.

Brigade Dump - C.29.a.8.9. (On N. side of No. 5 Track).

Advanced Dumps - BANK FARM, C.24.b.3.6.

POMMERN CASTLE, D.19.a.4.3.

LEFT BRIGADE.

Brigade Dump - C.23.c.3.1. (Junction of old German Front Line and WIELTJE - GRAFENSTAFEL Road).

Advanced Dumps - WINE HOUSE C.18.c.6.9.

POND FARM C.18.d.8.8.

SPREE FARM C.18.d.5.3.

Dug-Outs at C.18.d.7.5.

SOMME C.13.c.5.4.

Grenades, S.A.A., etc., will be drawn in the usual manner from the Divisional Bomb Store. Brigades will wire 55th Division "Q" by 9.30 a.m. daily stating what stores they require to draw.

/ R.E.Material

R.E. Material will be drawn from the Main Divisional R.E. Dump on application to the C.R.E.

The Divisional Emergency Dumps will only be drawn on in case of emergency on the authority of a Staff Officer.

The 166th Brigade will carry out the formation of all Brigade and advanced Dumps.

The 165th and 164th Brigades will notify direct the 166th Brigade the amounts of stores required to be held in each Dump, and will arrange to send an Officer to be attached to the 166th Brigade H.Q. to assist in their formation.

2. RESERVE OF RATIONS.

4,000 iron rations are held at the Divisional Emergency Dump and may be drawn upon in case of emergency on application to 55th Division "Q".

3. SUPPLIES.

On "W" day reserve rations consisting of biscuits, preserved meat, tea, sugar, jam and solidified alcohol will be issued to all Infantry Battalions, Machine Gun Companies and Light Trench Mortar Batteries on their trench strength for consumption on "Z + 1" day. These rations will be dumped well forward in selected sites in the vicinity of Brigade Dumps.

In order to curtail movement on "Y" day rations for consumption on "Z" day will be issued to all Units on "X" day.

4. WATER.

Brigades will hold at Brigade and Advanced Dumps sufficient water in petrol tins to fill the water bottles of all men twice.

[signature]

Lieut.-Colonel
A.A. & Q.M.G., 55th Division.

16-9-17.

5th R.Lanc. R.
10th L'pool R.
5th S.Lan. R.
5th N.Lan. R.

Reference map attached Brigade Instructions O/1, 16/9/17.-

Where '164 Brigade' is shewn please substitute '165 Brigade, and for 165 Brigade' amend to '164 Brigade.'

CAPTAIN,
17/9/1917. Brigade Major, 166th Infantry Brigade.

For Copy No 3

AMENDMENT No.1 to 166th Infantry Brigade Appendix 1 to O/1.

For line 3, para. 1,- read "YELLOW LINE" for "DOTTED RED LINE."

75

5th R.Lanc. R.
10th L'pool R.
5th S.Lan. R.
5th N.Lan. R.
166 M.G.C.
166 T.M.B.

Herewith map referred to in para.2, Appendix 1, issued with "Instructions for operations, O/1" dated 16/9/1917.

It should be superimposed on FREZENBERG 1/10,000 sheet.

CAPTAIN,

17/9/1917. Brigade Major, 166th Infantry Brigade.

SECRET.

166 INFANTRY BRIGADE.

APPENDIX NO. 4. to O/1.

ADMINISTRATIVE INSTRUCTIONS.

Duruing coming operations the following will be the administrarive arrangements.

1. SUPPLY OF S.A.A. GRENADES ETC.

5th R. Lanc. R. and 5th N. Lan. R. will obtain all S.A.A., Bombs, R.E. Material etc. from 164 and 165 Brigades respectively.

2. FIGHTING KIT.

Attached is a list of articles to be carried by Brigade (less 5th R. Lanc. R. and 5th N. Lan. R. who will receive orders later.),

With the exception of attached list, instructions laid down in S.S. 135, Secn. XXX are to be adhered to.

3. RATIONS.

Troops will carry 'Z' day's in addition to the Iron Ration. 'Z' plus 1 day's rations will be issued to units on 17th instant, and consist of Preserved Meat, biscuits, tea, sugar, and solidified alcohol.

These are to be made up into one man loads in sandbags, and dumped at a place to be notified later.

Rum will be issued daily.

4. WATER.

Onlym one water bottle per man will be available; these will be filled on Y/Z night. Water will be delivered in petrol tins to units on 'Z' night, and subsequently with rations.

5. BRIGADE CARRYING PARTY.

Each Battalion will detail 1 Officer, 1 N.C.O. and 20 Other Ranks to report to Staff Captain, at time and place to be notified later. They will be rationed by Brigade H.Q. on and after 'Z' plus 1 day.

6. NUMBER OF OFFICERS AND O.R. REMAINING OUT OF ACTION.

The numbers of Officers and Other Ranks which must be left behind will be as laid down in S.S. 135 Section XXX (as amended).

These numbers will include all details (Officers and Other Rabks) who are away from their units attending various courses of instruction, and the permanent staff of the Depot Battalion.

They will be accommodated at Units' Transport.

CAPTAIN.

17. 9. 1917. Staff Captain, 166 Inf. Brigade.

Issued to Signals 6 a.m. ....

Copy No.	1.	5th R. Lanc. R.
	2.	10th L'pool R.
	3.	5th S. Lan. R.
	4.	5th N. Lan. R.
	5.	166 M. G. C.
	6.	166 T. M. B.
	7.	B. T. O.
	8.	55th Division "Q" (for information).
	9.	B. G. C.
	10.	B. M.
	11.	S. C.
	12.	File.

ARTICLES TO BE CARRIED BY EACH BATTALION.

1. Pack will be worn on the back instead of haversack.

2. Heavy picks and shovels by 75% of Battalion, troops to be ready to dump them at short notice.

3. Entrenching tool and carrier will not be carried by men who go into action with heavy pick or shovel.

4. 1 Bandolier additional (total 170 rounds) per man, carried in the pack on top.

5. 200 each No. 23 and 24 Rifle Grenades (with rods and blank). Men not in possession of No. 23 will carry 1 Mills No. 5.

6. One aeroplane flare per man.

7. 3 tins of S.O.S. signals per platoon.

8. 2 sandbags per man.

SECRET. Copy No. 3

166 INFANTRY BRIGADE.

INSTRUCTIONS FOR OPERATIONS. O/1.

Reference attached map. B /9/1917.

1. V Corps is to attack on 'Z' day (to be notified later) 9th Division on right, 55th Division on left: 3rd and 59th Divisions in reserve. 58th Division (XVIII Corps) on left of 55th Division.

2. On the night 13th/14th the 27th Division which has been holding the front opposite to the Division was relieved by the 2nd Guards Reserve Division. An identification was obtained on the 14th September of the 91st R.I.R., 2nd Guards Reserve Division near HINDU COT.

It is probable that this Division holds the line on the same principles as the 27th Division, that is, all three Regiments in the line, with one Battalion of each Regiment in the front line, one in support and one in immediate reserve. Those in immediate reserve being located West of the PASSCHENDALE RIDGE, either in, close behind, or in front of the STADEN-ZONNEBEKE line.

3. Divisional and Brigade boundaries, frontages and objective are shewn on attached map. 165th Infantry Brigade with 1/5th N.Lan. attached, and 164th Infantry Brigade with 1/5th Kings Own attached, will attack on right and left respectively.

166th Infantry Brigade with Headquarters at WIELTJE (less two Battalions and M.G.Coy) will be in Divisional Reserve and will assemble as ordered subsequently.

4. Battalions of Divisional Reserve will be available to reinforce attacking Brigades if required to secure and maintain final objective. Hqrs 1/5 S.L. WARWICK Fm

5. Attack will be carried out by stages. Attacking Brigades will allot their own four Battalions to capture of areas up to RED DOTTED line in first instance, thence to Yellow, and thence to GREEN LINE. Capture and retention of HILL 37 is of supreme importance.

58th Division (174th Infantry Brigade) assisted by two Tanks will co-operate in capture of SCHULER FARM.

6. Leading Infantry will leave RED DOTTED LINE at Zero plus 80 minutes and YELLOW LINE at plus 165 minutes (approx. times).

7. 1/5th King's Own and 1/5th N.Lan. are intended to provide a reserve for each of the attacking Brigades as a striking force within easy reach of the final objective, for instant use if required to resist counter-attack and to crush any enemy who may attempt it. This is not intended to prevent their being used in case of necessity to ensure the attack being driven home should the forces in front of them prove unequal to their tasks.

8. The attack will be carried out under a creeping barrage, combined with a machine gun barrage, and a heavy bombardment of all known strong points and communications. The barrage (as at present arranged) will open 150 yards in front of the Infantry and will move by lifts of 50 yards. The first lift will be at ZERO plus 3 minutes. For the first 200 yards it will move at the rate of 100 yards in 4 minutes, thence at 100 yards in 6 minutes. When the protective barrage lifts from 150 yards beyond the RED DOTTED line the pace of the barrage will be at 100 yards in 8 minutes, with a pause of 40 minutes 150 yards beyond the YELLOW line.

9 The approximate position of strong points (to be constructed by Infantry Brigades) and of a supporting point (to be constructed by C.R.E.) are shewn on attached map. Further instructions will be issued as to co-operation of R.E. and Infantry in placing enemy strong points in a state of defence.

10. Details of Machine Gun barrage will form the subject of separate instructions. All machine guns of 164th Infantry Brigade and 165th Infantry Brigade are placed at the disposal of Brigadier Generals Commanding those Brigades. The 166th Infantry Brigade and 196th Machine Gun Coy's will be available for the machine gun barrage under orders of D.M.G.O.

11. Except as stated no details are yet available as to Tanks.

12. It is most important that on reaching any objective all troops taking it shall be re-organized as quickly as possible so that those not required for garrison purposes shouldbe capable of going forward again when more advanced positions have been captured by other troops.

13. For each enemy strong point certain definite parties will be told off beforehand -

(a) for mopping up - that is to capture or exterminate the whole of the enemy manning it

(b) as a garrison - to put it in a state of defence, organize fire from it so that it and other strong points, as captured, may be capable of supporting each other, and hold it to the last in the event of the enemy driving our troops back on it. The same body of troops may perform both task (a) and task (b) if considered desirable.

14. Instructions for signal communications, contact aeroplanes and other instructions in connection with the matters referred to on pages 6 and 7 of S.S.135 have been, or will be, issued separately to all concerned.

F. J. G. Lewis
13-9

Issued to Signals 6 am 17/9/17

166th Infantry Brigade.

Nopy No 1 5th R.Lanc. R.
2 10th L'pool R.
3 5th S. Lan. R.
4 5th N.Lan. R.
5 166 M. G. C.
6 166 T. M. B.

Copy No 7 B. G. C.
8 B. M.
9 S. C.
10 B. S. O.
11 War Diary
12 File

1/5 South Lancs.

SECRET.

166 INFANTRY BRIGADE.

APPENDIX 5 to O/1.

INSTRUCTIONS FOR SIGNAL COMMUNICATIONS.

Reference map sheet 28 N.W.
BELGIUM

1. Attention is drawn to S.S.148, the principles of which will be followed as closely as possible.

2. Brigade H.Q. 164, 165, & 166,- WIELTJE,
Brigade Forward Stations, 164, CAPRICORN KEEP
165, BANK FARM
Cable Head BRIDGE HOUSE
Pigeons, 4 birds each to 1/5thKing's Own and 1/5th N.Lan..
These will be delivered evening of 'Y' day.

Visual, existing Visual Station AUV in CALL SUPPORT (C.23.c.6.8) will receive from both Brigade Forward Stations and from the cable head.
Power Buzzers and Amplifiers will be installed as follows,-

BRIDGE HOUSE,	Code call N.1
CAPRICORN KEEP	,, N.2
BANK FARM	,, N.3

in addition to which 164 and 165 Brigades will each have two Power Buzzers to go forward.

Wireless Stations.- Code Call NV at dugout (C.24.a.2.4) near BRIDGE HOUSE.

A further wireless set will be at disposal of 164 Brigade to be sent forward if necessary, code call DU.

Runner posts between WIELTJE and BRIDGE HOUSE and BRIGADE FORWARD STATIONS will be located as follows,-

C.23.c.80.55
C.24.a.3.6
C.24.b.3.6
C.18.d.0.4
C.18.d.5.6

These will be marked by triangular notice boards.

3. Communications prior to Zero. In the forward area communications which are not urgent are to be made by runner. D.III telephones will not be used in front of WIELTJE-MILL COT before Zero.
Fullerphones may be used for URGENT messages but the telephone attached is to be used only by an officer and when absolutely necessary.

Visual Station (C.23.c.6.8) only receives D.D. messages until after Zero when messages may be sent forward.

Units will test LUCAS lamps for faults on Y day and report to Brigade Signal Officer any found faulty.

Dugouts at BRIDGE HOUSE and gun emplacement (C.24.a.15.40) are reserved entirely for Signal purposes.

4. Communications after Zero. All means of communication may be used to get messages through. Battalions should wait until there is a prospect of lines being maintained before they lay out cables.
Battalions will lay and maintain from Battalion Command Posts to Brigade Forward Station when latter is established.

* issued The latest code used by Fifth Army will be used.

All important messages will be sent in duplicate by different routes, and those of special importance in triplicate.

Diagram of communications attached.

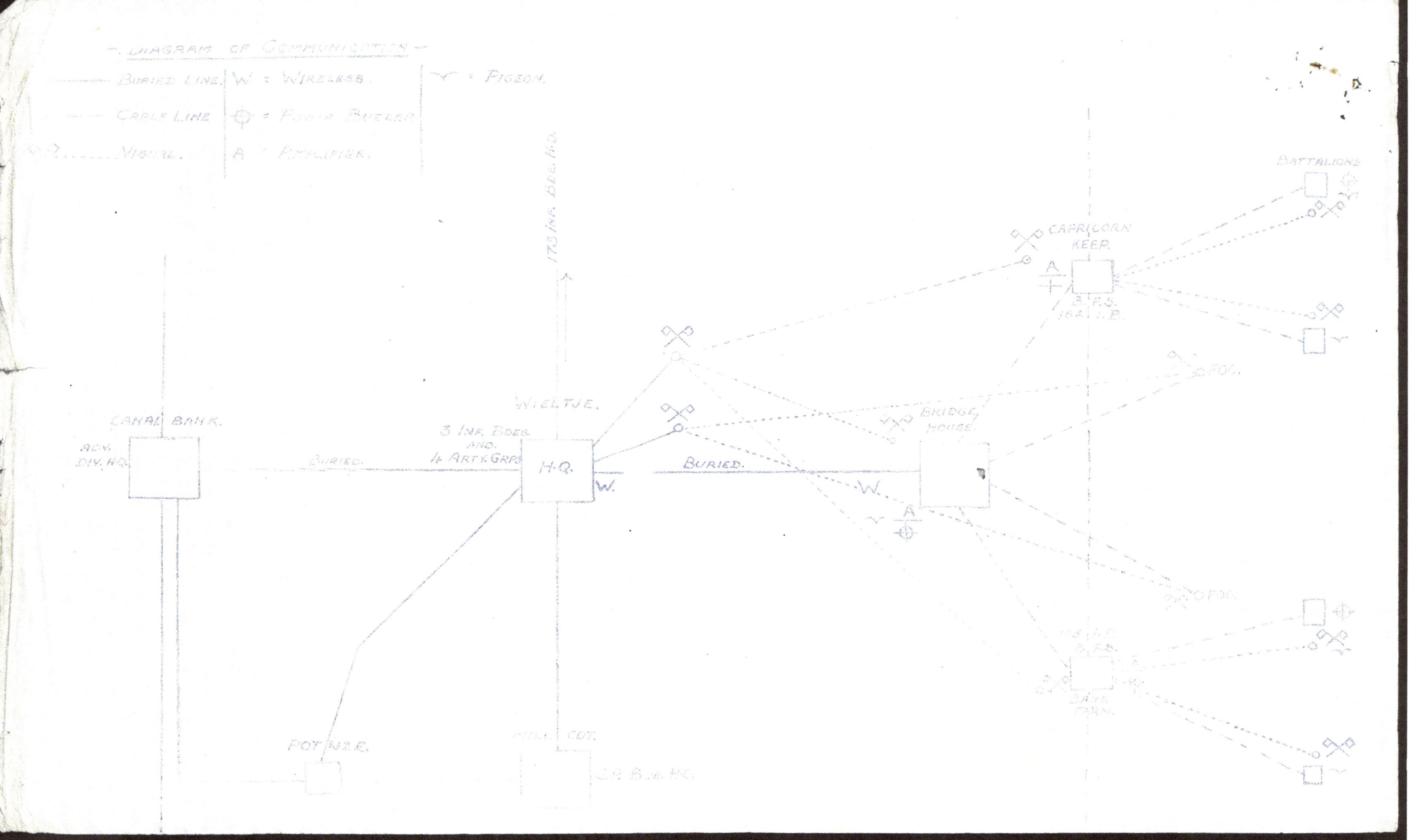

– DIAGRAM OF COMMUNICATIONS –

BURIED LINE. | W = WIRELESS. | = PIGEON.

CABLE LINE | = POWER BUZZER

VISUAL. | A = AMPLIFIER.

178 INF. BDE. H.Q.

CAPRICORN KEEP.

B.F.S. 164 I.B.

BATTALIONS

F.O.O.

BRIDGE HOUSE.

WIELTJE.

3 INF. BDES. AND 4 ARTY. GRPS.

H.Q.

W.

BURIED.

BURIED.

A

W.

A

CANAL BANK.

ADV. DIV. H.Q.

POT. N.Z.E.

HILL COT.

S.A. BDE. H.Q.

F.O.O.

165 I.B. B.F.S.

BANK FARM.

SECRET.   Copy No. 3

166TH INFANTRY BRIGADE ORDER NO. 97.

Ref:- FREZENBERG sheet
(Edn 3) 1/10,000, and
attached map.

Septr 17/1917.

1. Brigade will be relieved on W-X, X-Y, and Y-Z nights by 164th and 165th Infantry Brigades in accordance with attached table.

2. Attached map shows boundaries between 164th and 165th Brigades and approximate normal accommodation for information.

3. For purposes of relief on W-X night, areas will be commanded as under,-

A & B,	Major Pilkington, D.S.O, 1/5th S. Lan R.	H.Q., CAMBRAI reserve
C & D) R & S)	Lt-Col. A. WAYTE, 1/5th King's Own (R.L.R)	H.Q., WARWICK FARM.
P & Q,	Capt. RODDICK M.C. 1/10th Scottish (K.L.R)	H.Q., CALL RESERVE.

4 (a) On W-X and X-Y nights units of Brigade moving to YPRES area N, will march by GRAVENSTAFEL-ST.JEAN ROAD.
(b) Officers in charge of advanced parties of units moving on X-Y and Y-Z nights to ST.JEAN and YPRES area N. will report to Staff Captain, WIELTJE, 3 p.m. on day of move.

5. All further arrangements and details of guides for relief will be made between Commanding Officers concerned: Officers of incoming units will get in touch forthwith with officers named in para. 3.

6. All possible precautions will be taken to prevent enemy observation of troops, and during X & Y days movement will be reduced to a minimum.

7. Completion of all moves will be reported to Brigade H.Q. by code word "MORE." MORE

8. Command will pass on completion of relief on X-Y night

B. W. Thura
CAPTAIN,
Brigade Major, 166th Infantry Bde.

Issued to
Signals at 3 p m.

Copy No. 1 5th R.Lanc.R.
2. 10thL'pool R.
3. 5th S.Lan. R.
4 5th N.Lan. R.
5 166 M.G.C.
6 166 T.M.B.
7 55th Division
8 173 Infantry Brigade
No. 9 125 Infantry Brigade
10 275 Group R.F.A. Left
11 B. G. C.
12 B. M.
13 S. C.
14 B. S. O.
15 B. T. O.
16 War Diary
17 File
18 Major PILKINGTON, D.S.O. 1/
19 Capt RODDICK, M.C. 1/10th L.S.)
20 164 Inf.Bde
21 165 Inf.Bde

Issued with 166 Inf·Bde Order No·97

	Night	Outgoing units	In area	Goes to	Incoming unit	Remarks
1.	W-X	1/5th K.O. (R.Lanc.R)	C D E S	YPRES NORTH	7 K.L.R. 9 K.L.R. 1/4 R.L.R. 1/4 N.Lan.R.	All outgoing units will proceed by route march. No relief will commence before dusk.
2.		1½ Coys 1/5 S.Lan.R.	A B	,,	7 K.L.R. 9 K.L.R.	Relieving Battalions come under orders of B. G. C. on completion of relief.
3.		2 Coys 1/10 L.S.	P Q	,,	1/4 R.Lanc.R. 1/4 N.Lan. R.	
4.		-	R	-	165 M.G.Coy 165 T.M.B.	
5		-	T	-	164 M.G.Coy 164 T.M.B.	
6	X-Y	166 M.G.C.	Present front line & O.G. system	ST.JEAN area	164 M.G.C 165 M.G.C.	Relief of guns E of STEENBEEK must be completed by 2 a.m.
7		166 T.M.B.	Present front line & WIELTJE	YPRES NORTH	164 T.M.B. 165 T.M.B.	
8		1/5 S.Lan. (less 1½ Coys)	Present front line system	YPRES area N.	1/7 K.L.R. 1/9 K.L.R.	Arrangements will be made direct between Commanding Officers concerned. H.Q. 1/5th S.Lan.R. BANK FARM
9		1/10 L'pool R. (less 2 Coys)	,,	,,	1/4 R.Lanc.R. 1/4 N.Lan. R.	Reliefof troops E of STEENBEEK must be completed by 2 a.m. H.Q. 1/10 L'pool R: CAPRICORN KEEP
10		Bde H.Q.	WIELTJE	GOLDFISH CHATEAU	On completion of relief	Advanced H.Q. will remain WIELTJE dugout No. 4.
11	Y-Z	1/5 K.O. (R.Lanc.R)	YPRES area N.	O.G.system	As ordered by B.G.C.164 Inf.Bde	Battalion comes under orders of B.G.C. 164 Inf. Bde from 3 p.m. 'Y' day.
12		1/5 L.N.Lan.	CANAL BANK	,,	As ordered by B.G.C. 165 Inf.Bde	Battalion comes under orders of B.G.C. 165th Inf. Bde from 3 p.m. 'Y' day.
13		166 M.G.C.	ST.JEAN area	Selected points in forward area		Commence to move 11 p.m. and to be in position at 4.30 am under orders of D.M.G.O.

Copy No. 5

[illegible] INBORN

Operation Order No. 114

App. I

1. Intention.

Battalion will be relieved tonight by 7th and 9th R.I.R. in the right sector and will move into divisional reserve.

2. Relief.

B Coy will be relieved by A Coy 7th R.I.R.
[illegible] " " " " { Battalion 9th
[illegible] " " " " { [illegible] 9th
D " " " " by D Coy 9th

[illegible] B & C will each send 5 guides (1 per platoon and 1 Coy HQrs) to the junction of [illegible] track and old German front line at 6 pm where they will be met by guides of 7th who will commence relieving [illegible] at dusk. 9th guides (information later).

Movement.

On completion of relief Coys will move off by ½ platoons via the GRAVENSTAFEL – ST JEAN RD to camps at GOLDFISH Ch. Guides will be on the [illegible] [illegible] [illegible].

Lewis Guns

[illegible] will be dumped where OXFORD RD joins WIELTJE – GRAVENSTAFEL RD.

1 NCO & 1 man to be left in charge of each Coys guns and magazines. 2 guns taken over from [illegible] Bn will be brought out by "C" Coy. L G limbers will collect guns about 12 midnight.

5. **Stores**

Signed list of Stores (in duplicate) will be sent to O.R. as soon as possible. [illegible]

6. Completion of Relief will be notified to HQ by runner.

Acknowledge.

[illegible] Lt

18/9/17   A/Adjutant

"A" Form,
MESSAGES AND SIGNALS.

Army Form C.2121
(in pads of 100.)
No. of Message

Prefix Code m. Words Charge
Office of Origin and Service Instructions.
Sent
Sent At m. To By
This message is on a/c of: Service.
(Signature of "Franking Officer.")
Recd. at m. Date From By

TO 1/5 S. Lanc. Rgt.

Sender's Number	Day of Month.	In reply to Number.	AAA
* BM497	17		

W day is 17 Sept

From 166 Bde
Place
Time 1 PM

The above may be forwarded as now corrected.
Censor.
(Z)
Signature of Addressor or person authorised to telegraph in his name.

* This line should be erased if not required.

(710.) W W12093/M1217 50,000 pads. 1/17. D. D. & L. (E764.) Forms C/2121/11.

"A" Form. (In pads of 100.)

MESSAGES AND SIGNALS.

No. of Message ______

Prefix ______ Code ______ m.	Words	Charge	This message is on a/c of:	Recd. at ______ m.
Office of Origin and Service Instructions.	Sent		______ Service.	Date ______
Secret	At ______ m.			From ______
	To ______			By ______
	By ______		(Signature of "Franking Officer.")	

TO { ~~1/5 S.L.~~ ~~1/10 L.S.~~ ~~166 T.M.B.~~

Sender's Number	Day of Month.	In reply to Number.	AAA
* BM 507	17		

Following moves will probably take place on night 4/2

1/5 S Lancs to area (x) C & D – H.Q. Warwick Fm

1/10 L.S. " (x) R & S – H.Q. to be selected & reported on

166 TMB " (x) E

(x) see map attached 0 9 7

B[illegible] Capt.
Bde. Major

From 166 Bde.
Place
Time

The above may be forwarded as now corrected. (Z)

Censor. Signature of Addressor or person authorised to telegraph in his name.

* This line should be erased if not required.

(7107) Wt W12093/M1217 50,000 pads. 1/17. D. D. & L. (E764.) Forms C/2121/11.

"A" Form. MESSAGES AND SIGNALS.

Army Form C.2121 (in pads of 100.)

No. of Message

Prefix Code m. Words Charge

Office of Origin and Service Instructions.

SECRET.

Sent At m. To By

This message is on a/c of: Service.

(Signature of "Franking Officer.")

Recd. at m. Date From By

TO INSTRUCT, INSTIL, INBORN.

Sender's Number F 18 | Day of Month 17 | In reply to Number. | AAA

WARNING ORDER AAA INFANTRY IN O.B. AND O.G. SYSTEMS WILL PROBABLY BE RELIEVED TONIGHT BY TROOPS OF 164 AND 165 INFANTRY BRIGADES.

CAPTAIN

BRIGADE MAJOR.

INANE.

From

Place

Time

The above may be forwarded as now corrected. (Z)

Censor. Signature of Addressor or person authorised to telegraph in his name.

* This line should be erased if not required.

(7107) Wt. W12093/M1217 50,000 pads. 1/17. D. D. & L. (E764.) Forms C/2121/11.

SECRET.

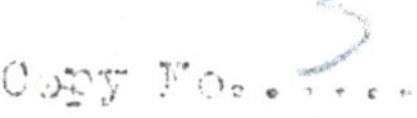

Copy No. 3

166 INFANTRY BRIGADE - APPENDIX NO. 6 to O/1.

MEDICAL ARRANGEMENTS.

The following will be the medical arrangements for the proposed operations :-

1. REGIMENTAL AID POSTS AT ZERO HOUR.

Each of the attacking Brigades will have two Regimental Aid Posts. The locations will be notified later.

Prior to the assault, the supporting battalions of the attacking Brigades will share the aid posts of the attacking battalions.

As the advance takes place, new R.A.Ps. will be selected by O.C's Units in consultation with their Medical Officers, and the new sites will be notified immediately to the Advanced Dressing Station, WIELTJE, by means of the R.A.M.C. Runners attached to Regimental M.Os. for communication purposes.

2. RELAY POSTS (for all R.A.Ps. except PLUM FARM.)

1.	BRIDGE HOUSE.	-	C.24.a.4.6.
2.	RAT FARM.	-	C.23.b.9.3.
3.	CALL FARM.	-	C.23.c.8.6.
4.	No. 44 DUGOUT.	-	C.23.c.3.1.

For PLUM FARM.

5.	UHLAN FARM.	-	C.29.b. Central.
6.	No. 6 DUGOUT.	-	C.29.a.8.5.

3. ADVANCED DRESSING STATION.	-	WIELTJE, C.28.a.9.5.
R.A.M.C. BEARERS ASSEMBLY POST.	-	CANAL BANK, I.1.b.7.7.
CORPS MAIN DRESSING STATION.	-	RED FARM, G.5.d.9.5.
SICK COLLECTING STATION.	-	MOATED FARM, H.2.d.7.2.
CORPS WALKING WOUNDED COLLECTING STATION.	-	VLAMERTINGHE MILL, H.8.a.9.9.

4. COLLECTION AND EVACUATION OF WOUNDED.

(a) From the Forward Area to Regimental Aid Posts.

By regimental stretcher bearers.

Each Battalion has already been ordered to maintain 32 regimental stretcher bearers, who are to be placed at the disposal of Regimental M.Os. prior to Zero.

Regimental M.Os. will arrange for the custody, and subsequent disposal of the rifles of any of the stretcher bearers who report to them with arms.

(b) From Regimental Aid Posts to the Advanced Dressing Station, WIELTJE.

By R.A.M.C. Bearers via the Relay Posts enumerated above, assisted when necessary by parties from the 200 infantrymen already detailed for duty as additional bearers.

Wheeled stretchers will be used to the fullest possible extent on the SHREE FARM - WIELTJE ROAD.

Motor Ambulances will be regulated by V Corps, and will clear Stretcher Cases from WIELTJE, and, as the operation progresses, from the neighbourhood of VON HUGEL FARM to the main dressing station at RED FARM.

5. WALKING WOUNDED.

Walking wounded will be directed by either tracks Nos. 4, 5 and 6, from the SPREE FARM - WIELTJE ROAD, or MILL COTTS, where, if possible, light railway trains will be available, for conveyance to CULLODEN SIDING (B.26.d.), and H.8 Central.

If no trains are available, walking wounded will be immediately directed via the POTIJZE - YPRES ROAD, or the ST. JEAN ROAD - SAVILE ROAD to MENIN ROAD CORNER - I.8.b.7.4. where they will be met by lorries, which will convey them to VLAMERTINGHE MILL.

The A.D.M.S. will arrange for the walking wounded routes to be marked with notice boards.

6. SPARE STRETCHERS.

Dumps of stretchers will be formed at Relay Posts and at the Advanced Dressing Station. Any stretchers salved, or not required, should be taken to one of the above places.

7. COMMUNICATION.

Close communication between all ranks on the chain of evacuation is essential and information regarding the number of casualties to be cleared ans the area where they are occurring should be constantly transmitted from Regimental M.Os. to the Officer in charge of bearer divisions.

For this purpose 2 R.A.M.C. Orderlies will be posted to each Regimental M.O. before the action to act as runners.

Bearers situated at Relay Posts must not be taken from these points except by the order of the officer in charge of bearers; otherwise the chain of evacuation will break down.

CAPTAIN.

18. 9. 1917. Staff Captain, 166 Infantry Bde.

Issued to Signals..........

Copy No. 1. 5th R. Lanc. R.
2. 10th L'pool R.
3. 5th S. Lan. R.
4. 5th N. Lan. R.
5. 166 M.G. Co.
6. 166 T.M. Bty.
7. B.T.O.
8. ~~55th Division 'Q' (for information)~~
9. B.G.C.
10. B.M.
11. S.C.
12. File.

Fifth Army.
I/2/40.A.

V Corps (I).

IGX 2/11
18th September 1917.

3rd Division.
9th Division.
42nd Division.
55th Division.
59th Division.
61st Division.

Examination of prisoners recently captured emphasises the following points :-

1. The creation of fresh shell holes is essential for the enemy's present tactics; shell holes quickly fill with water, especially in low-lying ground, necessitating frequent changes of position from old to new shell holes. Prisoners think that their present method of holding the line would become impossible on this front if we were to give up the use of H.E. or used only instantaneous fuze.

2. A close shrapnel barrage is more effective than H.E. against shell hole positions. This is confirmed by prisoners taken at VERDUN.

3. The large craters made by shells of heavy calibre have proved particularly useful to the enemy in defending his concreted blockhouses against minor attacks. Parties of the enemy crouching in the bottom of these craters are frequently passed unnoticed by the attackers; when a frontal counter-attack is made, these men come up and shoot at our men from behind, with the result that the position taken is lost by reason not of the counter-attack but of fire from behind.

4. Our instantaneous fuze is stated to be very effective and is much more feared than the ordinary fuze.

The conclusions to be drawn from the above would appear to be :-

1. The use of H.E. shell, especially of heavy calibres, to be reduced as much as possible, or instantaneous fuze to be used to a much greater extent.

2. The practice of prefacing minor operations against concrete blockhouses with bombardments with heavy calibres has the disadvantage of increasing the cover available and making the holding of the position, if taken, impossible without thorough mopping-up.

P. P. Hill-Dillon.

Capt. G.S.
for B.G., G.S.
V Corps.

1/5 S.L.
For information
166 Bde
18-9-17

B. Aitken, Capt.
Bde. Major

164
165
S
R
D
C
E
Wieltje
Argyle Fm.
White Cottage
29
DURHAM TR.
BILGE TR.
ADMIRALS TR.
MORMOUTH TR.
NEW
LONE ST.
STRAND
EDEN TR.
MILL TR.
CURZON ST.
SCOTTISH TR.
SCALE. 1:10,000
S.10. COPY No. 33

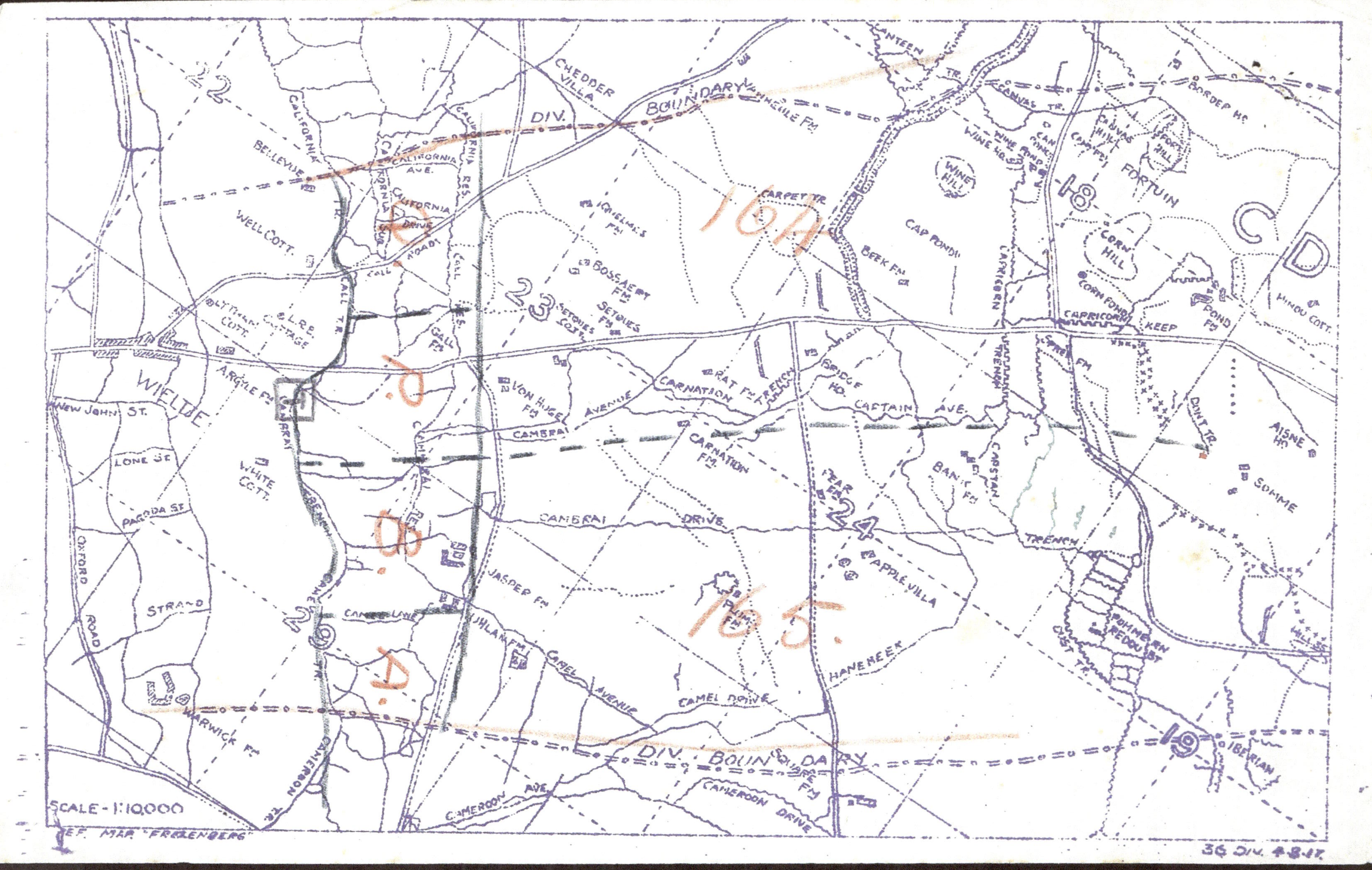

CHEDDER VILLA
DIV. BOUNDARY
FORTUIN
CORN HILL
WINE HILL
CAP POND
BEEK FM
CARPET TR.
CAPRICORN KEEP
CARPRICORN TRENCH
CAPTAIN AVE.
CAPSTAN
BANK FM
CARNATION AVENUE
CARNATION FM
CAMBRAI DRIVE
APPLE VILLA
PEAR FM
VON HUGEL FM
CALIFORNIA RES.
CALIFORNIA AVE.
CALL TR.
BELLEVUE
WELL COTT.
WHITE COTT.
WIELTJE
NEW JOHN ST.
LONE ST.
PAGODA ST.
STRAND
OXFORD ROAD
WARWICK FM
JASPER FM
CAMEL AVENUE
CAMEL DRIVE
HANEBEEK
CAMERON DRIVE
CAMERON AVE.
DIV. BOUNDARY
POMMERN REDOUBT
DIST TR.
DONT TR.
AISNE HO.
SOMME
IBERIAN
BORDER HO.
CANVAS TR.
CANTEEN TR.
164
165
Q. R. B. A.
C D
SCALE - 1:10000
REF. MAP "FREZENBERG"
3G DIV. 4.8.17.

Appx IV

S E C R E T. Copy No. 2

166 INFANTRY BRIGADE ORDER NO. 98.

Reference map issued with 166th Inf. Bde Order O/1. Sept 18/1917.

1.(a) Second and Fifth Armies will resume offensive on 'Z' day, ~~[illegible]~~
V. Corps will attack with 9th Division on right
55th Division on left
3rd & 59th Division in reserve
58th Division (XVIII Corps) on left of 55th Division.

(b) German lines opposite Divisional front are held by 2nd Guards Reserve Division. It is probable that all these Regts are in the line.,
one Bn of each Regt. in front line
One ,, ,, support
One ,, ,, immediate reserve, either W. of PASSCHENDAELE RIDGE or in vicinity of STADEN-ZONNEBEKE LINE.

2. Divisional and Brigade boundaries, frontages and objectives are shewn on map attached O/1.
165 Infantry Brigade with 1/5th L.N.L.Regt attached, and 164 Infantry Brigade with 1/5th King's Own (R.L.R.) attached will attack on right and left respectively.

166 Infantry Brigade (less two Battalions and M.G.C.) with "G" H.Q. at WIELTJE No. 4 dugout, and "Q" H.Q. CANAL BANK, No 46 dugout, will be in Divisional Reserve, and will assemble as detailed in order No.97.

3. It is the intention to capture and secure final objective (GREEN LINE).

4. Function of Divisional Reserve, is,-
(1) to reinforce assaulting troops
(2) if required, to secure and maintain final objectives.

5. Attack will be carried out by stages. Attacking Brigades will allot their own four Battalions to capture of areas up to RED DOTTED line, in first instance, thence to YELLOW and later t GREEN line. Capture and retention of HILL 37 is of supreme importance.

58th Division (173 Infantry Brigade) assisted by two Tanks will cooperate in capture of SCHULER FARM.

6. Artillery programme for 'Y' and 'Z' days,- see appendix No.9 barrage map (issued separately) shews timing.

7 Programme of Machine Gun barrage,- see Appendix No.11.

8. Contact aeroplanes will be over objective at
plus 60 min.
,, 120 ,,
,, 210 ,,
and subsequently as ordered.

9. Approximate position of strong points (to be constructed by Infantry Brigades) and of supporting point (to be constructed by R.E.) are shewn on map referred to.

(CONTINUATION)

166 Inf.Bde Order No.88.

10. Zero will be notified later.

11. 1/10th Liverpool Scottish and 1/5th South Lan. will each detail 1 Liaison Officer for Brigade to report to Brigade Intelligence Officer when Battalion moves from its assembly position.

12. All units of Brigade in YPRES AREA N. will send an officer to Divisional Headquarters, MERSEY CAMP to synchronize between 5.30 p.m. and 6 p.m. and between 7.30 p.m. and 8 p.m. 'Y' day.

166 M.G.C. will send similarly to Brigade Headquarters WIELTJE.

13. Separate instructions have been issued on following points,

(A) Cooperation of R.E. and Pioneers
(B) Aircraft
(C) Maps and Aeroplane Photographs
(D) Dumps & administrative instructions
(E) Medical arrangements
(F) Police
(G) Signalling arrangements
(H) Machine guns
(I) Artillery
(J) Prisoners of war.

B. Wilson
CAPTAIN,
Brigade Major, 166 Infantry Bde.

Issued [illegible] 8.30 p.m.
to Signals at

Copy No 1	1/10th L'pool R.	Copy No 7	S.C.
2	1/5th S.Lan. R.	8	B.S.O.
3	166 T.M.B.	9	B.T.O.
4	55th Division	10	War Diary
5	B. G. C.	11	File
6	B. M.		

ADDENDUM NO.1 to MOVEMENT TABLE accompanying 166 Inf.Bde Order No.97.

Serial No	Night	Unit	In area	To	Starting point	Time	Route	Remarks
14	Y-Z	1/5 S.L.	YPRES NORTH	C & D areas	H.12.b.4.7	10 p.m.	4 & 5 tracks	Move by platoons 100 yds distance H.Q.- WARWICK FM dugouts.
15	Y-Z	1/10 L.S.	,,	R & S areas	H.6.c.0.0	9.45 p.m.	Salvation Corner, No 6 track	Move by platoons 100 yds distance. H.Q.- ~~WARWICK FM.~~ BILGE TR. dugouts.
16	Y-Z	166 T.M.B.	,,	E area	Follow 1/5th S.Lan. Regt.			H.Q., CONGREVE WALK. C.28.C.4.1.
17	Y-Z	Brigade H.Q. (less Adv. Bde H.Q.)	GOLDFISH CHATEAU	CANAL BANK Dugouts 46-52	Dugouts will be taken over on vacation by 1/5th L.N.Lan. R.			Adv. Brigade H.Q., B.G.C., B.M., B.I.O., remain at No 4 dugout, WIELTJE.

SIGNAL ARRANGEMENT.

1. 1/5th S.Lan. will connect by telephone to WIELTJE-MILL COTTS lateral circuit, which is already laid into WARWICK FARM dugouts.
1/10th L.S. will connect up on circuit to WIELTJE already existing in BILGE TR dugouts.
166 T.M.B. communication will be by runners

2. Completion of all moves will be reported to ADV. Brigade H.Q. by code word "MORE."

B. Wilson
CAPTAIN,
Brigade Major, 166th Infantry Brigade.

19/9/1917.

Border Ho
Fort Hill
Corn Hill
Pond Fm
CAPRICORN KEEP
APPROXIMATE FRONT
PROTECTIVE
FINAL PROTECTIVE
Schuler Fm
Gallipoli
Zonnebeke
Iberian
Dova Fm
Martha Ho
Lilac
Carriage
VERY SECRET
REFERENCE
DIV BDY
BDE "
SUPP POINT
STRONG "
DIV. LIAISON Pt
BDE " "
NOTE TIMES SHOWN ARE TIMES OF LEAVING THE LINE.

1:10 000 K.3. EDITION 1. Parts of { 28 N.E. 28 N.W.

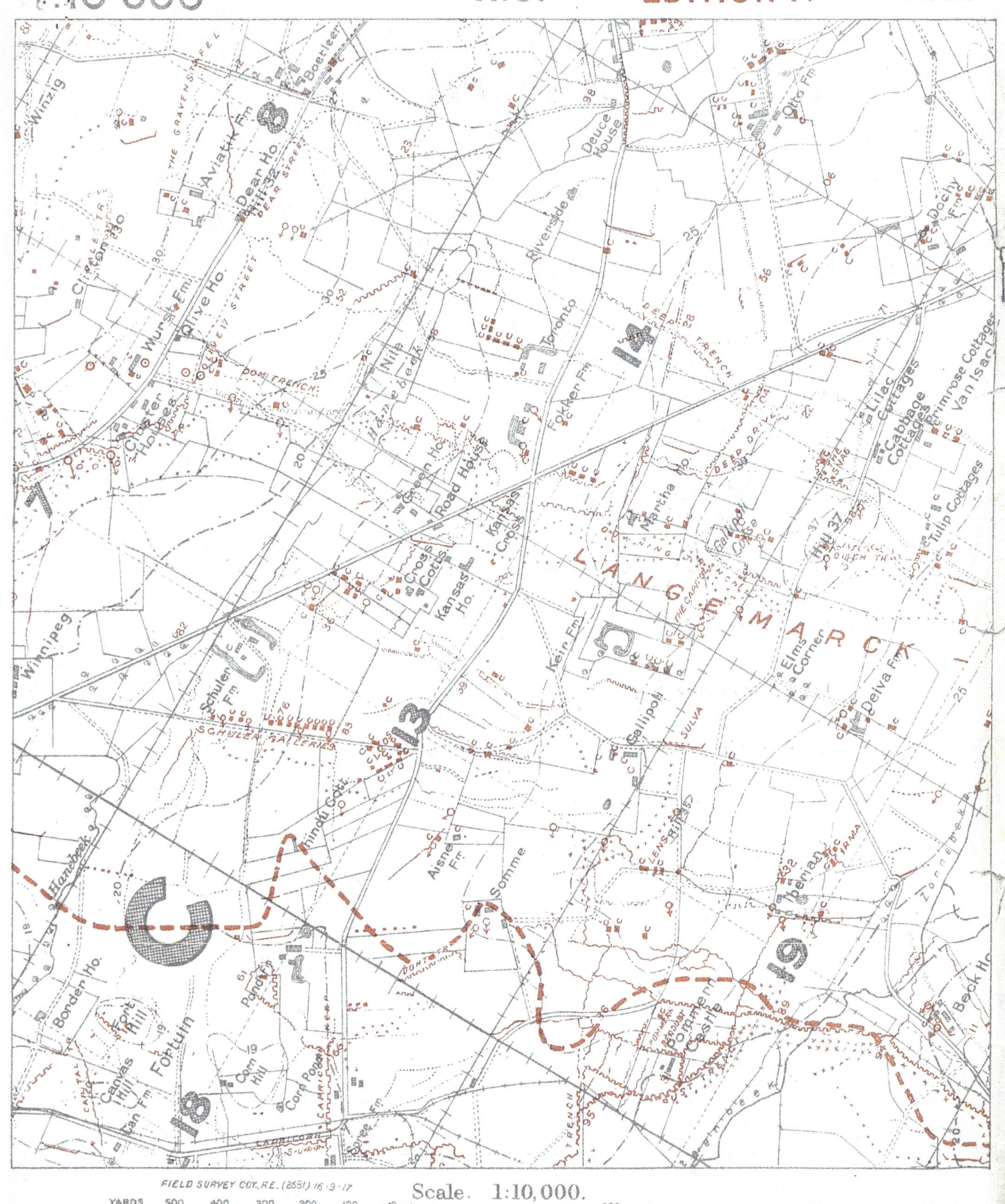

FIELD SURVEY COY. R.E. (2681) 16·3·17

Scale. 1:10,000.

YARDS 500 400 300 200 100 0 500 1,000 YARDS

Message Form.

.....................Division.

Map reference or mark own position on Map at back.

1. I am at..

2. I am at..and am consolidating.

3. I am at..and have consolidated.

4. I need :—Ammunition.
   Bombs.
   Rifle Grenades.
   Water.
   Very lights.
   Stokes shells.

5. Enemy forming up for counter-attack at....... ....

6. I am in touch with................................ on Right / Left at ....

7. I am not in touch on Right / Left

8. Am being shelled from...

9. I estimate my present strength at ....rifles.

10. Hostile {Battery / Machine Gun / Trench Mortar} active at..

Time.................................a.m. (p.m.) Name...

Date.. Platoon.................. Company............

Place... Battalion...

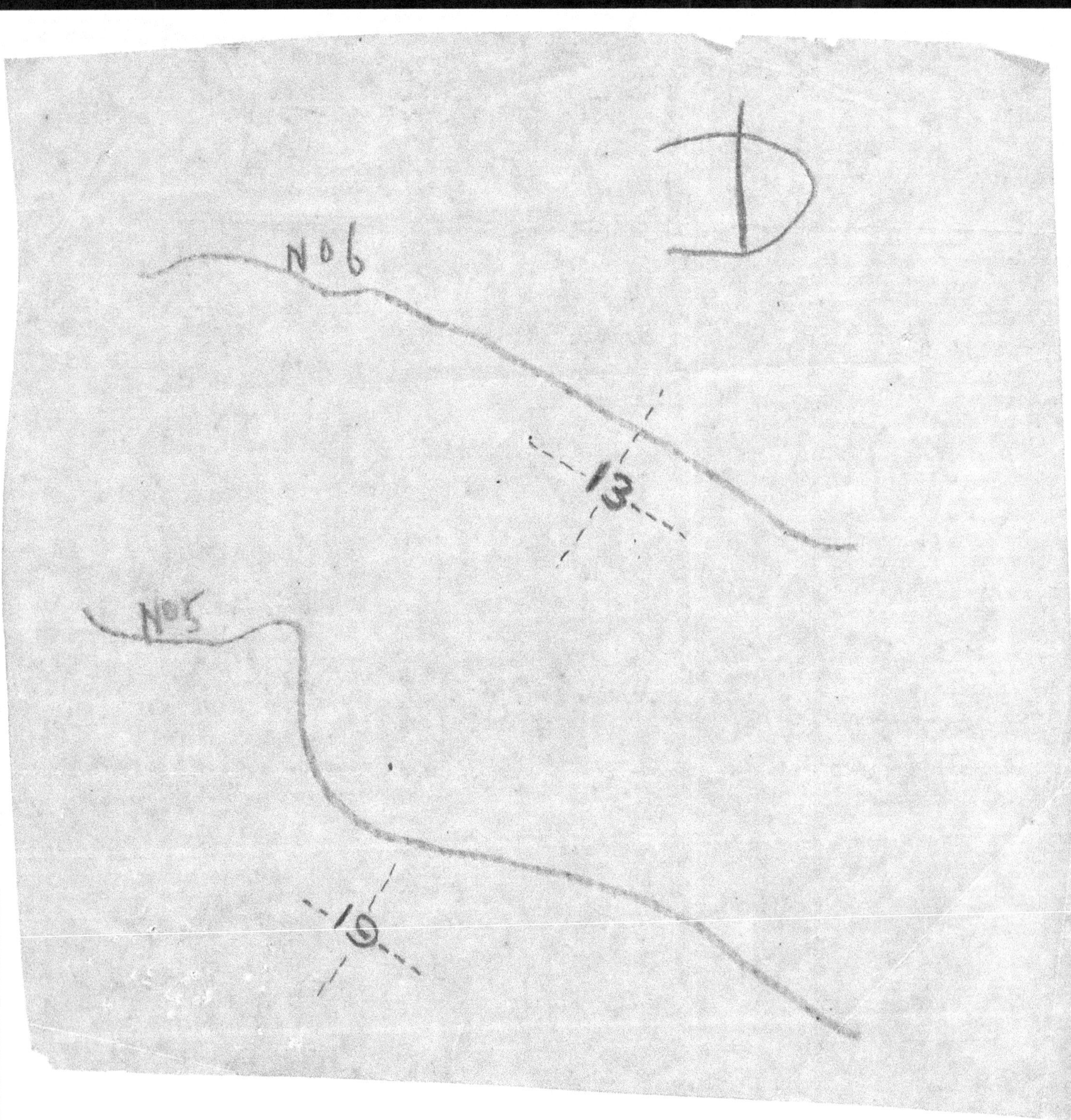

D
No 6
13
No 5
15

SECRET.

St

Addendum No.1 to Appendix 2 to O/1.-

1. Cancel para. 5.- Signal panels will not be used by Battalions.

2. Attached instructions are issued re protective aeroplanes. The signals will be used in the forthcoming operations.

B. Wilkinson Capt.

18/9/1917. 166th Infantry Brigade.

SECRET.

166TH INFANTRY BRIGADE.

Addendum No. 1 to Appendix 9 to O/1.

1. 4 salvoes of Smoke Shell will be fired at intervals of 8 minutes at a distance of not less than 400 yards from Infantry.

Table of Smoke Shell barrage.

Time	Objective on barrage line.
Zero plus 15 min.	1 hour 40 mins
Zero plus 23 min. & every 8 mins to 1 hour 29 min.	2 hours 48 mins.
Zero plus 1 hr 36 min	3 hours
Zero plus 1 hr 44 min & every 8 mins to plus 5 hours	Final protective line

2. At plus 5 hrs smoke will lift on line D.8.c.50.85 - D.9.c.80.25 and line D.21.d.5.4 - D.21.a.55.40. and ABRAHAM HEIGHTS D.15.b.

No smoke after Zero plus 4 hr 20 min.

B. Wilkinson

CAPTAIN.
Brigade Major, 166th Infantry Brigade.

19/9/1917.

"A" Form.
MESSAGES AND SIGNALS.

Army Form C.2121
(in pads of 100.)
No. of Message

Prefix Code m. Words Charge
Office of Origin and Service Instructions.
SECRET
Sent
At m.
To
By
This message is on a/c of:
Service.
(Signature of "Franking Officer.")
Recd. at m.
Date
From
By

TO			
	5 KO	5 SL	166 MGC
	10 LS	5 NL	166 TMB

Sender's Number.	Day of Month.	In reply to Number.	AAA
* AH1	19		

Addendum 1 to appendix 8 of Bde O/1 AAA
In paras 1-2-4 amend DIVISIONAL CAGE to READ ADVANCED DIVISIONAL CAGE PARA 3 - 2ND LINE add VIA MAIN DIVISIONAL CAGE I.7.b.15.50 AAA CANCEL PARA 5 AAA PARA 6 (b) ADD " HERE OFFICERS ONLY WILL BE SEARCHED AND THEIR EFFECTS PLACED IN SANDBAGS WITH LABEL ATTACHED GIVING OFFICERS NAME RANK AND REGT. AND TAKEN ON BY ESCORT TO CORPS CAGE

[signature] Capt
Brigade Major

From 166 Bde
Place
Time

The above may be forwarded as now corrected. (Z)
Censor. Signature of Addressor or person authorised to telegraph in his name.

* This line should be erased if not required.

(7107) Wt. W12093/M1247 50,000 pads. 1/17. D. D. & L. (E764) Forms C/2121/11.

S E C R E T.

166TH INFANTRY BRIGADE.

APPENDIX 2 to O/1.

AIRCRAFT.

1. No 21 Squadron R.F.C. is allotted to 55th Division for contact work.

2. Planes on contact work for the Division can be recognized by the following markings:-

(a) On both lower planes a rectangular attachment.

view from ground

(b) A white dumb-bell on either side of body of plane.

3. Signs to be used by infantry to show most advanced line held will be,-

(a) RED flares
(b) WATSON'S fans (as available)

Flares will be lit in the bottom of a trench or behind a parapet.

Watson fans will be used open and turned over at intervals of about 30 seconds so as to show alternately the white and coloured sides.

4. The signal for lighting flares or showing Watson fans will be a white Very light fired by an aeroplane. The Klaxon Horn will also be used by the aeroplane sounding a series of 'A's' in Morse. The Klaxon however may not always be audible. As this is the only occasion on which white Very lights will be fired from the air, flares must be lit or fans shewn immediately by the most advanced infantry on seeing this signal.

5. The signals panel as laid down in Appendix of S.S.135 will be used by units, care being taken to prevent their situation being discovered by the enemy's planes.

6. Dropping Station for Divisional Headquarters will be in the vicinity of SALVATION CORNER.

The exact location will be notified to No. 21 Squadron R.F.C. later.

7. The contact aeroplane will call for flares or fans at

ZERO plus 1 hour
ZERO plus 2 hours
Zero plus 2.30 hours

S E C R E T.   INBORN OPERATION ORDER Nº 116.   Copy Nº .....

III

1. OPERATION.

Battalion will move into Divisional Reserve in the OLD BRITISH FRONT LINE on night 19th September.

2. MOVEMENT.

Battalion will move forward at 10 p.m. as follows:-
Order:- A, C, B, D, H'Qrs. Platoons will move forward at 200 yards interval.
A, B, & H'Qrs by Nº 4 Track.
C & D Coys: by Nº 5 Track.
Headquarters: WARWICK FARM.

3. LEWIS GUNS.

O.C. Companies will send 1 N.C.O. and 1 O.R. per Company to load up their Lewis Guns, and 25 magazines per gun, at 6.30 p.m. in Camp, and these men will go with Limbers. Limbers will dump Companies' Guns where SAVILLE Road cuts Nº 4 & 5 Tracks.
A & B Guns Nº 4 Track.
C & D Guns Nº 5 Track.

4. STORES.

Companies will draw 16 Watson Fans from Q.M. in Camp now and explain their use to men.

All Officers' Valises, Men's Spare Kits, and Mess Boxes to be dumped at Q.M. Stores in Camp by 6.30 p.m.

5. CASUALTIES.

Companies will send in at once, estimated number of any heavy casualties they sustain (Battn. have to report immediately they have 50) and all officer casualties to be reported at once.

6. RUM.

Rum will be drawn from Battn. Ration Dump immediately Companies arrive in Line. 2 per Company & 1 for H.Qrs.
Dump will be notified.

7. COMPLETION OF RELIEF.

Companies will report immediately they are in position.

8. Officers not going forward will return to Transport Lines.

9. CARRYING PARTY.

Brigade Carrying Party will parade under 2/Lt. Young.
Battn. Carrying Party under Corpl. Gerrard. They will move up after Headquarters.

ACKNOWLEDGE.

2/Lt. Asst/Adjutant
for
Adjutant INBORN.

19th September, 1917

	Sent		
	At..................m.	.... *Service.*	Date..................
	To.......................		From..................
	By.......................	(Signature of "Franking Officer.")	By.....................

TO — [illegible]

Sender's Number.	Day of Month.	In reply to Number.	AAA
* BM 528	19		

Amend 1st Bde Order No 92 para 2 (b) read —

Contact aeroplane will call for flares at plus 80 mins plus 135 mins plus 210 mins and subsequently as ordered

10 Appendix 2 Ref para 7 add [illegible]

10 [illegible]

[illegible]

From 1st Bde.
Place
Time

The above may be forwarded as now corrected. **(Z)**

.... *Censor.*

Signature of Addressor or person authorised to telegraph in his name.

* This line should be erased if not required.

(3198.) Wt. W 12952/M1294. 375,000 Pads. 1/17. H. W. & V., Ld. (E. 818.)

Office of Origin and Service Instruc[tions]

SECRET

Sent	This message is on a/c of:	Recd. at .... m.
At..............m.	.... Service.	Date..............
To..............		From ....
By..............	(Signature of "Franking Officer.")	By..............

TO 1/5 S. Lanc. Regt ~~4th [illegible] [illegible] [illegible] [illegible] B~~

* Sender's Number.	Day of Month.	In reply to Number.	AAA
BM 526	19		

Reference "Addendum No 1 to Appendix 'E' of [illegible]"

Counter attack aeroplane signals

Should the special signal referred to be observed by the infy during the progress of or after the final protective barrage (beyond the GREEN line) has ceased, the S.O.S. signal will be sent up by the infy who observe it.

From 166 Bde.

Place

Time

B. A. Hume Capt

Bd. Major

The above may be forwarded as now corrected.

Censor.

(Z)

Signature of Addressor or person authorised to telegraph in his name.

* This line should be erased if not required.

(3198.) Wt. W 12952/M1294. 375,000 Pads. 1/17. H. W. & V., Ld. (E. 818.)

"A" Form.
MESSAGES AND SIGNALS.

Army Form C. 2121
(in pads of 100).
No of Message ....

Prefix .... Code .... m. Office of Origin and Service Instructions.	Words	Charge	This message is on a/c of:	Recd. at ......m
Secret	Sent At ......m. To ...... By		...... Service. (Signature of "Franking Officer.")	Date ...... From ...... By ......

TO INBORN

Sender's Number.	Day of Month.	In reply to Number.	AAA
* X322	19.		

Reference Appendix 4 Administrative Instructions para 5. –

The Officer of the Carrying Party will report to Staff Captain as soon as Battalion has orders to move from assembly position. N C O & men will remain in assembly positions until sent for. aaa Officer i/c carrying party to know position of ration dump.

Reference para 3 – Units will select a dump close to their assembly positions for Z plus 1 days rations and notify the location to B T O forthwith. Z plus 1 days rations together with water will be sent to these dumps today

From INANE "Q"
Place
Time

The above may be forwarded as now corrected.

Censor.

(Z) G B Davey Lt [illegible]

Signature of Addressor or person authorised to telegraph in his name.

* This line should be erased if not required.

100,000 Pads. W. 12093. M1217. McC. & Co., Ltd. 1/17. (E. 764). Forms C/2121/11.

SECRET. Copy No........3

166 INFANTRY BRIGADE - APPENDIX No. 7 to O/1.

POLICE ARRANGEMENTS FOR STRAGGLER POSTS.

The following Police Arrangements will be in force from midnight on Y/Z night :-

1. BRIGADE LINE OF POSTS.

Brigade Straggler Posts will be situated in the neighbourhood of the line SQUARE FARM, PEAR FARM, BRIDGE HOUSE, CARPET TRENCH.

164 and 165 Brigades will each maintain at least 2 Straggler Posts on this line, each post consisting of 2 Regimental Police.

The duty of Brigade Posts will be to collect all armed or unarmed stragglers seen moving to the rear through the Brigade line and to conduct them in formed bodies to the Divisional Stragglers Posts at C.28.b.1.3. (Junction OXFORD ROAD & WIELTJE - ST JEAN ROAD) where stragglers will be handed over to a Sergeant M.M.P.

All men on post duty must be acquainted with the following :-

(a) Next Brigade post on right and left.
(b) Nearest R.A.M.C. Collecting Post.
(c) Position of the advanced Prisoners of War cage (ST JEAN).

and will direct wounded men or prisoner's escorts accordingly.

2. DIVISIONAL STRAGGLER POSTS.

The line CAMBRIDGE ROAD - OXFORD ROAD has been taken as the Divisional line of posts by the V Corps, in whose area the following Divisional Straggler Posts will be maintained :-

(1) I.11.b.30.65. (9th Division).
(2) I.5.a.20.77. (9th Division).
(3) C.28.b.1.3. (55th Division).

The post to be found by 55th Division will consist of 1 N.C.O. M.M.P. and 3 O.R. to be detailed by the A.P.M. who is responsible for the working of the Divisional line of straggler posts.

The Divisional straggler post will be in possession of written orders issued for the last operations with Administrative Instruction No. 8 dated 9th July.

3. NEIGHBOURING POSTS.

The right Divisional straggler post of the XVIII Corps is situated at C.23.a.6.7.

The Left Divisional straggler post of the 1 ANZAC Corps (on right) is at I.17.b.2.8.

4. PATROLS.

The A.P.M. will arrange for patrols consisting of 2 men to be constantly working along the roads between 55th Divisional Post at C.28.b.1.3. and the posts on the right and left respectively.

Stragglers picked up by these patrols will be taken to the Divisional straggler post for disposal.

5. DIVISIONAL STRAGGLER COLLECTING STATION.

The Divisional Straggler Collecting Station will be in the dugouts at H.13.a.3.5.

At this station will be 1 Officer, 1 Sergt. and 6 Other ranks to be provided by the A.P.M.

Stragglers will be escorted in formed bodies by M.M.P. from the Straggler Post to the Divisional Colecting Station at regular intervals.

Stragglers will be equipped as fully as possible at the Divisional Collecting Station, given a hot meal and returned under escort to their first line transport from whom a receipt will be obtained.

The Officer i/c of the Divisional Stragglers Collecting Station will be in possession of written orders similar to those issuedwith 55th Division Administrative Instruction No. 8 dated 9th July.

The A.P.M. will arrange to collect at 12 noon on Z day, and afterwards at intervals of 12 hours, stragglers of this Division from the Collecting Post at the Prison, YPRES, and conduct them to the Divisional Collecting Station.

He will also arrange to send all stragglers of XVIII Corps to the latter's right straggler post at C.23.a.6.7. and stragglers of the 1 ANZAC Corps to the latter's left Divisional collecting post at I.16.b.3.4.

Any stragglers of the 9th Division will be sent to their collecting station at the Prison, YPRES.

6. EQUIPMENT OF POSTS.

The A.P.M. will arrange to draw and store at the Divisional Straggler Post and at the Collecting Station the same quantities of stores ordered to be maintained during the recent operations in para 5. of 55th Division Administrative Instruction No. 8 dated 9th July.

7. A return by units of stragglers collected during the last 24 hours will be submitted by the A.P.M. to Divisional H.Q. at noon daily.

CAPTAIN.

19/9/1917.

Staff Captain, 166 Infantry Brigade.

SECRET.   OPERATION ORDER Nº 115.   Copy Nº.......

by

Lieut. Colonel C.P. James, D.S.O. Commanding

1/5th SOUTH LANCASHIRE REGIMENT.

+++++++++++++++++++++++

1. V Corps is to attack on 'Z' day (to be notified later) 9th Division on Right, 55th Division on Left; 3rd and 59th Divisions in reserve. 58th Division (XVIII Corps) on left of 55th Division.

2. Divisional and Brigade Boundaries, frontages and objective are shewn on attached map. 165th Infantry Brigade with 1/5th N. Lan. R. attached, and 164th Infantry Brigade with 1/5th Kings Own attached will attack on right and left respectively.

3. 166th Infantry Brigade with Headquarters at WIELTJE (less two Battalions and M.G. Coy:) will be in Divisional Reserve and will assemble as ordered subsequently.

4. Battalions of Divisional Reserve will be available to reinforce attacking Brigades if required to secure and maintain final objective. Headquarters 1/5th S. Lan. R.:   WARWICK FARM.

5. AIRCRAFT.

(a) Nº 21 Squadron R.F.C. is allotted to 55th Division for contact work.

Planes on contact work for the Division can be recognised by the following markings :-

1. On both lower planes a rectangular attachment.

view from ground.

2. A white dumb-bell on either side of body of plane.

(b) Signs to be used by Infantry to show most advanced line held will be :-

(1) RED Flares.

(2) WATSON'S Fans (as available).

Flares will be lit in thebottom of a trench or behind a parapet. Watson fans will be used open and turned over at intervals of about 30 seconds so as to show alternately the white and coloured sides.

(c) The signal for lighting flaresor showing Watson fans will be a white Very Light fired by an aeroplane. The Klaxon horn will also be used by the aeroplane sounding a series of 'A's in Morse. The Klaxon however may not always be audible. As this is the only occasion on which white Very Lights will be fired from the air, flares must be lit or fans shewn immediately by the most advanced infantry on seeing this signal.

(d) The contact aeroplane will call for flares or fans at

ZERO plus 1 hour.

ZERO plus 2 hours.

ZERO plus 2.30 hours.

6. MAPS AND AEROPLANE PHOTOGRAPHS.

The following maps will be issued :-

Message form maps	-	on the scale of at least 3 to all officers and senior N.C.O's of fighting units.
Barrage maps	-	on the scale of one per officer and senior N.C.O's of fighting units.
GRAVENSTAFEL	-	1/10000 Trench Map.

OPERATION ORDER Nº 115 (Continued)   Sheet Nº 2.

7. (a) FIGHTING KIT AND RATIONS.
Instructions issued.

(b) WATER.

One water-bottle per man will be carried. When this has been filled IT MUST NOT BE TOUCHED ON 'Z' DAY.

Full Petrol Tins will be delivered to Units on evening of 'Y' day and these are to be carried forward to assembly positions for use on "Z" day.

The importance of keeping the water-bottle intact as long as possible must be impressed on all ranks.

(c) Brigade Carrying Party (2/Lt. Young, 1 N.C.O. & 20 Other Ranks) to report to Staff Captain at place to be notified later.

Trench Mortar Carrying Party (1 N.C.O. & 10 Other Ranks) will report to O.C. 166 Trench Mortar Battery at 2 p.m. on "Y" day, in billets YPRES N. Area.

Battalion Carrying Party (1 N.C.O. & 20 Other Ranks) will move up behind Battalion Headquarters. They will draw 10 YUKON Packs from the R.S.M.

(d) STRETCHER BEARERS.

The 32 Regimental Stretcher Bearers are under the orders of the Regimental Medical Officer. He will arrange for custody and safe disposal of rifles of any S.B's who report to him with them.

ACKNOWLEDGE.

..........................Lieutenant

A/Adjutant 1/5th SOUTH LANCASHIRE REGIMENT.

19th September, 1917.

Copies issued to :-

Nº 1. C. O.
2. 2nd in C.
3. Adjutant.
4. O.C. "A" Coy:
5. " "B" "
6. " "C" "
7. " "D" "
8. Transport Officer.
9. Intelligence Officer.
10. Signal Officer.
11. Quartermaster.
12. R.S.M.
13. File.
14. Medical Officer.

Issued at a.m. 19th September, 1917.

166 Bde A 84/27

55th Division AQC.670/7.

R. A.		
C. R. E.	166th Brigade,	Senior Chaplain C. of E.
164th Brigade,	196th M.G. Coy.	Senior Chaplain Non C.
165th Brigade,	1/4th S.Lan. R.	of E.
	A.D.M.S.	Div.Burial Officer.

BURIALS DURING HEAVY FIGHTING.

The arrangements for burial will remain as indicated in 55th Division Administrative Instruction No.1 issued prior to the last operations.

The Divisional Burial Officer is responsible for assisting units in the burial of their dead as far East as the line SQUARE FARM - BRIDGE HOUSE - VANHEULE FARM.

This line will be advanced when the situation renders it desirable.

Burials in front of this line of demarcation will be carried out by units. It is essential that all bodies lying near any trenches occupied by troops should be buried at the earliest possible moment.

Graves should be grouped together and clearly marked with a post or pile of bricks etc.

The personal effects and Red Identity disc of each body will be tied in a small bundle and those belonging to all officers and men buried in one grave will be forwarded together in a sandbag or sack to the Divisional Burial Officer's Office at the 55th Divisional Salvage Dump, VLAMERTINGHE together with the necessary certificate and inventory A.F.N.3190 and a statement showing :-

(a) Exact map reference of grave and location with reference to the neighbouring woods, houses, cross roads or other prominent objects.

(b) Any identification mark on grave.

(c) Nominal roll of men buried in the grave given in the order they are buried from left to right as viewed from the foot end of the grave.

(d) Date of burial and, if possible, the name of the Chaplain or officer officiating.

The Divisional Burial Officer will be responsible for sending the necessary particulars as to burial to the D.A.G., 3rd Echelon etc. through the Corps Burial Officer.

F. H. Eden

Lieut.Colonel,
A. A. & Q. M. G., 55th Division.

19/9/1917.

1/5th Battalion SOUTH LANCASHIRE REGIMENT.
NARRATIVE OF OPERATIONS
19th to 22nd September, 1917.

App V

The Battalion moved forward from GOLDFISH CHATEAU on the 19th September, 1917, at 10 p.m. to occupy Assembly Trenches in OB Line in Divisional Reserve. Headquarters: WARWICK FARM DUGOUTS.
Troops were in position at 1 a.m. Our Artillery opened at ZERO - 5.40 a.m. About 12 noon I was ordered to reinforce the 165 Infantry Brigade with two Companies (B & C), both under the command of Capt. J.H. Dickinson, M.C., were sent forward at 12.30 p.m. with instructions to report to Colonel Drew of the 9th Kings, Liverpool R.

At 1 p.m. I went to Brigade and received instructions to reinforce 165 Brigade with my two remaining Companies. I ordered these to move to shell holes round POMMERN CASTLE; Company Commanders to report to me (immediately they arrived) at BANK FARM. I moved to BANK FARM, arriving 2 p.m. Colonel Drew then informed me that my B & C Coys: had been ordered to attack GALLIPOLI COPSE and HILL 37. Instructions were then received from 165 Brigade that my two remaining Companies had to go in Support of the 2 Attacking Companies. GALLIPOLI COPSE and HILL 37 TO BE TAKEN AND HELD AT ALL COSTS. Captain H.G. Whitaker, M.C. was given the necessary instructions and placed in charge of both Companies. (A & D) A Company to be in Front Line. A wave of 4 Platoons in two lines. D Coy: behind in the same formation. Companies moved out at 3.30 pm. I went forward behind D Coy: Just as the Companies were passing SOMME, enemy dropped a heavy barrage. On pasing SOMME I met Captain Dickinson coming back wounded, who informed me that HILL 37 had been taken at 4 p.m. I sent word back to BANK FARM. On arrival at GALLIPOLI COPSE about 5 p.m. I found a number of my men in possession with 2 Lewis Guns. The enemy then commenced to shell GALLIPOLI very heavily, and working backwards placed a heavy barrage round and about GALLIPOLI COPSE. The men were ordered to move slightly forward in the shell holes to avoid this fire, one Lewis Gun remaining in THE CORNER OF THE building to bring flanking fire to bear. At 5.30 p.m. the enemy were seen moving forward behind barrage to Counter-Attack. I joined my Companies at HILL 37. The attack was repulsed by Rifle and Lewis Gun Fire, the enemy on the Right getting very close to within about 20 yards; on the Left to within about 50 yards. At this time, I sent messages back to BANK FARM, explaining the situation, and asking for Reinforcements and Ammunition, as both flanks were in the air, there was a danger of the enemy enveloping us.

At 7.30 p.m. I sent my Adjutant back to BANK FARM to explain the situation. By this time, with the exception of desultory shelling and short bursts of Machine Gun Fire, the line was fairly quiet. There being no communication to the rear and having received no messages, I left HILL 37 at 9 p.m. and returned to BANK FARM.

Owing to the close proximity of the enemy in the counter-attack, all messages received and sent since ZERO, Maps and B.A.B. Code Book were destroyed, so they might not fall into the enemy's hands. This now interferes with giving correct sequence of times. Up to the night of the 21st inst., things were fairly quiet. Rations, Water, and Ammunition were sent forward at dusk. Owing to the Machine Gun Fire and Sniping, it was impossible for any movement to be made forward of GALLIPOLI with the exception of occasional runners. Enemy again heavily countered at 6.30 p.m. night of the 21st. This attack was broken up by the excellent barrages which our Artillery put down. The Liverpool Scottish reinforced with 2 Platoons one on either flank of our position. On the night of the 22nd inst., we were relieved by the 2/6th South Staffs: Relief was carried out quickly and without casualties. Before we left, Visual Communication was opened by us from HILL 37 to SOMME. This would simplify the difficulty of getting messages down from the Front Line.

(sd) C.P. JAMES, Lieut. Colonel
Commanding 1/5th Battalion SOUTH LANCASHIRE REGIMENT.

"C" Form.

MESSAGES AND SIGNALS.

Army Form C. 2123.
(In books of 100.)

No. of Message..............

Prefix SM Code MHPA Words 14

Received From 1RZ By Rawlins

Sent, or sent out At ......m. To ...... By ......

Office Stamp. FB 27/9/17

£ s. d.

Charges to collect

Service Instructions.

Handed in at 1RZ Office ......m. Received 1.30 a m.

TO ~~1RZone Divisional ...~~
~~inbone ...~~

*Sender's Number	Day of Month	In reply to Number	AAA

following from GOC
18 DIVN aaa
Splendid Well done

FROM 1RZ
PLACE & TIME 11.55 pm

* This line should be erased if not required.

(S.O. 1065) Wt. 7496—M 857 125,000 Pads. McC. & Co., Ltd. 10/16 (E 489) Forms C/2123/2

Army Form C. 2123.
(In books of 100.)

"C" Form.

MESSAGES AND SIGNALS.

No. of Message..............

Prefix.........Code.........Words.........	Received	Sent, or sent out	Office Stamp.
£ s. d.	From	At ......m.	
Charges to collect	By	To	
Service Instructions.		By	

Handed in at ...... Office ......m. Received ......m.

TO Infantry

*Sender's Number	Day of Month	In reply to Number	AAA
	22nd		

Major Gen congratulates & thanks all ranks for their brilliant defeat of yesterdays heavy counter attack aaa They must have dealt the enemy a severe blow

FROM General Boyd Moss
PLACE & TIME

* This line should be erased if not required.

(S.O. 1065) Wt. 7496—M 857 125,000 Pads. McC. & Co., Ltd. 10/16 (E 489) Forms C/2123/3

"A" Form.

Army Form C. 2121.
(In pads of 100.)

MESSAGES AND SIGNALS.

No. of Message..............

Prefix............Code..............m	Words.	Charge.	This message is on a/c of:	Recd. at ....m.
Office of Origin and Service Instructions.	Sent		......................Service.	Date..............
	At..............m.			From..............
	To..............			
	By..............		(Signature of "Franking Officer.")	By..............

TO { 5 S Lanc. | INBORN

Sender's Number.	Day of Month.	In reply to Number.	AAA
* G.11	21		

Following	from	Division	begins
Corps	Commander	congratulates	
KING	and	[illegible]	and
thanks	them	for	their
success	today	ends	

IRON

From

Place

Time

The above may be forwarded as now corrected. (Z)

.... *Censor.*

Signature of Addressor or person authorised to telegraph in his name. Major

* This line should be erased if not required.

(3198.) Wt. W 12952/M1294. 375,000 Pads. 1/17. H.W.&V., Ld. (E. 818.)

"C" Form (Duplicate).
Army Form C. 2123.
(In books of 50's in duplicate.)

MESSAGES AND SIGNALS.

No. of Message ....

	Charges to Pay.	Office Stamp.
SM BLAM 45	£ s. d.	
Service Instructions. 1RZ		

Handed in at .... Office .... m. Received .... m.

TO: Inform that instruct instrument

Sender's Number	Day of Month	In reply to Number	AAA
BM 470	21		

Army and Corps Commanders congratulations & thanks to all ranks for splendid efforts in todays battle aaa Co operation between Infantry artillery & Flying corps has been excellent & very important successes have been gained all along the Front

50
50
40
40
200

1040
1040

370
40
410

108
120
120
112
460

FROM: Irvine

PLACE & TIME: 2.10 am

230
5th

Wt. 492—M437 500,000 Pads. H W V 5/16 Forms C.2123.

"A" Form.

Army Form C. 2121.
(In pads of 100.)

MESSAGES AND SIGNALS.

No. of Message..............

Prefix.........Code............m	Words.	Charge.	*This message is on a/c of:*	Recd. at.........m.
Office of Origin and Service Instructions.	Sent		.... *Service.*	Date...............
	At..............m.			From ....
	To................			
	By................		(Signature of "Franking Officer.")	By..................

TO IN BORN

Sender's Number.	Day of Month.	In reply to Number.	AAA
* G.18	20		

wire	from	Fifth	Army
begins	aaa	The	Army
Commander	wishes	to	thank
all	arms	and	ranks
for	their	splendid	efforts
in	todays	battle	aaa
Co-operation	between	Infantry	Artillery
and	Flying	Corps	has
been	excellent	and	very
important	successes	have	been
gained	all	along	the
line	ends		

From IRON
Place
Time

The above may be forwarded as now corrected. (Z)

[signature] Major

Censor.

Signature of Addressor or person authorised to telegraph in his name.

* This line should be erased if not required.

(3198.) Wt. W 12952/M1294. 375,000 Pads. 1/17. H. W. & V., Ld. (E. 818.)

55th (WEST LANCASHIRE) DIVISION ORDER OF THE DAY.

****

1. The following telegrams have been received :-

"Fifth Army wire begins aaa The Army Commander wishes to thank all arms and all ranks for their splendid efforts in todays battle aaa Co-operation between Infantry Artillery and Flying Corps has been excellent and very important successes have been gained all along the front aaa Ends aaa".

"Corps Commander thanks Field and Heavy Artillery for their good work and the F.O.Os for the very useful and timely information sent in aaa Ends aaa".

"Corps Commander congratulates 9th and 55th Divisions and thanks them for their success today aaa Ends aaa".

2. The Major General Commanding wishes to add his thanks and congratulations to all arms and ranks of the Division.

There is no doubt whatever that in addition to making a very substantial advance over difficult ground stubbornly defended, well organized, and liberally provided with strong cover, artillery, and machine guns, the Division, aided most ably by the Corps Heavy Artillery, succeeded in dealing the enemy a very heavy blow, and causing him severe losses.

Success was due to the fine determination shown by all ranks and the hearty co-operation of Artillery, Engineers, Infantry, Machine Gun Companies, Trench Mortars and R.A.M.C. with each other, which is the sign of a united and disciplined Division.

(Sd) T. ROSE PRICE.

Lieut-Colonel.

General Staff, 55th Division.

55th Division H.Q.,

21st September 1917.

55th (WEST LANCASHIRE) DIVISION.
****

ORDER OF THE DAY.

The following telegram has been received from GENERAL SIR HERBERT PLUMER G.C.M.G., G.C.V.O., K.C.B., commanding the Second Army :-

"GENERAL JEUDWINE, Commanding 55th Division.

Many congratulations to you and your Division on your success yesterday aaa You must have accounted for a great many

GENERAL PLUMER."

Lieut-Colonel,
General Staff, 55th Division.

55th Division H.Q.
22nd September, 1917.

55th (WEST LANCASHIRE) DIVISION ORDER OF THE DAY.

The following telegrams from the V Corps have been received ;-

"The Commander-in-Chief visited Corps Headquarters this evening and expressed himself very pleased in the work of both Divisions and sends them his congratulations and thanks".

"Fifth Army wire begins aaa Please congratulate 55th Division on the gallant defence of HILL 37 yesterday and upon the energy and resource displayed by Commanders on the spot in organising counter attacks aaa Ends aaa".

T. Rees Price

55th Division H.Q.,

23rd September, 1917.

Lieut-Colonel,

General Staff, 55th Division.

55TH (WEST LANCASHIRE) DIVISION.
****

ORDER OF THE DAY.
================

The following telegram has been received from The Right Honourable E.G.V. Earl of DERBY, K.G., G.C.V.O., C.B., Secretary of State for War :-

"GENERAL JEUDWINE, 55th Division Hdqrs. B.E.F.

Well done 55th West Lancashire Divn accept my most hearty congratulations I sincerely trust your losses are not heavy

DERBY."

T. Rose Price.

Lieut-Colonel,
General Staff, 55th Divn.

55th Division H.Q.
24th September, 1917.

1.L.

SECRET

SMOKE SIGNAL FROM COUNTER-ATTACK AEROPLANES WITHOUT THE MARKINGS OF CONTACT AEROPLANES.

1. A small number of smoke bombs are available for use by Counter-attack aeroplanes without the markings of contact aeroplanes, in forthcoming operations.

2. They will be used to draw the attention of the attacking infantry to any signs of an enemy counter-attack developing.

3. The procedure will be as follows :-

   (a) Counter-attack Plane will sound one long blast on the Klaxon horn.

   (b) The smoke bomb will be discharged.

4. The bomb will burst about 100 feet below the machine, into a white parachute flare which descends slowly leaving a long trail of brown smoke about 1 ft. broad behind it.

5. The supply of these bombs is very limited at present, so too much reliance must not be placed on this method of communication.

S E C R E T.

166TH INFANTRY BRIGADE.

APPENDIX 1 to O/1.

EMPLOYMENT OF R.E. AND PIONEERS.

1. One supporting point will be constructed at or about ELMS CORNER (D.20.a.05.65) as soon as our troops have moved forward after the pause on the ~~DOTTED RED line~~. YELLOW LINE

A garrison of ½ platoon, one machine gun and one Lewis gun will be found by 165 Infantry Brigade.

2. One Field Company and two Companies of Pioneers will be detailed for the marking and making of certain tracks forward from the OLD BLACK LINE. The routes chosen for these tracks will be as shewn on a map (to be issued later).

3. One Company of Pioneers will be detailed for the improvement of the WIELTJE-GRAVENSTAFEL ROAD.

4. C.R.E. will arrange mutually with Brigadier Generals Commanding 164th and 165th Infantry Brigades for the allotment of R.E. and Pioneers for work on selected enemy strong points.

S E C R E T.

166 INFANTRY BRIGADE.

APPENDIX 3 to O/1.

MAPS AND AEROPLANE PHOTOGRAPHS.

1. The following maps have been issued on the scale of one per officer,

WESTROOSEBEKE	1/10,000 Trench Map
ST JULIEN	,,
ZONNEBEKE	,,
FREZENBERG	,,
PASSCHENDAELE	,,

2. The following maps will be issued,-

GRAVENSTAFEL	1/10,000 Trench Map
Message form maps	- on the scale of at least 3 to all officers and senior N.C.Os of fighting units
Barrage maps	- on the scale of one per officer and senior N.C.Os of fighting units.

3. Oblique aeroplane photographs and panoramas are also being issued on a large scale.

4. The maps mentioned in paragraph 2 will be carried by all concerned.

S E C R E T

166 INFANTRY BRIGADE.

APPENDIX 8 to O/1.

PRISONERS OF WAR.

1. Divisional Cage W. of ST.JEAN on S. side of YPRES-ST JEAN road at I.3.a.6.6.

2. Prisoners of War will be escorted by fighting troops to Divisional Cage and there handed over to officer i/c Guard who will give a receipt. Escort will not exceed 10% of prisoners but will never be less than 2 men.

3. A.P.M. will arrange for escort of prisoners in batches to the Corps Cage.

4. Prisoners will be escorted to the Divisional Cage by SPREE FARM - WIELTJE - ST.JEAN Road, or tracks no 4, 5 or 6 to JUNCTION Rd and thence to Cage.

These routes of evacuation will be cleared by marked by notice boards from CALL TRENCH-CAMBRAI TRENCH line to Cage.

5. 1/10th Liverpool Scottish will detail 1 runner to report to Divisional Intelligence Officer at Divisional Cage at 9 p.m. Y day.

6. Searching of prisoners.

(a) All prisoners will be searched immediately captured to ensure they have no weapons concealed.

(b) No personal effects such as decorations, watches, trinkets etc, identity discs, pay books, mess tins, water bottles, haversacks etc, will be taken from prisoners nor will they be searched for papers of tactical importance by the fighting troops, whose only duty in this connection will be to see that papers are not done away with by prisoners before they reach the Divisional Cage.

7. Wounded prisoners will be evacuated to Cage in the ordinary way and will not be retained for examination at the Dressing Stations.

8. Only officers of the General Staff, Provost Staff and Intelligence Corps are allowed to converse with prisoners.

All escorts will take steps to ensure that prisoners do not converse with unauthorised persons.

S E C R E T APPENDIX NO.9 to O/1.

166 INFANTRY BRIGADE.

A R T I L L E R Y.

1. Artillery supporting 55th Division.

3rd Divisional Artillery
55th Divisional Artillery
108th, 3?th, 86th and 232nd Army Brigade R.F.A.

2. Positions of Headquarters. As follows,-

3rd Divisional Artillery H.Q. 18.b.3.8.
55th ,, ,, H.Q. MERSEY CAMP, H.1.a.5.5.
Liaison Officer and Right Main Group Commander
(Lieut-Col. W.J.K.RETTIE. D.S.O.) H.Q. WIELTJE DUGOUTS
Liaison Officer and Left Main Group Commander
(Lieut-Col. T.E.TOPPING, C.M.G.,D.S.O.) H.Q. WIELTJE DUGOUTS

3. S.O.S.

When S.O.S. is received all batteries will openfire at a rapid rate for 5 mins, and at reduced rate for 10 more minutes. They will then cease fire until call or signal is repeated. For 24 hours after capture of final objective S.O.S. barrage will be that detailed for protective barrage.

(4. Barrage. Will consist of three parts.

(a) Creeping barrage, 18 batteries, 18-pdr (shrapnel giving 40% bursts on graze will be employed). Barrage will be thickened on more important Objectives. Lifts 50 yards.

(b) Searching barrage 6 batteries 18-pdr and 7 batteries 4.5" Hows. will search and sweep their lanes from 100 yds to 500 yds in advance of Creeping Barrage.

(c) Secondary barrage, 5 batteries 6" Hows, 3 batteries 60-pdrs will cover area from 450 to 1200 yds in advance of Creeping Barrage.

(d) Protective barrages will be found as under,-

1. Guns of creeping barrage will form a line in a 150 yds in advance of RED and YELLOW lines and 230 yds in advance of GREEN line when this is gained.

2. Guns and Hows. of Searching Barrage will search and sweep their lanes from line of Creeping Barrage forward [illegible] [illegible] for 300 yds, and on RED and YELLOW lines, 18 pdrs will fire one round every 3 minutesof Smoke Shells (provided wind is West)

3 Guns and Hows. of Secondary Barrage will also fire.

5. Parties of 2 F.O.O's. will be held in readiness to push forward as opportunity offers to more forward observation posts.

6. Previous bombardment will be divided into seven continuous periods between 3 a.m. 'Y' day to Zero,-

(Sheet 2, Appendix 9 to O/1)

Period 1. 3 a.m. to 5 a.m. 'Y' day on hostile front systems; in two 10 minute bursts; 75% H.E. will be used.

Period 2, 5 a.m. to 5.45 a.m. Actual barrage on Divisional front as programme on 'Z' day. 18-pdrs fire 100% Shrapnel.

Period 3. 5.45 a.m. to 9 a.m. 6.45 a.m. draw-net barrage on GREEN line (300 yds E of final objective). Barrage will shorten, 100 yds at a time and move at rate of 100 yds in two minutes till it reaches RED DOTTED line D.7.c.55.15 - D.19.d.70.60.

Period 4 & 5. 9 a.m. to 12 noon, and 12 noon to 6 p.m. as in period 1.
At 5 p.m. Draw-net barrage on DOTTED GREEN line as in Period 3.

Period 6, 6 p.m. to 9 p.m. Searching and harassing fire maintained in two bursts of 20 minutes each, 18-pdrs with H.E.
4.5" Hows. on strong points as far back as GREEN DOTTED line.

Period 7. 9 p.m 'Y' day to Zero hour, as in period 1, the independent bursts every half hour, last burst starting at Zero minus 20 mins. with all available 18 pdrs and 4.5" Hows.

18 pdrs cease fire at Zero minus 5, so that opening of attack barrage may be a distinct signal. 4.5" Hows will continue till Zero hour to deceive enemy as to hour attack.

S E C R E T.

APPENDIX No.11
to O/1.

166 INFANTRY BRIGADE.

ACTION OF MASSED MACHINE GUNS.

Preliminary arrangements for the action of Machine Guns in carrying out Barrage and Supporting fire, and S.O.S. Lines,-

1. BARRAGE and SUPPORTING FIRE will be carried out by

166th Infantry Brigade	16 guns
196 th M. G. C.	16 guns

2. ORGANIZATION.
(a) Machine guns will be organised into batteries of 8 guns each. Two batteries will form a Group and one Group will be allotted to each Brigade front.
(b) An Officer will command each Group and will be situated at a position to be notified later.
(c) The approximate positions of batteries are shewn on the attached tracing "A"
They will be designated from right to left as follows,

O.C. 196 M.G.C.	("P" Battery (8 guns) ("Q" ,, (8 ,,)		Right Group.
O.C.166 M.G.C.	("R" ,, (8 ,,) ("S" ,, (8 ,,)		Left Group

3. It is intention
(a) to cover infantry advance to RED line, to put down protective barrage during pause on RED line
(b) to support advance from RED line to YELLOW line, and to put down protective barrage forward of YELLOW line during pause
(c) to support advance from YELLOW to GREEN line and to put down protective barrage forward of GREEN line during consolidation.
(d) to lay on S.O.S. lines forward of GREEN line in case of counter attack.

4. CONTROL.
(a) Guns will operate under Divisional control
(b) The programme will not be departed from so long as the attack proceeds as planned. In the event of any portion of the line being unable to move forward the barrage lines will be re-arranged under Divisional orders.

5. COMMUNICATION and LIAISON.
(a)Group Commanders will be in communication with their batteries by telephone or runner
(b) Liaison with Divisional Headquarters will be maintained through Brigade Headquarters.

6. AMMUNITION.
A dump of 120,000 rounds S.A.A. is being made behind each battery, under Divisional arrangements.

7. CALCULATION FORMS are being issued and willbe filled in vy Battery Commanders.

8. TRAVERSE. The limit of traverse of each gun will be 4°.

Z 29

WO 95/2922

Confidential

War Diary

of

1/5th BATTALION

South Lancashire Regiment

From 1st October 1917.

To 31st October 1917.

Volume 38.

Instructions regarding War Diaries and Intelligence Summaries are contained in F. S. Regs., Part II. and the Staff Manual respectively. Title pages will be prepared in manuscript.

WAR DIARY
or
INTELLIGENCE SUMMARY.

1/5th South Lancashire Regt.

(Erase heading not required.)

Army Form C. 2118.

Place	Date	Hour	Summary of Events and Information	Remarks and references to Appendices
EPEHY	1 Oct		Battalion in Brigade Reserve. Providing working parties approx 7/350 O.R.	
[illegible]	12th		employed on widening, deepening, revetting and fire stepping front line about	
[illegible]			FAWCUS AVE; carrying parties, work on shelters etc all under R.E. supervision.	
	12/13th		Relieved by 1/5th Kings' Liverpool Regiment; entrained where Railway crosses	
			road on ST EMILIE – VILLERS FAUCON RD for TINCOURT, where we took over billets	
TINCOURT			in empty houses.	
	13		Cleaning of clothing and equipment, baths and Company inspections	
	14/		Company Drill. Working parties to be provided daily under R.E	
	15		supervision, improving billets and shelters, pioneers making beds etc.	
	15		Lts A.V. Gliffe and H.G. Ayway – Leicester Regt. joined for duty.	
	16		Lt Colonel proceeded on 3 weeks special leave to the United Kingdom.	
			Major [illegible] [illegible] DSO took over command and Capt H.G. Whitaker M.C. assumed	
			duties of Second in Command.	
	17/21		Proceeding with Training, improving billets, inspections by G.O.C. Division and	
			Major-General WRIGHT USA FORCES who also witnessed demonstrations of Platoon	
			in the Attack by platoons of B Company under 2nd Lt FRANCIS.	
	22	3/30 pm	Marched out of TINCOURT, entrained at HAMEL on Light Railway for	

A6945 Wt. W11422/M1160 350,000 12/16 D. D. & L. Forms/C./2118/14.

Instructions regarding War Diaries and Intelligence Summaries are contained in F. S. Regs., Part II. and the Staff Manual respectively. Title pages will be prepared in manuscript.

WAR DIARY ~~or~~ ~~INTELLIGENCE~~ SUMMARY.

(*Erase heading not required.*)

Army Form C. 2118.

2.

Place	Date	Hour	Summary of Events and Information	Remarks and references to Appendices
RIGHT	22		Forward Area where we relieved 1/6th (RIFLE) BN KINGS LIVERPOOL REGT	
SUB-SECTOR			in the RIGHT SUB-SECTOR of the LEFT BRIGADE FRONT, with C and D Companies	App I
			in Line, "A" Company in Support "B" Company in Reserve, and	
			Headquarters at LEMAIRE RD F.4.D.0.4.	
	23		Quiet day. Patrols out at night but no enemy seen or heard.	
	24	7am	4 aeroplanes passed over OSSUS WOOD flying very low dropped 18 bombs on	
			enemy trenches and then returned. Our Artillery shelled enemy lines	
			whole of morning with 18 pounders and 4.5.	
			Slight trench mortar activity by enemy in the afternoon, our Stokes & 2" mortar replied.	
	25		Quiet day and night throughout.	
	26		Our field guns shelled enemy trenches in the morning, also slight enemy	
			artillery activity.	
	27.	3.30am	A concentration shoot was carried out by field guns and Howitzers on enemy	
			trenches and communications also Gas projectors discharged against	App II
			enemy line.	
		10.15am	9 hostile planes crossed our lines and hovered over for 20 mins. One	

A6945 Wt. W11422/M1160 350,000 12/16 D. D. & L. Forms/C./2118/14.

Instructions regarding War Diaries and Intelligence Summaries are contained in F. S. Regs., Part II. and the Staff Manual respectively. Title pages will be prepared in manuscript.

3.

WAR DIARY
or
~~INTELLIGENCE~~ SUMMARY.
(*Erase heading not required.*)

Army Form C. 2118.

Place	Date	Hour	Summary of Events and Information	Remarks and references to Appendices
	27 Oct		Enemy artillery slightly active in the afternoon.	
		7pm	Inter Company relief:- "A" relieved "C" Coy in LEFT FRONT. "B" Coy relieved "D" in RIGHT FRONT. "C" Coy moved to support and "D" into RESERVE.	App II.
	28 Oct		Hostile artillery active from 9am to 12 noon, and again in the afternoon from 1.40pm to 3.30pm. 1 OR wounded (T.M. Bomb) The following officers reinforcements reported:- 2/Lts I.C. PEARSON, W.R. SCROGGIE, A.E. EMBERSON, C.S. GILLESPIE, 4th Loyal North Lancs R.	
	29	10am	Enemy carried out a concentrated shoot on the sub-sector between 10 and 11am using all calibres 5.9s, 4.2s, 77mm, also heavy and light trench mortars, on our front system. A barrage was also put down on EAGLE QUARRY, SNIPE and QUAIL QUARRY with heavy Trench Mortars, and BIRD LANE with 5.9 shells. 1 OR Killed, 1 Off Wd. 2 OR wounded	
		7pm	Relieved by 1/4th BN LOYAL NORTH LANCASHIRE R. and moved into BRIGADE RESERVE in relief of 1/5th KINGS OWN ROYAL LANCS and 7th BN KINGS OWN YORKSHIRE LIGHT INF. at VAUCELLETTE FM AREA 13.G.	App IV.
	30/31		Supplying working parties under R.E. supervision 6 Offrs 272 OR.	

[illegible] Major
Cmdg. 1/5th South Lancashire Regt

A6945 Wt. W11422/M1160 350,000 12/16 D. D. & L. Forms/C./2118/14.

S E C R E T.   OPERATION ORDER № 120.   Copy № 14...

App I

by
Major W.N. Pilkington. D.S.O. Commanding
1/5th SOUTH LANCASHIRE REGIMENT.
+++++++++++++++++++++++

1. OPERATION. 1/5th SOUTH LANCASHIRE REGIMENT will relieve the 1/6th (Rifle) Bn. Kings Liverpool Regiment in Left Sector (Right Sub-Sector) on-night22/23rd October.

2. DISPOSITIONS.
"C" Coy: in left front in relief of "C" Coy: 6th K.L.R.
(plus 1 Lewis Gun Team from "B")
"D" Coy: in right front in relief of "D" " "
(plus 1 Lewis Gun Team from "B")
"A" Coy: in Support ~~front~~ in relief of "A" " "
in HEYTHROP and CRUCIFORM POSTS.
"B" Coy: (less 2 L.G. Teams) in Reserve, relieve "B" Coy: 6th K.L.R.
HEADQUARTERS:- LEMEIRE ROAD.

3. MOVE. Battalion will entrain 5 p.m. at K.13.d.8.3.
Companies and H.Q. will move independently to arrive 4.45 p.m.
2/Lt. FRANCIS will act as Entraining Officer, and will report at Station at 4.30 p.m.
Detrain at EPEHY F.7.b.9.7. where Companies will move forward by Platoons at 100 yards interval. Guides of 6th K.L.R. (1 per Company and 1 Battn.H.Q.) will meet them at W. end of PRIEL CUTTING at 6 p.m., and take to Bn. H.Q., where 1 guide per post will be waiting.

4. ADVANCE PARTY. Advance Party of 1 Officer and C.S.M. per Company, №s 1 of Lewis Gun Teams (A C, & D Coys:) Also 2/Lt. Ingham, L/Sgt. Myers, 3 Snipers, Sgt. Mutch and 1 Signaller per Company, will report outside Battalion Headquarters at 10 a.m.

5. TAKING OVER. All Defence Schemes, Work in the Defence, in progress, and proposed will be taken over.
Great care will be exercised in taking over Stores, including gum boots, stoves, braziers and petrol tins. Lists will be forwarded to Bn. H.Q. by 7 p.m. day of relief.

6. STORES. Blankets will be dumped at Q.M. Stores by 9.30 a.m. Valises, Mess Boxes, etc. by 1 p.m.

7. BILLETS. All Billets in TINCOURT will be handed over in a scrupulously clean condition and certificate to this effect will be ~~obtained from relieving Companies~~. rendered to O/Room

8. CARE OF FEET. All feet will be washed and treated with whale oil, and certificate to this effect will be rendered to Orderly Room by 2.30 p.m.

9. COMPLETION OF RELIEF. Will be notified to Battalion H.Q. by the Code Word "TAG".

ACKNOWLEDGE.

L. Kirkbett[illegible]
2/Lieut.
A/Adjutant 1/5th SOUTH LANCASHIRE REGIMENT.

21st October, 1917.

Secret

Operation Order No 121
by
Major W. M. Pilkington D.S.O. (Comdg)

1.

A concentration shoot will be carried out by Field guns and Howitzers on selected targets in enemy trenches and communications on Brigade Front on morning of 27th October. Divisional M.G. Coy will co-operate.

At the same hour 'G' Special Company R.E. will discharge 600 gas projectors if wind is favourable (between N.N.W. and S.S.W.)

300 from X 17a 40.35
300 from X 17c 25.75

If wind is unfavourable discharge will be postponed to night 27/28 Oct.

2. O.C. Companies will ensure that all necessary precautions are taken and that all working parties are withdrawn to their normal positions by 2.45 am.

Sentries will be reduced to a minimum consistent with safety between 3.30 am and 4.30 am.

No patrols will be out after 3 am.

3. Watches will be synchronized at Battalion H.Q. at 12 midnight

4. O.C. "G" Special Coy R.E. will decide as to whether conditions are favourable for discharge or otherwise.

Following code word will be used
Discharge will take place as ordered - HALLINES
Discharge cancelled ROISEL

5. Zero hour will be at 3.30 am.

Acknowledge.

Copies to
No 1. OC A Coy
" 2. " B "
" 3 " C "
" 4 " D
" 5 Int: Ofr.
" 6 } War Diary
" 7 }

26/10/17

2nd Lieut
A/Adjutant.

[illegible] No. 9

[illegible]

[illegible]

1. Relief.

[illegible] night 24th [illegible] 1916 [illegible]

2. Move

[illegible]

A. Company will relieve [illegible]

B. " " " [illegible]

[illegible] C. Company [illegible] [illegible] on moving [illegible] [illegible] in [illegible]

On completion of relief

C. Company will [illegible]

D. " [illegible]

[illegible]

Details of relief will be [illegible] concerned.

3. Taking Over

[illegible] relieving [illegible] [illegible] [illegible] details of [illegible] proposed

[illegible] visit [illegible] working parties, fatigues etc [illegible]

4. Stores

[illegible] stores [illegible]

5. Rations

Rations [illegible]

A. Coy
B. "
C. "
D. "

[illegible]
[illegible]
[illegible]

6. Completion of relief will be notified to Bn H.Q. by code word OCT.

Acknowledge [illegible]

Secret

Operation Orders No. 123 copy No.
by
Major W.R. Pilkington D.S.O. Comdg
1/5 South Lancashire Regt

Ref: French Maps Nos 77 and
1/20,000 62c N.B.

27th October, 1917.

1. Operation

The Battalion will be relieved in the Right Sub-sector on the night of 28/29th October by 1/4th Batt. Royal North Lancashire Regiment.

Companies will be relieved as follows.

A. Coy 1/4 L.N.L will relieve B. Coy 1/5 S.L.R. on Right front
B " — " — " " A " " Left "
C " — " — " " C " " in support in Heythrop and Cruciform Post
D " (less 2 L.G. teams) " D Coy (less 2 LG teams) } 1/5 S.L.R. in reserve in Brill Bank.

2. Move - On completion of relief Battalion will move into Brigade Reserve in relief of 1/5 Kings Own Royal Lancaster R. Companies will move independently as under

A. Company to Vaughan Bank
B " " Meath Post
C " " Limerick Post
D " " Kildare Post
H.Q " " Vaughan Bank.

3. Guides 1 guide per Platoon and 1 from Bn. H.Q will be at N end of Brill Cutting to guide Coys of 1/4 L.N.L in by 6 pm. Guides for posts will be waiting at junction of Bird Lane and Oldham St.

4. Defence Schemes

Work and Stores - All Defence Schemes Details of work in the defences in progress and proposed will be handed over work and wire pro-formas must be handed over complete to date to 1/4 L.N.L and copies forwarded to Bn. H.Q. by 4 pm. O.C. C Coy will ensure that all details of work on Cruciform and Heythrop posts are also very carefully handed over. Lists of Trench Stores to be handed over will be prepared and forwarded to Bn. H.Q by noon and receipts by 9 am morning following relief. Great care will be exercised in handing over. Every care must be taken to render accurate lists.

5. Transport

T.O will make necessary arrangements for conveyance of Medical Stores, Mess boxes, Signalling Equipment, Orderly Room boxes and valises into Reserve Area.

6. Advance Party.

1 Offr. and 1 N.C.O per Coy and R.S.M for HQ will take over billets and Stores.

H.Q Gas N.C.O and 1 Gas N.C.O per Coy will accompany party, and take over Anti-Gas Stores

7. Lewis Guns

L.G. Teams of D Coy attached to front line Coys will rejoin their Companies on completion of relief.

8. Handing Over

Trenches and billets will be handed over in a scrupulously clean condition and a certificate to this effect obtained from incoming unit.

9. Relief Complete

Completion of relief in Right Sub-sector will be notified to Bn. H.Q. by code word ... ITA
in Brigade Reserve by code word ... SIN

Acknowledge

[signature] 2nd Lieut
A/Adjutant 1/5 South Lancs.

Issued at 11/55 pm
Copy No 1 1/4 Loyal North Lancs R
2 1/5 Kings Own Royal Lancs R
3 O.C A Coy
4 " B "
5 " C "
6 " D "
7 C.O
8 2.O. [illegible] QM
9 R.S.M.
10] War Diary ✓
11]
12 File.

War Diary

of the

1/5 S Lanc R

for the period

1st to 30th November

1917

November 1917

Army Form C. 2118.

Instructions regarding War Diaries and Intelligence Summaries are contained in F. S. Regs., Part II, and the Staff Manual respectively. Title pages will be prepared in manuscript.

WAR DIARY
or
~~INTELLIGENCE SUMMARY.~~
(*Erase heading not required.*)

Place	Date	Hour	Summary of Events and Information	Remarks and references to Appendices
Oct 31st / Nov 1st			Relieved 1/5 Loyal North Lancs Regt in Centre Sub Sector of Left Brigade Front. Dispositions D + C Companies Front Line, B Coy Support in SHERWOOD LANE. A Company in reserve in GLOSTER RD.	
November 6th			Inter Company relief. New Dispositions A + B Companies Front Line C Company in support in SHERWOOD LANE, D Company in reserve in GLOSTER ROAD.	
November 12th			Relieved by 1/5 Bn Loyal North Lancashire Regt and moved into Brigade Reserve. Dispositions A Coy MEATH POST, B Coy KILDARE + LIMERICK POSTS, Battalion Headquarters together with C + D Companies at VAUCELETTE FM.	
November 16th			Battalion took over fresh dispositions in Brigade Reserve Battalion Headquarters moved to 14 WILLOWS ROAD. D Company moved to HIGH STREET and came under orders of O.C 1/5 Kings Own Royal Lancaster Regt, Coy H.Qrs + 2 Platoons C Coy moved SHERWOOD LANE, 2 Platoons C Coy moved to 14 WILLOWS RD. Dispositions A + B Coys same as before	

D. D. & L., London, E.C.
(A7883) Wt W809/M1672 350,000 4/17 Sch 52a Forms/C/2118/14

Instructions regarding War Diaries and Intelligence Summaries are contained in F. S. Regs., Part II, and the Staff Manual respectively. Title pages will be prepared in manuscript.

WAR DIARY
or
INTELLIGENCE SUMMARY.
(Erase heading not required.)

Army Form C. 2118.

Place	Date	Hour	Summary of Events and Information	Remarks and references to Appendices
November	25/26th		Relieved 1/5 Kings Own Royal Lancs Regt in left sub sector of Brigade front. Dispositions B & D Companies in Front Line. C Coy in support in GEORGE STREET, A Company in reserve in HIGH STREET at Battalion Headquarters.	
November	28th		Heavy massing of enemy troops on our front reported.	
November	30th		Enemy attacked about 7.20am in great numbers and broke through North of VILLERS-GUISLAIN. At once large numbers worked down Southwards and attacked the battalion in rear. Not an officer or man of the battalion came back and, long after the enemy had advanced on our front were seen to be fighting round Battalion Headquarters. The fighting qualities of the Regt were displayed at their best and a wonderful example has been given to the new battalion.	
			The approximate strength of the battalion in the line was 21 Officers – 540 other ranks.	
			[illegible]	

D. D. & L., London, E.C. (A7883) Wt W869/M1672 350,000 4/17 Sch 52a Forms/C/2118/14

Secret

Amendment to O.O. 123 [illegible] 76

Para 2 is cancelled

Substitute

Move

On completion of relief, Battalion will move into Brigade Reserve.

Bn. Hqrs. and B. Coy to Vaughan Bank

A. Coy - Meath Post (2 platoons forming permanent garrison)

C. Coy Vancellette Farm area X.13c

D. Coy (less 2 platoons) Limerick Post } forming
2 Platoons Kildare Post } permanent garrisons

Acknowledge

[illegible] 2/Lieut
A/Adjt. 1/5 South Lancs. R.

Copies to all recipients of O.O. 123

Vol 24

War Diary

of the

1/5th S. Lan. R.

for the period

1st to 31st December 1917.

Z 31

December 1917

Army Form C. 2118.

Instructions regarding War Diaries and Intelligence Summaries are contained in F. S. Regs., Part II. and the Staff Manual respectively. Title pages will be prepared in manuscript.

WAR DIARY
or
~~INTELLIGENCE~~ SUMMARY.

(*Erase heading not required.*)

Place	Date	Hour	Summary of Events and Information	Remarks and references to Appendices
December	1st		Reinforcing platoon from transport lines attacked MEATH POST and LIMERICK POST but were unable to gain ground owing to heavy enemy barrage and machine gun fire. The attacking force withdrew to its original position which was held until relieved by 21st Division during night 1st/2nd December	
December	2nd		Reinforcing platoon moved back to billets at BUIRE.	
December	2nd/4th		Resting at BUIRE. Capt D Nisbett assumed command of the battalion.	
December	5th		Moved by march route to FLAMICOURT and were billeted in Carnatton? huts	
December	6th/7th		Devoted to the cleaning of the mens' clothes & equipment	
December	8th		The Bn. fell in at 6.45 am, marched to FLAMICOURT station and entrained at 8 am. Detrained at AUBIGNY at 4.30 pm and marched seven kilometres to IZEL-LES-HAMEAU where we took over billets	
December	9th/10th		Carried out ordinary training.	
December	11th		The Battn paraded 9.45 am and marched to BETHENCOURT a distance of three miles. on the march the Bn was inspected by Brig. Gen Kentish & G.O.C 55th Div. Men smartly turned out and marching very good. Landed BETHENCOURT 11.30 am & took over billets	

A7092 Wt. W128 9/M1293. 750,000. 1/17. D. D & L. Ltd. Forms/C2118/14.

December 1917

Instructions regarding War Diaries and Intelligence Summaries are contained in F. S. Regs., Part II. and the Staff Manual respectively. Title pages will be prepared in manuscript.

WAR DIARY
or
INTELLIGENCE SUMMARY.

(Erase heading not required.)

Army Form C. 2118.

Place	Date	Hour	Summary of Events and Information	Remarks and references to Appendices
December	12th		Moved by march route to VALHOUN commencing 9.30 am arriving at destination 1.40 pm. Distance 9 miles. Weather good	
December	13th		Moved by march route at 10.0 am to PALFART and LIVOSSART, distance 9 miles. Marching heavy & weather unsettled.	
December	14th		Moved by march route to LAIRES, distance 5 Kilometres. Marching very heavy & weather very bad.	
December	15th/16th		~~Day~~ Devoted to improving billets and cleaning of the mens kits	
December	17th		Heavy snow fell, which cancelled all parades.	
December	18th/24th		Training under Brig General Lentish on Brigade Parade Ground	
December	25th		Church Parades. Remainder of day devoted to the mens' comfort. Dinner served to the men in village estaminets at noon.	
December	26th/31st		Devoted to training. 31st Major von Pilkington DSO returned from one months leave and assumed command of the Battn	

[illegible] 2/Lt ~~Capt~~ Adjt
for Cmdt 1/5th South Lancs Regt

A7092 Wt. W128 9/M1293. 750,000. 1/17. D. D & L. Ltd. Forms/C2118/14.

Vol 25

War Diary

of the

1/5th S Lan R

for the period

1st to 31st January

1918

Z 32

Army Form C. 2118.

Instructions regarding War Diaries and Intelligence Summaries are contained in F. S. Regs., Part II, and the Staff Manual respectively. Title pages will be prepared in manuscript.

WAR DIARY
or
INTELLIGENCE SUMMARY.
(Erase heading not required.)

H.Q. 166TH INFANTRY BDE. No. .... Date 4.2.18

Place	Date	Hour	Summary of Events and Information	Remarks and references to Appendices
Field	1918 Jan	1st	Holiday. Football league games. The Bn had a dinner in Estaminets	
	2–4		Training.	
		4	Lt Col J McCarthy O'Leary took over command of the Bn.	
	5	8	Training.	
		8	Draft of 300 OR arrived. Not sufficient billets in LAIRES for the whole Bn. D Coy on detachment to LIVOSSART.	
	8–31		Training	

S. Gibson 2Lt
Adjt. 1/5 South Lancs Regt

D. D. & L., London, E.C. (A7283) Wt W809/M1672 350,000 4/17 Sch 52a Forms/C/2118/14

Vol 26

War Diary

of the

15th S. Lan. R

for the period

1st to 28th Febry

1918

Instructions regarding War Diaries and Intelligence Summaries are contained in F. S. Regs., Part II. and the Staff Manual respectively. Title pages will be prepared in manuscript.

Army Form C. 2118.

WAR DIARY
~~or~~
~~INTELLIGENCE SUMMARY.~~

(Erase heading not required.)

Place	Date	Hour	Summary of Events and Information	Remarks and references to Appendices
	1918 Feby	1	On the breaking up of the 2nd Line 4 Officers & 100 O.R. were posted to this unit.	
	2	- 8	Training	
		9	The Bn left LAIRES @ 10.9 am & marched to FLECHIN where they took over billets for the night	
		10	Left FLECHIN @ 8.35 am & marched to BURBURE & took over billets.	
		11	Rest at BURBURE	
		12	Left BURBURE @ 11.30 am & marched to BUSNETTES & took over billets.	
		13	Third Anniversary of the Bn Landing in FRANCE General Holiday	
		14	Left BUSNETTES @ 11.15 a.m. & marched to FERME DU ROI near BETHUNE. Here the Bn was in DIVISIONAL Reserve.	
	15	- 23	Training & Reconnaissance by parties of Officers & NCOs of defences.	
		24	Stood by to take up position in rear defences at short notice.	
		25	Moved up & relieved the 6th K.L.R. in support of left Brigade. Relief complete @ 4 p.m.	
	26	- 28	Bn H.Q. @ WINDY CORNER A Coy in O.B. LINE B " GIVENCY REDOUBTS VILLAGE LINE C " D " HERTS REDOUBT WINDY CORNER KEEP	

S Gilson 2Lt [illegible]
1/5 SOUTH LANCS REGT

A7092 Wt. W128 9/M1293 750,000. 1/17. D. D & L. Ltd. Forms/C2118/14.

Vol 27

War Diary

of

1/5th S. Lan. R.

for period

1st to 31st March

1918

Z 34.

G 4 ?

Instructions regarding War Diaries and Intelligence Summaries are contained in F. S. Regs., Part II. and the Staff Manual respectively. Title pages will be prepared in manuscript.

WAR DIARY
or
INTELLIGENCE SUMMARY.
(Erase heading not required.)

Army Form C. 2118.

Place	Date	Hour	Summary of Events and Information	Remarks and references to Appendices
March 1st/3rd			Battalion in Support	
March 4th			Bn took over Right sub sector of Brigade front. Dispositions D Coy PRINCES ISLAND B Coy BARNTON TEE. A Coy O B line. C Coy LE PLANTIN N + S. Bn HQ ARA 5.2	
5th/6th			B Coy heavily shelled + gaps made in the breastwork	
7th			5am Heavy bombardment opened on our Divisional front + a box barrage round BARNTON TEE. A raiding party of 3 officers 120 OR entered our line at BARNTON TEE. No 3 Post (2Lt J Burgess) repulsed them + took two wounded prisoners. No 1 Post (2Lt J A Forbes) also repulsed them but lost 7 men missing. No 2 post under Sergt W Box was captured. C Coy relieved B Coy	
8th			A quiet day	
9th			Heavy firing on left from 4.10 am. Heavy firing on right from 4.45 am at 6/15 am all quiet.	
10th			German attack expected on Portuguese front. Heavy firing heard from 5.30 am to 6.15 am	
11th			Usual artillery activity. A Coy relieved D in PRINCES ISLAND. D Coy took over O B line.	
12/13th			Enemy artillery active	
14th			B Coy relieved 3 Platoons C Coy in BARNTON LOCALITY. C Coy occupied LE PLANTIN N+S.	
15th			D Coy relieved A Coy in PRINCES ISLAND	
16th			Usual artillery activity.	

A7092 Wt. W128.9/M1293. 750,000. 1/17. D. D & L. Ltd. Forms/C2118/14.

Army Form C. 2118.

Instructions regarding War Diaries and Intelligence Summaries are contained in F. S. Regs., Part II. and the Staff Manual respectively. Title pages will be prepared in manuscript.

WAR DIARY
or
~~INTELLIGENCE SUMMARY.~~

(Erase heading not required.)

Place	Date	Hour	Summary of Events and Information	Remarks and references to Appendices
March	17th		Battalion on our left carried out a raid at 5 am.	
			HQrs. A B & C Coys relieved by 1/6th KLR at 10 am. D Coy relieved 7.30pm	
			Took over billets HQrs B & D Coy at ESSARS A & C at LES CHOQUAUX.	
	18th		Cleaning up and inspections.	
	19th		Inspection by BGC	
	20th		Working parties, cable burying.	
	21st		Working parties. Capt T.D. Lee reported for duty 2/Lt Mackenzie to England on Six months tour of duty.	
	22nd		Inspection by Lieut Gen Haking, Cmdr XI Corps. GOC Division + BGC present	
	23rd		Training, COs inspection.	
	24th		Moved up to BUSTLE positions at CORRE with Bn HQrs at the Chateau	
			Returned to billets at ESSARS at 11 am	
	25th		166 Inf Bde took over new front south of LA BASSEE CANAL from 137 ~~Bde~~ Inf Bde and 2½ Coys 139 Inf Bde. Dispositions	
			Right Bn: 1/5th Kings Own + B & D Coy 1/5th South Lancs Regt attached	
			Left Bn 1/10th Kings Liverpool Regt. Support Bn 1/5th South Lancs (less 2 Coys) at LE PREOL	

A7092 Wt. W128:9/M1293. 750,000. 1/17. D. D & L. Ltd. Forms/C2118/14.

Instructions regarding War Diaries and Intelligence Summaries are contained in F. S. Regs., Part II. and the Staff Manual respectively. Title pages will be prepared in manuscript.

WAR DIARY
or
INTELLIGENCE SUMMARY.
(Erase heading not required.)

Army Form C. 2118.

Place	Date	Hour	Summary of Events and Information	Remarks and references to Appendices
March	26th		Battalion moved up to CAMBRIN LOCALITY in close support. C+D Coy. rejoined on redistribution of Bde front.	
	27th		A+B Coys moved up to the reserve line A Coy attached to 1/10th Kings Liverpool Regt B " — " — 1/5th Kings Own (R L) Regt	
	28/31	31	Battalion engaged each night on wiring in front of Reserve Line. Work also carried on improving the CAMBRIN defences. Enemy very quiet	
			[signature] Lt Col Cmd 1/5th South Lancs Regt	

A7092 Wt. W128.9/M1293. 750,000. 1/17. D. D & L. Ltd. Forms/C2118/14.

166th Brigade.

55th Division

1/5th BATTALION

SOUTH LANCASHIRE REGIMENT

APRIL 1918.

Vol 29

War Diary

of

1/5 Glos R.

for period

1st to 31st May

1918

236

15

166/55

Instructions regarding War Diaries and Intelligence Summaries are contained in F. S. Regs., Part II. and the Staff Manual respectively. Title pages will be prepared in manuscript.

WAR DIARY
or
INTELLIGENCE SUMMARY.
(Erase heading not required.)

1/5 S. Lancs

Vol 28

Army Form C. 2118.

Place	Date	Hour	Summary of Events and Information	Remarks and references to Appendices
	1/4/18		C.O. + 4 Coy. Commdrs attended lectures at Bde. H.Q. by [illegible]. 4 of our observation balloons brought down.	
	3/4/18		Relieved 1/5 King's Own in CAMBRIN N. Sector. Relief quiet + completed by 5-30 a.m.	
	4/4/18		XI Corps Commdr visited our trenches. Quiet day.	
	5/4/18		Quiet day.	
	6/4/18		Gas projectors discharged by Battn. on left 164 Inf. Bde. at 1 a.m. [illegible] Coy Commdrs of relieving Bde (2nd Inf. Bde.) viewed trenches.	
	7/4/18		Shoot on enemy trenches at 5 am. very little retaliation. Battn. relieved by 1st Northants Regt. + moved back to billets at BEUVRY.	
	8/4/18		Placed 1/5 K.L.R. in Divisional [illegible] Battn. moved to billets at ESSARS	
	9/4/18		At 4-15 a very heavy bombardment and at 5-30 the order BUSTLE arrived. A + C Coys under Major Pilkington [illegible] moved to an assembly position N.W. of GORRE + the remainder of the Battn. took up positions in the LE PREOL [illegible] locality. Both parties had casualties when moving to their positions. Shell fire all day. A + C Coys came under the command of 165 Bde. + B + D Coys under the command of 164 Bde. D + B Coys [illegible] LOISNE CENTRAL which was occupied by 1½ Coys. of the 1/10 K.L.R. [illegible] B Coy dug in in rear [illegible] at LOISNE CHATEAU. At 5-30 pm [illegible] ordered to reinforce 1/4 L.N.L. (the left Bn.) A Coy reinforced 4 K.O.R.L. with 2 platoons in DEATH + GLORY SAP + CHEYNE WALK, the other 2 platoons reinforcing 1/4 L.N.L.	
	10/4/18		Boche attempted to surround LOISNE CENTRAL held by [illegible] 1/10 K.L.R. a counter attack arranged by Major PILKINGTON D.S.O. [illegible] led to the	

A7092 Wt. W125.9/M1293. 750,000. 1/17. D. D & L. Ltd. Forms/C2118/14.

Army Form C. 2118.

Instructions regarding War Diaries and Intelligence Summaries are contained in F. S. Regs., Part II. and the Staff Manual respectively. Title pages will be prepared in manuscript.

WAR DIARY
or
INTELLIGENCE SUMMARY.

(Erase heading not required.)

Place	Date	Hour	Summary of Events and Information	Remarks and references to Appendices
	1/4/18		capture of 21 prisoners & 2 M.G.s [illegible] 2/Lt Dymond who led his platoon was killed.	
	11/4/18		2 Platoons of B. Coy relieved 2 platoons [illegible] Fusiliers & a line of [illegible] taken over from NEWCOT EXTENSION down GRENADIER ROAD to WINDY CORNER.	
	12/4/18		On night of 12/13 [illegible] Coy took over [illegible] LE PLANTIN S. and GRENADIER ROAD as far as its junction with NEWCOT EXTENSION. This line was held [illegible] under heavy [illegible] BLACK WATCH [illegible]	
	13/4/18		[illegible] took over [illegible] of LOISNE CENTRAL [illegible] with A Coy in support [illegible] on the night of 15/16 April.	
	15/4/18		Battn. [illegible] into [illegible] at BURBURE [illegible] of 15/16 and B & D. Coys on night 16th April.	
	16/4/18		Re-organisation & refitting at BURBURE	
	20/4/18		Moved on sudden orders to VERQUIN where [illegible]	
	21/4/18		The Battn. [illegible] to Right sector of Bde. front [illegible] 2nd WELSH REGT, 3rd Bde. leaving behind 4 officers & 100 [illegible] under MAJOR PILKINGTON D.S.O. [illegible] FOUQUIÈRES [illegible] BURBURE ALLOUAGNE & [illegible] the Battn. [illegible] VERQUINEUL. Relief complete 2 am [illegible] in FESTUBERT SECTOR:- Front line D. Coy LE PLANTIN NORTH A. Coy FESTUBERT B. Coy CAILLOUX [illegible] Coy [illegible]	

A7092' Wt. W128 9/M1293. 750,000. 1/17. D. D & I. Ltd, Forms/C2118/14.

Army Form C. 2118.

Instructions regarding War Diaries and Intelligence Summaries are contained in F. S. Regs., Part II. and the Staff Manual respectively. Title pages will be prepared in manuscript.

WAR DIARY
or
INTELLIGENCE SUMMARY.
(Erase heading not required.)

Place	Date	Hour	Summary of Events and Information	Remarks and references to Appendices
	22/4/18		Route A [illegible] by 1/5 K.O.R.L.R. [illegible] left [illegible] by the enemy.	
			Normal day on Battn. front.	
	23/4/18		Normal day with usual shelling of village line. [illegible] to [illegible] our flank between GAILLOUX [illegible] K.O.L.R.	
			Unsuccessful attempt by 1/5 K.O. [illegible]	
	24/4/18		Normal day. Usual harassing shelling of village line.	
	25/4/18		Route A [illegible] by 1/10 LIVERPOOL SCOTTISH [illegible] [illegible] by 1/5 K.O.R.L.R.	
			on our left. Battn. [illegible] [illegible]	
			[illegible] LE PLANTIN NORTH [illegible] D [illegible]	
			FESTUBERT & GAILLOUX with [illegible]	
			1/5 KINGS OWN [illegible] South of CANAL in Bde Reserve.	
	26/4/18		Route A [illegible]	
	27/4/18		Heavy enemy shelling of FESTUBERT at 2.30 am. [illegible]	
			[illegible] S.O.S. [illegible]	
			Bde relieved at night by 165 Bde. 1/5 LIVERPOOL [illegible]	
			[illegible] 1/5 SOUTH LANCS.	
	28/4/18		Relief complete 2 am. Battn. [illegible] VERQUIGNEUL	
			on arrival coming into Div. Reserve.	
	29/4/18		In Div. Reserve.	
	30/4/18		" "	

J MacCarthy [?] Lt Col
Comdg. 1/5th South Lancs Regt
1/5/18

A7092 Wt. W128 9/M1293 750,000. 1/17. D. D & L. Ltd. Forms/C2118/14.

NARRATIVE.

1/5th BATTN. SOUTH LANCASHIRE REGT.

On the night of the 8th/9th April 1918, the Battalion was billeted in ESSARS and adjoining villages.

2. A bombardment opened over the whole area at about 4.15 am on the 9th.

3. The order BUSTLE was received at 5.15 am and by 6.15 am all Coys. were on the move to their positions.
A. & C. Coys. under Major W.N.PILKINGTON, D.S.O. to an assembly position N.W. of GORRE.
Battn. H.Q., B. & D. Coys. to LE PREOL Locality North.

4. At 1 pm A. & C. Coys. were placed under orders of G.O.C. 165 Bde. (See report from Major PILKINGTON, D.S.O. attached.)

5. Battn. H.Q., B. & D. Coys. moved forward and held the line of breastworks from the CANAL to TUNING FORK. They were heavily shelled on the way and suffered some 20 casualties.

6. This line was heavily shelled until about 3 pm when the fire slackened.

7. At 5 pm Battn. H.Q. B. & D. Coys. were placed at disposal of G.O.C. 164 Bde.
Battn. H.Q. was ordered to join 164 Bde. H.Q. and was used for carrying ammunition and rations to the front line.
B. & D. Coys. were ordered to move, carrying bombs and ammunition, to GIVENCHY to reinforce 1/4th LOYAL NORTH LANCS and 1/4th K.O. ROYAL LANCASTERS.

8. B. Coy. (with 1/4th LOYAL NORTH LANCS) was located as follows :-
3 Platoons in PICCADILLY and UPPER CUT. under orders of O.C. D. Coy. 1/4th L. N. LANCS.
1 Platoon in GRENADIER ROAD under Capt. LEE (O.C. B. Coy. 1/5th S. LANCS), who, reinforced by 2 platoons LANCASHIRE FUSILIERS, had command of this locality.

On the 10th inst. 2 of his platoons from PICCADILLY relieved the LANCASHIRE FUSILIERS in GRENADIER ROAD.

From 3 am 14th inst. B. Coy. held -
LE PLANTIN SOUTH.
GRENADIER ROAD.
~~XXXXXXXXX~~.NEW CUT EXTENSION.
until relieved on the night of the 16th by the 1st Battn. BLACK WATCH.

During this period (9th to 16th) the Company was heavily shelled at intervals suffering -
1 Officer and 35 O.Rs. casualties.

D. Coy. was located as follows :-
13 & 14 Platoons in DEATH OR GLORY SAP & CHEYNE WALK.
15 Platoon CAMBRIDGE TERRACE.
16 Platoon OXFORD TERRACE.

On 10th inst. 15 Platoon was moved to OXFORD TERRACE.

On 11th inst. 15 Platoon occupied original front line exploring WARLINGHAM CRATER.

On 13th inst. 13 & 14 Platoons under Capt. HILL held PONT FIXE. 15 & 16 Platoons WINDY CORNER.

From 14th inst. the whole of D. Coy. (under Capt. HILL) held WINDY CORNER until relieved on the night of the 16th by 1 Bn. Camerons.

From 9th to 16th inst. D. Coy. suffered 42 casualties.

The Band, Pioneers and Concert Party were sent up from ESSARS to reinforce GIVENCHY on the morning of the 9th They did duty ~~xh~~ in the trenches there until the 15th inst.

suffering 4 casualties.

(Sd) J.MACARTHY O'LEARY.

18th April 1918.

Commanding 1/5th Bn. SOUTH
LANCASHIRE REGT.

OPERATIONS. APRIL 9th to 14th/15th.

A. & C. Coys. 1/5th Bn. S. LANCS after assembling in field behind GORRE were ordered up to LOISNE CHATEAU to help 1/10th L'pools who were holding LOISNE CENTRAL. The companies took up positions astride the road in front of the CHATEAU up towards the KEEP. Shelling had been going on all day but eased up at night. At 6.15 pm Lt. FRODSHAM Coy went up to see dispositions of 1/10th L'pool R. A report came round that enemy were in dugout in left rear. FRODSHAM and I ~~gmx~~ crawled out through the houses and got back to supporting platoon which was sent up at once under 2/Lt. DYMOND.

Taking the enemy in rear the attack was at once successful and most of enemy were taken prisoners. The attack was brilliantly led by DYMOND and his Platoon Sergeant who took on his men firing from the hip in face of heavy M.G. fire. Rfn. HOLCROFT single handed captured an M.G. killing two and capturing four others of the crew. The remainder of the Company were driven back and it was during this that DYMOND was killed. The enemy had waded down the drain on the S. side of the KEEP and were quickly establishing themselves in a gunpit and ruined houses. Many of them were storm troops and evidently it was a determined attempt to cut off the KEEP. That night ditch was blocked with wire and a night and day L.G. post placed to command it. It was reported that enemy were cutting our wire. Bursts of L.G. fire were directed on it. At 8 am on 11th barrage was put down on front and supports and an attack towards LOISNE N. was dissipated by artillery. Enemy artillery very active in afternoon. A prisoner captured on our wire said attack was to be launched next morning. Steps were taken at once to get artillery to fire on farms where enemy were expected to mass.

The morning broke misty but there was no attack. Enemy shelling more intermittently in short bursts.

13th 1/10 were taken out of garrison which was No. 1 Company in KEEP and one in support. Wire was put out to flank towards LOISNE N. Nothing further happened until relieved night 14th/15th.

During the tour a large amount of sniping was done towards TOURET. One Sgt. (CARR) claiming 55 hits, and gaining very valuable information for artillery targets.

(Sd) W. N. PILKINGTON, Major,

1/5th S. LANCASHIRE REGT.,

April 17th 1918. in Command of A. & C. Coys.

NARRATIVE OF EVENTS AFFECTING LETTER 'A' COMPANY OF THE 5th BATTN. SOUTH LANCASHIRE REGT. DURING THE OPERATIONS 9th to 16th APRIL 1918.

On the morning of the 9th April 1918, 'A' Coy. was billeted at LES CHOQUAUX in Divisional Reserve.

At about 4 am a warning order was received to prepare to "BUSTLE" and about ¾ of an hour later, one to "BUSTLE".

The Coy. moved off about 5.30 am with 'C' Coy., under the Command of Major N. PILKINGTON, D.S.O.

Route followed to positions of assembly ~~xxxxx~~ at X.27.c.60.25. :-
From LES CHOQUAUX past ROBY DUMP on main road towards LOCON until turning to right at MANCHESTER ROAD (came under shell fire at about X.13.d.4.9. and then broke up into artillery formation by sections), crossed CANAL DE LA LAWE at bridge X.13.d.7.8. and proceeded in diamond formation between LOISNE Stream and road running from LES GLATIGNIES to LE HAMEL, clearing LE HAMEL on the N.E. side to cross roads in X.27.a. Thence to BUSTLE point.

ACTION TAKEN ON ARRIVAL AT BUSTLE POINT.

We took up temporary positions in shell holes about 7 am, issued picks and shovels, and despatched two patrols, one through GORRE and one towards LOISNE to get in touch with the situation.

About 9.30 am the fog lifted a little and we moved in a N.E. direction taking up a position and digging in about X.27.d.05.85. to X.27.d.20.50. with two platoons, keeping the other two platoons in reserve at X.27.c.80.60. At about 2 pm I had orders to report to Brigade H.Q. LOISNE CHATEAU and received instructions to take up a position covering the CHATEAU from the N.E.

I reconnoitred the ground and had the Company in position by about 4.30 pm, and proceeded to dig in (as per sketch map). These positions were held until the night of 13th/14th April, during which time we consolidated positions and wired the front facing N.E. and around the posts.

On the night of the 13th/14th we sent 3 Platoons forward and relieved our 'C' Coy. in shell hole positions running from X.22.a.90.10. to X.22.d.3.4. with Coy. H.Q. at post at X.22.d.25.15. These positions were held until relieved by "A" Coy. 2nd Battn. S.W. Bordrs. (1st Division) on the night 15th/16th, and on relief proceeded to BURBURE.

Trench strength of 'A' Coy. about 136.

CASUALTIES. 9 killed.
28 wounded.

(Sd) NAYLOR. Capt.

O.C. 'A' Coy. (9th - 16th April).

C.M. STAFFORD, 2/Lt.
O.C. No. 4 Platoon (9th - 16th April).

1st August 1918.

BRIEF ACCOUNT OF THE PART TAKEN BY "B" COY. 5TH SOUTH LANCS. REGT. IN OPERATIONS 9th - 16th APRIL, 1918.

On the night of 8th/9th April the Battalion was billeted at ESSARS.

About 4.30 a.m. on the 9th April the enemy bombardment opened and the billets of the Coy. came under shell fire. The Coy. fell in, and on receipt of the order to proceed to 'BUSTLE' positions, moved off to LE PREOL N Defences, taking the route LA CROIX DE FER - LA BASSEE CANAL, and being under shell fire of varying intensity all the way. On arrival at the wood the defences from ROUTE 20 to the CANAL BANK at F.11.c.5.7. were occupied and touch was obtained with GLOUCESTERS on S. of the CANAL and with 'D' Coy. of 5th South Lancs. N. of ROUTE 20. About noon, the shell fire and M.G. fire which had been coming from the N. slackened in intensity. During the morning a Straggler's Post on the CANAL BANK had guided a large number of men mostly T.M.Battery into the defences which were there very fully manned.

About 5.30 I received orders to withdraw the Coy. from the defences and report to 164 Bde.H.Q. to which 'B' Coy. was to be attached, and acting on further orders received from G.O.C., 164 Bde. took my Coy. up to GIVENCHY to reinforce 1/4th L.N.Lancs.Regt. carryingup with us supplies of S.A.A. and bombs. On reporting to Lt-Col. CRUMP Commanding 1/4th L.N.Lancs. I was instructed to hand over three platoons to Company Commanders of his Battn. as reinforcements for duty in NEW CUT - PICCADILLY etc., and to take the remaining platoon to GRENADIER ROAD to form along with 2 platoons of the Lancashire Fusiliers a defensive flank from the top of NEW CUT EXTENSION down GRENADIER ROAD to WINDY CORNER. I was placed in charge of all the troops on this defensive flank.

The night was quiet, but next day the trenches were steadily shelled. There were no shelters or dugouts for the men, who were compelled to live in the trenches day and night, but they behaved magnificently and shewed a splendid spirit.

On the evening of 10th the 2 platoons of Lancashire Fusiliers in GRENADIER ROAD were withdrawn and replaced by 2 of the other platoons of 'B' Coy. and on the 12th, the 4th platoon also rejoined the Coy. on the defensive flank referred to above.

On the night of 13th/14th 'B' Coy. was relieved of the section of NEW CUT EXTENSION that we had been holding and took over LE PLANTIN S instead, and dispositions remained there until relief by 1st Black Watch on night of 16th/17th.

Of the behaviour of all ranks I cannot speak too highly. In a trench where they were without shelter, even from the weather, under almost constant shell fire, often unable to get their meals or food of any sort for considerable periods, and without the satisfaction of being able to retaliate since they were so placed as to have no view of the enemy, they were one and all cheerful and ready for any emergency at all times. The behaviour of the stretcher-bearers in particular was beyond all praise and doubtless saved many lives by the promptitude which they attended to all casualties under shell fire.

(sd) J.D.LEE, Capt.
O.C. 'B' Coy. 5th S.Lancs.R.

REPORT ON ACTION FROM APRIL 9th to 16th.

On the morning of the 9th April 'BUSTLE' came through at 5 a.m. and at 6 a.m. the Company moved out from ESSARS to occupy a part of the SAILLY LABOURSE LINE. On the way the Company came under heavy shell fire, about 16 casualties being incurred. At 7.15 a.m. the Coy. was in position from F.5.a.1.0. to F.10.b.9.8. At times shelling was intense especially on the left occupied by No. 16 Platoon. At 5.30 p.m. orders were received to move to vicinity of 164 Bde. H.Qrs. and from that time came under the orders of that Bde. being attached to 1/4th K.O.R.L. and 1/4th L.N.Ls.

The 2 platoons attached to 1/4th K.O.R.L.R. moved up immediately and occupied DEATH AND GLORY SAP and CHEYNE WALK.

One of the other two platoons attached to 1/4th L.N.Ls. occupied S.1. Locality whilst the other moved along FINCHLEY ROAD and took up an outpost position extending to WARLINGHEM CRATER. This continued until the 12th when the two platoons attached to the 1/4th K.O.R.L. moved back and occupied PONT FIXE defences, whilst the other two platoons occupied WINDY CORNER defences. On the 14th the whole Coy. moved into WINDY CORNER to occupy the defences and to form a defensive flank to the North.

At both PONT FIXE and WINDY CORNER the Coy. was exposed to the heaviest shell fire but never flagged until the relief on the evening of the 16th by the 1st Camerons.

About 45 casualties were incurred.

(sd) J.E.H.HILL, Capt.
O.C., 'D' Coy.

NARRATIVE OF EVENTS AFFECTING No. 4 PLATOON, 'A' COMPANY, of the 5th BATTALION, SOUTH LANCASHIRE REGIMENT, during the OPERATIONS 9th to 16th APRIL, 1918.

On the morning of the 9th April 1918, No. 4 Platoon was billeted at LES CHOQUAX in Divisional Reserve. At about 4 a.m. a warning order was received to prepare to 'BUSTLE' and about ¾ hour later one to 'BUSTLE'.

The platoon moved off about 5.30 a.m. with 'C' Coy. under the command of Major N.PILKINGTON, D.S.O. Route followed to position of assembly at X.27.c.60.25. from LES CHOQUAUX past RUBY DUMP on main road towards LOCON until turning to right at MANCHESTER ROAD (came under shell fire at about X.13.d.4.9.)and then broke up into artillery formation)by sections) crossed CANAL DE LA LAWE at Bridge X.13.d.3.8. and proceeded in diamond formation between LOISNE STREAM and road running from LES GLATIGNIES to LE HAMEL, clearing LE HAMEL on the N.E. side to cross roads in X.27.a. Thence to Bustle point.

Action taken on arrival at Bustle point.
The platoon took up a temporary position in shell holes about 7 a.m. Picks and shovels were issued. A patrol was sent out in the direction of LOISNE to get touch with the situation. About 9.30 a.m. the fog lifted a little and the platoon moved in a N.E. direction taking up a position and digging in about X.27.d.05.85. Two platoons were held in reserve at X.27.c.40.60. Here the platoon awaited further orders from the Company Commander. Up to this period of the operations the platoon had six casualties.

At about 3 p.m I had orders to move the platoon and to take up a position covering the chateau from the N.E. The platoon was in position by about 4.30 p.m. Every advantage of improving our defences was taken. A patrol was immediately despatched ina N. direction to get in touch with the Regt., on my left.

The position was held until the night of the 13th/14th April, during which time I consolidated and wired the front facing N.E. and around the post (as per attached sketch map).

On the night of the 13th/14th the platoon moved forward and relieved a platoon of our 'C' Coy. in shell hole positions at about X.22.a.9.1. to X.22.d.2.9. Company H.Q., at X.22.d.25.15.

(The shelling which up to this period was very heavy now became normal. E.A. were active during the following days up to the 15th). This position was ~~relieved~~ held until relieved by "A" Company, 2nd Battn. S.W.B. (1st Division) on the night 15th/16th April and on relief the platoon proceeded to BURBURE.

(sd) C.M.STAFFORD, 2/Lt.
O/C. No. 4 Platoon, 'A' Coy.
5th S.Lancs.R.

On the night of the 8th/9th April my Company were in rest billets in ESSARS. About 4.15 a.m. we were aroused by heavy firing on the front system and at 5 a.m. we received orders to "BUSTLE". We immediately turned out and 6 o'clock left ESSARS to take up positions in the SAILLY LABOURSE LINE E. of GORRE. We got there and reported that we were in position by 7 o'clock with 12 casualties. This was due I think to our getting away from billets quickly as the Bosche put down a heavy barrage on GORRE and roads leading from it. We remained in this position until 5 p.m. during which time we were subjected to most intense shell fire and many rumours as to the position in front. About 5 p.m. we drew our rations and supply of bombs and S.A.A. and went forward to reinforce R. Brigade, my platoon took up a position along CHEYNE WALK and DEATH AND GLORY SAP, here we stayed until 12th when the coy. joined again and took over the WINDY CORNER defences being relieved by the 1st Camerons on the night of the 16th.

During the 14th and 15th we were shelled with some very heavy howitzers and I was jolly thankful when we were relieved.

(sd) 2/Lt.
14 Platoon 'D' Coy.

DIARY OF EVENTS.

APRIL 9th.

On the night of the 8th/9th my company were on Divisional rest at LOCON. At 4.30 a.m. we received "BUSTLE". The company formed up on the LOCON - BETHUNE Road. At 5.30 a.m. we received orders to take up a position W. of GORRE WOOD. We marched off by platoons under shell fire, through LE HAMEL, then to our position where we formed up into artillery formation. On the 9th we had orders to take up another position South of LOISNE STREAM about X.27.b.60.70. and consolidated. My platoon were on the right of the Company front and was holding bridge X.27.b.60.60.

On the 10th we received orders to reinforce the 1/10th Scottish Regt. who were holding LOISNE CENTRAL KEEP. To get to this position we went through a very heavy barrage.

On the 11th the enemy was passing our fronts E. and N. of the Keep and was simply mowed down by our L.Gun and rifle fire. He tried with two M.Gun sections to get behind our position he was driven back by a counter attack and suffered heavy casualties. We captured three M.Guns and about 30 prisoners. We held this keep until the 13th and was then relieved by the 1st S.W.B.Regt.,

(sd) F.WALLINGTON, 2/Lieut.
'C' Coy.,
South Lancs. Regt.,

2930

1/5th Battalion, The King's Own Royal Lancaster Regiment.

Summary of Events from 9th - 14th April, 1918.

Monday 8th April.

The Battalion arrived from CAMBRIN Sector at LOCON and was billetted in neighbourhood of LA TOMBE WILLOT.

Tuesday 9th April.

At 4 a.m. a very heavy bombardment began and LOCON was heavily shelled.

At 5.50 a.m. Battalion received order to "Bustle". This was cancelled about 7.30 am. when troops were told to "Stand By".

At 8.15 am. orders received from Bde. "Carry on with Bustle".

Coys. were told off to their localities and proceeded independently, the 1st Company (A) leaving at 8.20 a.m.

Headquarters moved through LOCON and over the Bridge at MESPLAUX and temporary H.Q. established on the bank of the ditch 100 yards N. of where the stream runs under the RUE DU BOIS X.20.b.92.50. They were afterwards moved to a house on the RUE DU BOIS X.20.b.75.15. Very heavy shelling all morning. In the afternoon and not before, messages were received from all Coys. that they were in position, but touch by A Coy. with troops on its flanks was not established. Only one message received from this Coy..

During the day numbers of Portuguese and British R.G.A. troops, who stated that they had no rifles to fire with kept streaming down the RUE DU BOIS. I diverted about 200 Portuguese and ordered them to dig in along the line of the ditch running from RUE DU BOIS to LAWE CANAL (afterwards known as the switch line) where my H.Q. Platoon were already established.

About 6 p.m. a Lance Corporal came and stated that Germans had attacked EMPEROR ROAD locality in force and it is feared that all were killed or captured.

The night was comparatively ~~calm~~ quiet. We were reinforced by 2 Coys. 1/4th Seaforth Highlanders.

Wednesday 10th April.

Very heavy shelling started 5 a.m. Heavy casualties. During the day 'B' Company under Captain FORSHAW, M.C., were heavily attacked 3 times at LE TOURET, but held on to their positions. 'D' Company on their right was also attacked. Reports from 'C' Company (Capt.BRIGGS) at LOISNE WEST POST said no attack developed.

At 5 p.m. Major BUCKLE and H.Q., 1st Northumberland Fusiliers arrived and shared H.Q. with me.

1 Company of this Battalion relieved 'B' and 'D' Coys at night, and the 2 Companies were withdrawn to the Switch Line. 'C' Company remained in present position.

Tonight we have had some little artillery support. Yesterday there was no reply to the German Artillery. Quiet night.

Thursday 11th April.

At 8.30 a.m. owing to the heavy shelling and congestion with 1st N.F. I moved Headquarters to LES GLATIGNIES. Quiet morning until 12 noon when S.O.S. went beyond MESPLAUX FARM. I saw about a Company of Seaforths coming towards us. I immediately rallied every available man at H.Q. and we manned fire positions and awaited events. The Seaforth retirement stopped and position became normal. Portuguese interpreter came with Commandant and said there would be trouble if his men were not sent away. I ordered them to go informing Brigade. Their position was taken by some R.E.

Our casualties are now 12 Officers and 240 O.R. Evening quiet.

Friday 12th April.	Went round Switch Line 6 a.m. During morning Germans attacked MESPLAUX FARM but were beaten off. The day was fairly quiet on the whole. My Companies were not engaged.
Saturday 13th April.	An abnormally quiet morning. Thick fog. 'B' Company dug a defensive flank on S. side of CANAL during the night and were joined by 2/Lt. YARES party from 251 Tunnelling Company. At 3 p.m. the whole switch line and Bn. H.Q. heavily bombarded. Sgt.BARROW and Pte.HOWARD killed. Germans attacked other side of CANAL but were repulsed. Bn.H.Q. moved at 6.30 to a farm at X.19.b.9.3. 'B' and 'D' Coys. relieved 1/4th S.Lancashire Regt., at MESPLAUX. Relief reported complete by 12.30 a.m.
Sunday 14th April.	Much colder - morning quiet. In the afternoon 'B' and 'D' Coys. at MESPLAUX heavily bombarded with guns and T.Ms. causing some casualties. No infantry action followed. Night quieter. The Battalion was relieved by 1st N.F. and 4th Royal Fusiliers. Relief complete by 1 a.m. Coys. marched independently to near VENDIN where lorries were waiting and proceeded to billets at RAIMBERT ARRIVING ABout 5 a.m.

Total casualties 15 Officers and 271 O.R.

(sd) A.WAYTE, Lt.Colonel,
Commanding 1/5th K.L.O.R.L.R.

18th April,1918.

Operations 9th/13th April, 1918.

2nd Lieut. W.T.YARE 'A' Coy. 1/5th K.O.R.L.R.

On the 9th, 10th and 11th April I was attached to 170th Tunnelling Coy. R.E. at VERQUIN together with 40 O.R. of 'A' Coy. 1/5th K.O.R.L.R. I was recalled to join my unit and reported to 166 Bde. H.Q. at ECLUSE D'ESSARS taking my party of 40 men and 16 men of 1/5th South Lancs. Regt., About noon 12th I received orders to take up a position in the line commencing on the LAWE CANAL (about pt. X.13.d.35.10.) and running Southeast. On my right was the 251 Coy. R.E. On my left the Shropshire Light Infantry. No shelling on this position.

Carried S.A.A. to front line for N.Fs. during night 12th/13th April.

The morning of 13/4/18 was very foggy and fairly quiet. At 1 a.m. 13/4/18 I joined 'B' Company 1/5th K.O.R.L.R. and formed a defensive flank of shell hole posts along the S.W. bank of LAWE CANAL from X.13.d.35.10. to Switch Line.

At 3.45 p.m. 13/4/18 the enemy put down a very heavy 5.9 barrage in X.13.d. and X.20.a. Barrage ceased 6.30 p.m. Rumour s of enemy advance N. of CANAL not confirmed.

At 10.45 p.m. 13/4/18 my party together with 'B' Company 1/5th K.O.R.L.R. took over posts N.E. and S.E. of MESPLAUX FARM. MESPLAUX FARM shelled from for 3 hours during 14/4/18.

Relieved night 14th/15th by R.F.s.

(sd). W.YARE, 2/Lieut.

Operations 9th to 14th April.

'C' Company, 1/5th K.O.R.L.R.

'C' Company was in billets N. of LOCON when the alarm was received at 4.30 a.m. April 9th. The Company fell in on the Battalion Alarm Post and after a hurried breakfast moved off via LE CASAN, MESPLAUX, and LES FACONS to LOISNE North Keep at X.22.a.5.5. which was held by two platoon and Coy. H.Q. The remaining two platoons dug in on the North side of the Keep to fill a gap between 'C' Coy. and 'D' Coy. Touch was eventually obtained with the 1/10th L'pools at LOISNE CENTRAL but no men were available to stop the gap which existed, but arrangements were made to cover the ground with L.G. fire from the Keep.

The whole operation was carried out under heavy shell fire.

During the afternoon the enemy was engaged with L.G. fire when he became visible around LE TOURET CENTRAL and the farm at X.16.d.75.10.

During the night 10th/11th April the line on the left was withdrawn and the Company holding it together with my two platoons was relieved by a company of Northumberland Fusiliers. With these two platoons I attempted to stop the gap between myself and the 1/10th L'pools but found I was unable to do so as I had too few men so I filled the gap between LOISNE KEEP and 1/5th South Lancs. who were in support to 1/10th Liverpools The Coy. held these same dispositions until relieved.

No infantry attack actually developed against my Coy. but during the whole tour I was heavily shelled each day. At first the shells were principally heavies, but towards the end they were field guns firing at practically point blank range.

Very few casualties occurred as a result of this shelling and the Company came out of action on night 14th/15th April with less than thirty casualties.

Each night patrols went out to front and flanks to keep in touch. Touch was kept with Battn. H.Q. by lamp signals and runners.

(sd) W.N.BRIGGS, Capt.
O.C., 'C' Coy.
1/5th The King's Own.

Account of Operations April 9th - 14th, 1918.

'D' Coy. 1/5th The King's Own R. L. Regt.,

n.. During the night 8th/9th April, the Coy. was in scattered billets in LES LOBES. The heighbourhood was shelled all night and at 3 a.m. this increased in intensity. There was much gas. At 5.30 a.m. I received orders to 'BUSTLE'. At 6.45 a.m. The Company was on parade awaiting orders to move off. I received these at 8 a.m.

My Bustle positions were - to occupy a line between 'C' Company in LOISNE E. and 'B' Coy. in LE TOURET E. KEEP. The route takes was Cross Rds. R.32.c. - LE VERT LANNET - LE CASAN - LES FACONS - ROUTE C. The villages en route were being heavily shelled.

About X.22.a. central I halted the Coy. and they laid out in artillery formation owing to a severe barrage along a line from X.16.c.05.40. to LOISNE.

I went forward and made a personal reconnaissance and found 'C' Coy. in LOISNE W. and B Coy. in LE TOURET CENTRAL KEEP. I also saw enemy moving about in the vicinity of CHATEAU DU RAUX and was fired on by M.Gs. I determined to connect up between these two companies.

The Coy. moved forward and dug slits on an irregular line between the two Keeps.

I kept one platoon in reserve.

Fire positions had been created by 11.30 a.m.

About 2 p.m. the enemy advanced in extended lines. Rapid fire with rifles and Lewis guns checked him and he occupied a ditch or dead ground about 300 yards away. Not long afterwards large numbers of troops were seen in A.16.a. moving towards LOCON. My patrols informed me that they were Germans. They were about 2000 yds away.

A lot of T.M. fire was heard in LE TOURET against the left of 'B' Coy. Patrols at night reported enemy digging and wiring. We kept up L.G. fire throughout the night to disperse him.

April 10th. About 5 a.m. a heavy bombardment was again opened but this was ineffective owing to the scattered slits occupied by my men. Small parties of enemy (presumably) M.G. crews) attempted to push forward to points of vantage but these were stopped. This was the enemy programme throughout the morning.

About 1.45 p.m. a violent bombardment took place against LE TOURET KEEP and my left. About 20 minutes later about 100 enemy attempted to outflank LE TOURET KEEP but were stopped. We had good targets. We could not see what was happening on the left of 'B' Coy. owing to the houses but rapid rifle fire was heard.

About 2.30 p.m. some men of 'B' Coy. (about a platoon strong) came down the road. I took command of these men and intended to use them with my counter attack platoon. The enemy could be seen in LE TOURET KEEP.

I was harassed by T.Ms. and snipers from the houses throughout the evening. I was relieved at night by the 1st N.F.

April 11th, 12th, 13th. Attached to the N.Fs. and 4th Seaforths as counter attack company and occupied part of the Switch Line.

13th/14th - 14th/15th April. I relieved the 4th S.Lancs. in the front line in MESPLAUX between the FARM and LAWE CANAL. The night was fairly quiet but several casualties came from enemy snipers enfilading the positions. At dawn next morning 3 sections (each about 9 men) were seen leaving houses on CANAL BANK at X.8.c. They were a good target for our L.Gs. which effectually disposed of them. Much movement was done by the enemy during the morning around the houses in LE CASAN. Our L.Gs. and snipers had a busy time.

About 12.10 p.m. in response to his S.O.S. the enemy opened out a violent bombardment of T.Ms. and 5.9s. These fell short. In response to a light signal he lengthened his range and we had a very severe bombardment for an hour. This died away about 4 p.m. The Keep and vicinity were practically obliterated. No enemy infantry action followed.

I was relieved by the 4th R.Fs. at night.

(sd) W.METCALFE, Capt.
O.C., 'D' Company.

1-8-18.

'B' Company.

.....On the morning of the 9th April at about 7.30 a.m. we were ordered to "stand to" and be ready to move off at a moment's notice. We moved down to the Battalion parade ground and were then told to "stand by" and that what had been supposed to have been an attack had proved to be only a raid on a large scale, and that the Division on our left had driven the enemy back. Breakfasts were being served when we received orders to move to our "Bustle" positions at once.

We moved off by platoons at 200 yards interval, but had soon to split up into ½ platoons and then quickly into sections owing to the heavy bombardment by the enemy. "B" Coy. moved up to LE TOURET and held the horse shoe line of defences in that village, 'A' Coy. moving forward to LE TOURET North. Shortly after getting into position heavy rifle fire and L. G. fire gave us the "cue" that 'A' Coy. were in the thick of it, but owing to the mist we could not see what had taken place.

Shortly afterwards, a force of about 3 platoons of the enemy came forward to attack our right and 'D' Company. We allowed them to advance as far as the MAISON ROUGE Road when we opened fire. 3 or 4 only of the enemy were seen to get back. In the mean-time we inflicted heavy casualties on their supports, who had been formed up in mass in a small wood.

The night went by quickly, but early next morning (10th) our left two platoons were attacked in force, but held the enemy back inflicting heavy losses on the enemy. Again and again did they attack our left two platoons, each time being driven back, until at the 6th time of attacking they managed to get round our left flank and caused havoc among our left two platoons. Those who were not killed or wounded being taken prisoners.

The right now became untenable and the order "line the road" was given, we attempted to do so, but found the enemy forces too great for us, then we were ordered to get down the RUE DU BOIS as best we could and join up 'D' Coy. and the Seaforths, 3 Officers and 31 men gathered in the shell holes just behind 'D' and dug in according to orders.

Later we were drawn back to the main line of resistance and had the unpleasant experience of our own 18 pdrs firing at us at point blank range. We dug in and later were ordered to form a defensive flank, which we had just completed when we received orders to relieve the garrison at MESPLAUX FARM. After a very uncomfortable 2 days in this place under heavy shell fire, we were at last relieved after a very strenuous 6 days of hard fighting and digging and forming defensive flanks.

We were in action with the enemy on the left of MESPLAUX FARM on the 12th and 13th.

(sd) H.V.TRINGHAM, 2/Lieut.
'B' Coy. 1/5th K.O.R.L.R.

'D' Company.

On the morning of the 9th April 1918 a very heavy bombardment opened out about ~~xxxxxx~~ 3.30 a.m. and a number of shells fell near to our billets in LE TOMBE WILLOT. As the bombardment continued, I got up and dressed and went round to my Company Commander, who gave me the order to pass the word round to "Stand To". The men were got ready and later in the morning we got the order to "BUSTLE". We moved on to the Battalion Parade Ground at LE TOMBE WILLOT where we received the information that a big raid had taken place up North and that everything was alright but we must 'Standto' and await orders. Whilst the men were having their breakfasts we received orders to move off and take up our positions on the South side of LE TOURET. We advanced in platoons about 200 yards interval but as the shelling was bad we had to split up into sections and later into artillery formation. We arrived at the RUE DE BOIS and passed a number of Portuguese who were alongside the road. We hurried passed them and the Company Commander gave orders to take as much cover as possible in a field South of the RUE DE BOIS - the Company still being in artillery formation. The Company Commander and myself went forward to reconnoitre the ground and see the best place to dig in. We returned and orders were then given for the Company to advance and where each platoon would dig in. We dug a trench on the South side of the ~~XXXX~~ RUE DE BOIS our left being just behind the LE TOURET VILLAGE. We linked up with 'C' Company on our right but not being able to get in touch with anybody on our left we swung a platoon round which faced almost due North. The enemy made repeated attempts to attack but were repulsed on our front by rifle and Lewis gun fire and seemed to take shelter in the buildings of LE TOURET. We were in various positions on the front as ordered by HQ., but never did we allow the Boshce to get near enough for hand to hand fighting and on many occasions did we inflict very heavy losses on him.

We were relieved on the night of the 15th from MESPLAUX FARM.

Our casualties were fairly heavy most of them being caused whilst at MESPLAUX FARM with shell fire.

(sd) H.CORLESS, 2/Lieut.
'D' Company.
1/5th K.O.R.L.R.

'D' Company.

On the morning of April 9th 1918 we were in billets at LE TOMBE WILLOT and were aroused early in the morning by a very heavy bombardment.

We got our men dressed, and waited orders, which arrived later in the morning, and we were ordered to stand by on the square at LOCON.

Whilst there information was given us that it was only a big raid up North, but we breakfasted on the square, and then got hurried orders to take up positions on the right of LE TOURET. We found all approaches heavily shelled and moved across country, first by platoons, then by sections in artillery formation.

We passed fugitive Portuguese but got no information as to what had happened, and we carried on until we reached our objective.

We dug a new trench joining up on right with our 'C' Company but our left flank at LE TOURET was unprotected, so one platoon swung round on this flank facing almost due North.

Enemy attempted to advance against us but our men did not allow them to come within 200 yards, and they caused heavy casualties in the enemy ranks.

Later in the afternoon we were heavily shelled by all calibres including a heavy percentage of 5.9 shells.

Dates of the various moves we made in this front have gone now beyond my recall, but we moved to various positions, on orders received from H.Q., never at all at the will of the enemy, as we never lost a post.

On the evening of the 15th we were relieved from positions at MESPLAUX FARM, and from there on the left to LAWE CANAL.

Our casualties were fairly heavy mostly by shell fire.

We had a few sniped, but the enemy never approached close enough for hand to hand fighting.

(sd) J.H.BAIRD, 2/Lieut.
O.C., 13 Platoon,
'D' Company,
1/5th K.O.R.L.R.

1/8/18.

No. 9 PLATOON 'C' COY. 1/5th S.LANCS.REGT.,

DIARY OF EVENTS.

APRIL 9th - 16th, 1918.

APRIL 9th.

5.30 a.m. In rest billets at LES CHOQUAUX and orders were received to 'BUSTLE'. No. 9 Platoon moved off at 6.10 a.m. and proceeded to just E. of LE HAMEL, here it remained in sections (well apart) till 10.30 a.m., during this period the platoon had several casualties from shell fire, heavy shells and gas shells were being sent all round, and GORRE was being very heavily shelled.

10.30 a.m. The Company moved forward and took up a position just S. of the LE HAMEL - LOISNE road, and here consolidated. No. 9 platoon were on the left of the Company and were in touch with Portuguese stragglers until night time when the Portuguese departed and details of the 165 Brigade took up their vacated position.

The night of April 9th/10th was spent here without anything out of the ordinary happening. The position was shelled (slightly) throughout the night.

APRIL 10th.

At 9 a.m. the Company moved up to LOISNE CENTRAL KEEP and remained here till the night of relief April 15th/16th by the 1st S.W.B.

During the five days in the keep, many enemy were killed by snipers and L.Gs. as they appeared to be lost and odd Germans came on lost and were captured by the garrison of the keep.

The keep was heavily shelled during the 10th, 11th and 12th but quietened down between the 12th and 15th.

The enemy tried to raid the KEEP about 5 p.m. on April 10th, but were driven off leaving 23 prisoners, and several dead in our hands.

(sd) M.F.DODDS, 2/Lieut.
O.C., No. 9 Platoon,
'C' Coy.
1/5th S.LANCS.REGT.

1/8/18.

'X' Company Operations Against Enemy,
April 9th - 16th.

5 Platoon.

On the morning of the 9th the Coy. being in rest billets at LE HAMEL were awakened by heavy artillery fire along the whole divisional front at 3.30 a.m. the shells falling dangerously close to the billets. On realising the nature of the shelling the men stood to and awaited orders. Acting on O.C., Coy. orders the men moved up to their Bustle positions in the TUNING FORK LINE by 6.30 a.m. in platoons, being heavily shelled the whole way up. The bulk of the heavy enemy attack being directed against the 55th Division which they repulsed magnificently, the mist making matters very difficult. During the 9th, 10th the Coy. were continuously shelled, the casualties being heavy. On these days the enemy tried to advance, but was driven off by the harassing fire of our L.Gs. and M.Gs. On the night of 10th/11th the Company moved forward and established ORCHARD POST. At 8 a.m. the morning of the 11th the enemy opened a hurricane bombardment on our positions for about 20 minutes during which we lost our officer in charge and a L.G. team, command being taken over by the Senior N.C.O. who was in command until the arrival of an officer. The 11th/12th passed quietly until 12 midnight on the 12th when we had to take the Tower, a position occupied by thr enemy S.E. of ROUTE A KEEP, our Company attack proved successful, 5 enemy killed, 9 prisoners 1 M.G. . At 4 a.m. on the 13th the Coy. were relieved by the 13th K.L.R. going down to T.F.L. After a quiet day we proceeded to FESTUBERT at 10 p.m. to relieve a Coy. of the 13th King's for 48 hours, which passed fairly quiet, finally getting relieved 11 p.m. 16/4/18.

(sd) Corporal DIXON,
5 Platoon X

Instructions regarding War Diaries and Intelligence Summaries are contained in F. S. Regs., Part II. and the Staff Manual respectively. Title pages will be prepared in manuscript.

WAR DIARY
or
INTELLIGENCE SUMMARY.
(Erase heading not required.)

Army Form C. 2118.

Place	Date	Hour	Summary of Events and Information	Remarks and references to Appendices
In the Field	MAY 1st 1918		In Divnl: Reserve.	
	2nd		Moved from VERQUIGNEUL to support position for left Brigade. Bn HQ in LE PREOL WOOD. A & D Coys in LE PREOL N. defences & B & C Coys in TUNING FORK SWITCH. Relieved the 1/6th KLR.	
	3rd		Quiet Day	
	4		Nos 6 & 7 Platoons re-inforced the 1/5th KORL	
	5		Quiet Day	
	6		Nos 6 & 7 Platoons returned and the Battn relieved the 1/10th KLR in the Left sub-sector with Bn HQ in MARAIS E. B & D Coys in frontline. A & C in support.	
	7		Quiet Day.	
	8		Warned that a big hostile attack was expected on night 9th/10th. Thinned out B & D Coys in front line.	
	9		Further thinned out the Coys in Front Line	
	10		Bn HQrs @ MARAIS E handed over to the 1/10 KLR & removed to TUNING FORK S. ROAD	
	11		Quiet Day	
	12		-do-	
	13		-do-	
	14		Relieved by 1/6th KLR & the Battn took up "BUSTLE" (alarm) position till 7.30 pm after which they moved to billets in VERQUIGNEUL	
	15		Divisional Reserve	
	16		-do-	
	17		-do-	
	18		-do-	
	19		-do-	
			-do-	

A7092. Wt. W128:9/M1293. 750,000. 1/17. D. D & I. Ltd. Forms/C2118/14.

Instructions regarding War Diaries and Intelligence Summaries are contained in F. S. Regs., Part II. and the Staff Manual respectively. Title pages will be prepared in manuscript.

WAR DIARY
or
INTELLIGENCE SUMMARY.
(Erase heading not required.)

Army Form C. 2118.

Place	Date	Hour	Summary of Events and Information	Remarks and references to Appendices
In the Field	May 20th 1918		Moved into support positions of Right Brigade & took over from 1/5 KLR. D Coy had 12 casualties by one shell when leaving VERQUIGNEUL.	
	21st		Quiet day in support.	
	22		— do —	
	23		— do —	
	24		Moved forward & relieved the 1/10 KLR (Scottish) in the left sub-sector. Bn HQrs in SOUTH TUNING FORK ROAD with A & C Coys in Front line D in support & B in reserve.	
	25		Consistently shelled from 10 am to 3 pm around Bn HQrs.	
	26		A & D Coys HdQrs shelled with Heavies.	
	27		Bn HQrs moved to ADDISON RD & MARRIS ST.	
	28		D Coy relieving A Coy & A Coy taking over D Coys position. B Coy relieved C Coy, C Coy taking over B Coys position.	
	29		Quiet day.	
	30		At 2.25 am heavy hostile barrage on CAILLOUX & our artillery replied to SOS. Enemy attempted raid on Battn on our left but got caught by wire leaving 1 prisoner & many dead. Our casualties 1 Died 3 wounded.	
	31		No change. Quiet day.	

[signature] 2/Lt [illegible]
[illegible]

A7092 Wt. W125.9/M1293. 750,000. 1/17. D. D. & L. Ltd. Forms/C2118/14.

O.S. — Suppl. No. 4 5

2929

166 BDE

Raid on Enemy Trenches

North of GIVENCHY on June 10th

1918 at 1.10 am by 1/5th S Lancs R

1918 JUNE

Vol 30

War Diary

Of

1/5 S. Lan. R.

for period

1st to 30th June 1918

Z 37

Instructions regarding War Diaries and Intelligence Summaries are contained in F. S. Regs., Part II. and the Staff Manual respectively. Title pages will be prepared in manuscript.

WAR DIARY
or
~~INTELLIGENCE SUMMARY.~~
(*Erase heading not required.*)

Army Form C. 2118.

5 South Lancs Regt
June 1918

Place	Date	Hour	Summary of Events and Information	Remarks and references to Appendices
[illegible] (Battle Field?)	1918 June 1		Quiet day but several casualties through Gas. Relieved by 1/7 KLR	
	2		The Battalion proceeded to 'BUSTLE' (alarm) position till 5 pm and then to No 2 Camp at VAUDRICOURT. in Divisional Reserve.	
	3		Divisional Reserve	
	4		— do —	
	5		— do —	
	6		— do —	
	7		— do —	
	8		— do — The Battalion left VAUDRICOURT camp & relieved the 1/7th KLR in support LE PLANTIN SUBSECTOR	
	9		Bn Head Quarters Gas shelled in early morning.	
	10		Quiet Day	
	11		— do —	
	12		Relieved the 1/10 KLR in Brigade Subsector. A & C Coys with 2 platoons in front line & 2 in support. B & D in Reserve line. Lt Col C E Thompson DSO MC took over command of Battalion	
	13		Quiet Day.	
	14		— do —	
	15		— do —	
	16		Inter Company Relief. B & C Coys exchanged dispositions. A & D Coys exchanged dispositions	
	17		Quiet Day.	
	18/19		A Battalion raiding party of 2 Officers (Lt [illegible] & 2/Lt [illegible]) + 60 O.Rs carried out a raid on a portion of the enemy front line system at [illegible]. The party was covered by a very heavy artillery & machine Gun barrage & reached its objective. No Germans were found and the party returned to our lines.	

Army Form C. 2118.

Instructions regarding War Diaries and Intelligence Summaries are contained in F. S. Regs., Part II. and the Staff Manual respectively. Title pages will be prepared in manuscript.

WAR DIARY
or
INTELLIGENCE SUMMARY.
(Erase heading not required.)

5 S LANCS REGT

JUNE 1918

Place	Date	Hour	Summary of Events and Information	Remarks and references to Appendices
In the Field	18/19	June (Contd)	A Battalion of the Division on our left carried out a raid at 12-35 am the same night & captured 3 prisoners.	
	19/20		The Battalion on our right (2/5 Lancs Fus – 164 Bde) made a raid on the enemy's line at 11-50 pm under a heavy artillery barrage.	
	20		Relieved by the 5th KLR. The Battalion occupied alarm positions till 5 am & then marched to camp at DROUVIN. 2 platoons of A Coy were left as garrison to VAUXHALL Bridgehead. 2 Platoons of C Coy were left behind as garrison to WESTMINSTER Bridgehead.	
	21		In Divisional Reserve	
	22		— do —	
	23		— do —	
	24		— do —	
	25		— do —	
	26		The Battalion relieved the 1/7th KLR in the left Subsector, B & D Coy in the Front line, A & C in Support. FESTUBERT SUBSECTOR.	
	27		A Quiet Day & No Change.	
	28		— do —	
	29		— do —	
	30		A Coy relieved D Coy in FESTUBERT and C Coy relieved B Coy in CAILLOUX	

C G Thompson
Lt Col Comdg
5 S Lancs Regt

A7092 Wt. W128;9/M1293. 750,000. 1/17. D. D & L. Ltd. Forms/C2118/14.

C O P Y.

****

166th Inf.Bde No G.11/54.

1/5th R.Lanc.R.
10th L'pool R.
1/5th S.Lan.R.
166th T.M.Bty.

---

1. The Major General has directed that the 165th and 166th Infantry Brigades will carry out at least one raid each before coming out of the line: this because identifications are urgently required.

2. The 1/5th South Lancashire Regt is selected to carry out this raid, and the Commanding Officer will reconnoitre the front held by the Brigade and submit proposals and place for the raid, which can either be a silent raid or one with an Artillery programme.

3. The Officers Commanding 1/5th King's Own (R.Lanc.R) and the 10th King's (Liverpool Scottish) will also submit similar proposals with a view to carrying out a raid should that of the 1/5th South Lancashire fail in its object.

4. The B.G.C. impresses on Commanding Officers the necessity of the Coy Officers who are selected to carry out the raid, making a very thorough reconnaissance of the ground over which they are to operate.

5. Commanding Officers when making their reconnaissance of the ground are reminded of the necessity of ensuring that the place of the enemy's line selected is under good observation of the Artillery, before coming to a decision.

(sd) R.J.KENTISH.

BRIGADIER GENERAL
Commanding 166th Infantry Brigade.

9th June 1918.

SECRET

166th Inf.Bde No G.11/54/1

CA 950 pm 17/6/18

55TH DIVISION.

Reference your No G.S.1059 dated 8/6/18.- and this Office G.11/54 of 9/6/18 (copy attached)

The 1/5th South Lancashire's will raid the enemy trenches in the O.B. Line on the night of the 18th/19th inst. The orders for the operation together with full particulars regarding the Artillery, M.G. and T.M. programmes will be forwarded you tonight ~~or early tomorrow~~.

R J Kentish

BRIGADIER GENERAL,
Commanding 166th Infantry Brigade.

16th June 1918.

Headquarters,
166th Infantry Brigade,
17th June 1918.

Dear General,

I am sending you a rough copy of orders which I have not gone through yet. I am sending them to you however as promised tonight. Tomorrow morning we can make any alterations necessary.

Yours v. sincerely
R. J. Kentish

Major General Sir H.S.Jeudwine, K.C.B.
Commanding 55th Division,
B.E.F.

D R A F T.

166TH INFANTRY BRIGADE ORDER NO -

Ref. Map FESTUBERT
Section, 1/10,000.

-th June 1918.

1. At Zero hour night 18th/19th June a Battalion Raiding party of 2 Officers (Lt R.L.LEAKE and 2ndLt H.W.FRIGHT) and 45 O.R. will assault a portion of the O.B. Line after clearing enemy shell hole positions in front of it. The object of the raid is to kill Germans within the area of attack - less about half a dozen required as prisoners for identification purposes.

The Raid will be covered by a strong concentration of Field Artillery.

2. OBJECTIVE.
Enemy shell hole positions and Posts within the area A.2.d.45.43 - A.2.d.15.75, A.2.d.58.78 - A.2.d.60.65, including the portion of the O.B. Line between the two last named points.

3. ASSEMBLY.
The Raiding Party will be assembled by 12.30 p.m. Z night in shell holes and old trenches immediately East of the ditch running S.E. from the bend in LLOYD'S AVENUE at A.2.c.95.32.

4. ARTILLERY PROGRAMME.
The accompanying maps shew
"A" the flank barrages of 18-pdrs maintained throughout the operation;
"B" the movement of the creeping 18-pdr barrage.

The flank barrages open at Zero - also one Battery of 4.5" Hows plus 1 Section firing 106 fuze on to O.B. Line wire from A.2.d.60.65 to A.2.d.58.78. The wire-cutting Hows cease fire at 0 plus 3 and switch or lift to selected targets. Remaining available Hows engage probably enemy M.G. positions from Zero to conclusion of operation.

At 0 plus 3 - 18-pdr creeper on the line A.2.d.45.43 to A.2.d.15.75,
0 plus 6 - lift 100 yards,
0 plus 8 - lift on to O.B. line,
0 plus 10 - lift clear of O.B. line and form protective barrage in rear - less 1 Battery switching to right flank barrage and 1 Battery to left flank barrage.
0 plus 30 - cease fire.

Rate of fire.- Maximum for first 10 minutes, i.e.-
4 rds per gun 18-pdr - 3 rds per How.
0 plus 17 to 0 plus 25 - rate of fire to quicken.

5. PLAN OF ATTACK.

At O plus 3 when creeping barrage begins, the Raiding Party begin to move and close up to it. During the advance the party will keep as close to the barrage as possible, searching all shell holes and old trenches traversed so far as time permits, but taking special care that the barrage is followed as closely as possible.

Formation of party will be in four sections, plus a central section under immediate command of O.C. Raid.

The left section will swing outwards across LLOYD'S AVENUE to deal with isolated shell hole about A.2.d.17.70. After clearing this up it will turn inwards towards the rest of the party which moves South of LLOYD'S AVENUE.

The O.B. Line will be entered between A.2.d.60.65 and A.2.d.58.78. The O.B. Line will be left not later than O plus 17. Lieut LEAKE will arrange whistle signal for withdrawal. He will arrange that this signal will sounded by certain of his subordinate Commanders at any time during the operation after prisoners have been secured.

6. EQUIPMENT.

Steel helmets, box respirators, rifles with bayonets fixed, 9 rounds in magazine one in breach, 20 rounds in the pocket. Selected N.C.Os carry revolvers and two selected men per section carry two bombs each.

7. O.C. "D" Coy will arrange to dispose his Front Line Posts as required by O.C. Raid. O.C."D" Coy will move up one of his Supporting Platoons, or a portion of one if necessary. The Posts of "D" Coy will not be advanced beyond the general line of the Raiding Party's assembly position.

8. From 12 midnight "Z" night until the Raiding Party has returned, a forward Aid Post will be established at double Coy H.Q. F.6. c 75.35. Captain G.L.IRWIN, R.A.M.C, will arrange.

9. Synchronised time will be sent to O.C. Raid at double Coy H.Qrs F.6. c 75.35 at 10.30 p.m. 18th June.

10. Prisoners will be despatched under escort of Raiding Party direct to Battalion H.Qrs.

11. Machine Guns and Stokes Mortars will engage selected targets under orders issued direct to the Officers Commanding concerned.

S E C R E T

Copy No......23

55TH (WEST LANCASHIRE) DIVISION ORDER No. 197.

18th June, 1918.

1. 166th Infantry Brigade will carry out a raid N. of GIVENCHY tomorrow morning, June 19th.

2. ZERO hour will be 1.10 a.m.

3. Objectives - Enemy shell hole positions within the area A.2.d.45.43. - A.2.d.15.75. - A.2.d.58.78. - A.2.d.60.65. including the portion of the O.B.LINE between the two last named points.

4. The raid will be covered by flanking, creeping and protective Field Artillery barrages, as arranged between B.G.C., 166th Infantry Brigade and O.C., Left Group, 55th Divisional Artillery.

5. (a) 1st Divisional Artillery are assisting with a feint barrage from A.16.a.35.72. to A.16.a.73.30.

   (b) 3 6" T.Ms. are to fire on hostile T.Ms. in A.16.a. and c. (N. of CANAL).

6. Watches will be synchronised by an Officer from Divisional Headquarters at 166th Inf.Bde. H.Q., BEUVRY MILL at 7 p.m. and at CANAL HOUSE at 7.30 p.m.
   Liaison Officer Corps H.A. will synchronise time at 55th Div. H.Q., at 6.30 p.m.

7. ACKNOWLEDGE.

T. Rose Price.

Lieut-Colonel,
General Staff, 55th Division.

55th Division H.Q.,
Issued at 3.30 p.m.

Issued to:-

No. 1. Div. Artillery.
2. Div. Engineers.
3. 164th Inf.Bde.
4. 165th Inf.Bde.
5. 166th Inf.Bde.
6. 55th Bn.M.G.C.
7. Div. Signals.
8. A.D.M.S.
9. I Corps.
10. I Corps H.A.
11. C.B.S.O. I Corps.
12. 1st Divn.
13. 46th Division.
14. File.
15. War Diary.
16. War Diary.
17. G.S.
18. G.O.C.
19. 'Q'.

Raid nil that 6th hours would also coop.

SECRET.

Copy No 9

166TH INFANTRY BRIGADE ORDER NO 165.

Ref.Map FESTUBERT Sec.
1/10,000.

18th June 1918.

1. The 1/5th South Lancashire Regt. will carry out a minor operation tomorrow morning against the enemy Front Line between A.2.d.50.78 and A.2.d.80.65. The details of this operation are contained in the attached Battalion Order (vide Appendix I).

2. The 55th Divisional Artillery under orders of the O.C. Left Group will cooperate in accordance with the orders issued by that Officer (vide Appendix II). (sent C.R.A)

3. The 1st Corps Heavy Artillery will cooperate by concentrating certain Batteries on the enemy Front Line immediately E. of FESTUBERT and the 1st Divisional Artillery and the Divisional T.M.Battery by concentrating certain Batteries and T.M's on the enemy front line immediately N. of the LA BASSEE CANAL.

4. The Machine Guns and the 166th Infantry Brigade Light T.M. Battery will cooperate under orders which have been issued verbally.

5. Zero hour will be at 1.10 a.m. and watches will be synchronized as follows.-

(a) At Divisional Headquarters (DROUVIN) at 6.30 pm.
1st Corps Heavy Artillery.
1st Divisional Artillery.
(b) At Left Brigade Headquarters (BEUVRY HILL) at 7 p.m.
166th Infantry Brigade,
Left Group, 55th Divisional Artillery,
Left Group, 55th Bn. M.G.C.
(c) At Right Brigade Headquarters (CANAL HOUSE) at 7.30 pm.
1/5th South Lancashire Regt ,
Right Group, 55th Divisional Artillery,
6" T.M. Battery,
166th T.M.Battery.

6. Acknowledge.

Issued to
Signals 6 p.m.

CAPTAIN,
Brigade Major, 166th Infantry Brigade.

Copy No		No	
1	1/5th S.Lan.R.	11	138th Infantry Brigade
2	1/5th R.Lanc.R.	12	164th ,,
3	10th King's (L.S)	13	1st Corps H.A.
4	166th T.M.Bty	14	1st Div'l Artillery
5	Left Group, 55th D.A.	15	B.G.C. & B.M.
6	Right Group ,,	16	S.C.
7	Left Group, 55th Bn MGC	17	B.T.O.
8	55th Bn M.G.C.	18	B.S.O.
9	55th Division,	19	War Diary,
10	C.R.A., 55th Division	20	File.

SECRET.

Copy No

Ref. Map FESTUBERT SECTION
1/10,000.

5TH S. LANCS. R. ORDER NO. 30.

1. At 1.10 a.m. on night 18/19th June a Battalion raiding party party of 2 Officers (Lt R.L.LEAKE and 2nd Lieut H.W.[illegible]) and [illegible]0 O.R. will assault a portion of the O.B. Line, after clearing enemy shell hole positions in front of it. The object of the raid is to kill Germans - within the area of attack, less about half a dozen required as prisoners for identification purposes. The Raid will be covered by a strong concentration of Artillery.

2. OBJECTIVE. Enemy shell-hole positions and Posts within the area - A.2.d.45.43 - A.2.d.15.75 - A.2.d.58.78 - A.2.d.60.65, including the portion of the O.B. Line between the two last named points.

3. ASSEMBLY. The raiding party will be assembled by 12.45 am 19/6/18 in shell holes and old trenches immediately East of the ditch running S.E. from the bend in LLOYD'S AVENUE at A.2.c.95.32 The raiding party will trickle into position by parties of 5 or 6 in absolute silence.

4. ARTILLERY PROGRAMME.

At Zero until 0 plus 5 - two batteries of 4.5 Hows firing 106 fuze cut wire in front of O.B. line from A.2.d.60.65 to A.2.d.58.78.

At 0 plus 3 - 18-pdr creeping barrage on line A.2.d.45.43 to A.2.d.15.75,
At 0 plus 6 - Lift 100 yards
At 0 plus 8 - Lift on to O.B. Line,
At 0 plus 10 Lift clear of O.B. line and form protective barrage in rear, less one battery switching to right flank barrage and one battery to left flank barrage,
At 0 plus 30 Cease fire.

From Zero to Zero plus 30 flank barrages are maintained. The area between the flank barrages through which the party can advance is shown on attached map (to 166th Infantry Brigade and Lieut R.L.LEAKE only).

Rate of fire:- All 18-pdrs 0 to 0 plus 10, 4 rounds per gun per minute,
0 plus 10 to 0 plus 30, 3 rounds per gun per minute.

5. PLAN OF ATTACK.

Infantry begin to move at 0 plus 3 and close up to creeping barrage. During the advance the party will keep as close to the barrage as possible searching all shell-holes and old trenches traversed. Special parties of 1 N.C.O. and 6 each will be detailed to clear and occupy

(a) isolated shell-hole North of LLOYD'S AVENUE about A.2.d.17.70;
(b) Shell hole group about A.2.d.36.70.

These parties will not withdraw until the main body reaches them on its way back from O.B. line.

Formation of party will be in four sections, plus a central section under the hand of O.C. Raid. Mopping up party for (a) will be attached to left section. Mopping up party for (b) will be attached to left-centre section.
The O.B. Line will be entered between A.2.d.60.65 and A.2.d.58
The O.B. Line will be left not later than 0 plus 17. 70
Lieut R.L.LEAKE will arrange whistle signal for withdrawal.

6. EQUIPMENT. - Steel helmets - box respirators - rifles with bayonets fixed - 9 rounds in magazine, one round in breach - 20 rounds S.A.A. in pocket. Selected N.C.Os carry revolvers - and 2 selected men per section carry 2 bombs each. Wire cutters - not less than 4 pairs per section including 2 large size per section.

7. COVERING ASSEMBLY. As soon after dark as possible, O.C."D" Coy will establish posts on the flanks of the assembly position of raiding party - as verbally arranged. These posts will remain in position until the raiding party has returned. These flank posts must be on the alert for any attempt by the enemy to get round the flank barrages and take the raiders in rear. They must not hesitate to advance and attack any enemy making such an attempt.

8. MEDICAL.
From 12 midnight 18/19th June - forward Aid Post will be established at double Company Headquarters at F.6.c.75.35.

9. PRISONERS - will be sent direct to Battalion H.Q. under escort of raiding party.

10. SYNCHRONISED TIME - will be sent to O.C. Raid at F.6.c.75.35 at 10.30 p.m. 18th June.

11. MACHINE GUNS and STOKES MORTARS are cooperating under orders of 166 Brigade.

12. Acknowledge.

(sd) S.GIBSON,
2nd Lieut and Adjutant,
5th South Lancs. R.

Issued at
2 p.m. 18th June/18.

Copy No 1 166 Infantry Brigade,
2 "A" Coy,
3 "B" "
4 "C" "
5 "D" "
6 Lieut R.L.LEAKE.
7 1/10th K.L.R.
8 2/5th Lan.Fus.
9 M.G.Coy (Left Group)
10 166 T.M.B.
11 File
12 War Diary.

ACCOUNT OF MINOR OPERATION BY 1/5TH S.LAN.R. 19TH JUNE 1918.

At 1.10 a.m. a party of 2 Officers and 60 O.R. under Command of Lieut R.L.LEAKE from the Right Battalion (1/5th S.Lan.R.) raided the O.B.L. between WILLOW ROAD and YELLOW ROAD under cover of an Artillery, T.M. and M.G. barrage.

The party succeeded in entering the O.B.L. but found the trench badly knocked about and no enemy there.

The enemy fired a very large number of lights - white, double green, double red, and double orange - the majority of which were fired from behind the O.B.L. The hostile Artillery reply was slight, being chiefly directed against A.7.b.8.7. and A.8.a.2.8. An enemy M.G. firing from A.2.b.9.8. (approx) was active throughout the operation; fortunately the majority of the bullets were high.

Our casualties were 1 killed, 3 missing and 15 wounded, including 2nd Lieut H.W.FRIGHT, who although hit in the thigh stayed with Lieut LEAKE until the end of the operation.

All was quiet by 1.40 a.m.

Two Germans were seen by left flanking party in a shell-hole Post close to LLOYD'S AVENUE. They threw a bomb wounding 4 of our men and then made off, our men being prevented from following them by a belt of apron wire reinforced by trip wire.

The wire in front of O.B.L. seemed to have been neglected and no signs of recent work were seen in the breastworks.

The support given by the Heavy and Field Artillery was excellent.

R Macdonald
LIEUT.

19th June 1918. Intelligence Officer, 166th Infantry Bde.

for Brigadier General
Commanding

Ent. 11.15pm. 19.6.18.

166th Inf.Bde No G.11/67/3.

55TH DIVISION.

The return showing the casualties received in the Raid this morning has since turned out to be incorrect. The O.C. 1/5th S.Lancs. Regt. reported at 4.30 p.m. that the total number of casualties is 20 and not 12 as previously reported, and that included in the number are 4 missing and not 1 as previously reported. That this number of men should have been missing unbeknown to the Commanding Officer, and to the Officers who took part in the Raid, for the best part of a day is inexplicable.

I have ordered the Officer Commanding the Battalion to make every endeavour to recover the bodies, and so to remove what must, if they are left in NO MAN'S LAND, remain a slur on the good name of his Battalion.

R. J. Kentish

BRIGADIER GENERAL,
Commanding 166th Infantry Brigade.

19th June, 1918.

Cl 750/k 19/6/18

S[illegible]CRET.

B.H. 4/490.

Headquarters,
18th Brigade, R.G.A.(2)
44th Brigade, R.G.A.(4)

Reference Map WILLOW ROAD 1/10,000. 30/5/18.

1. The 166th Infantry Brigade. 55th Division, are carrying out a raid in A.2.d on night 18th/19th June.

2. H.A., I Corps will co-operate as in attached Schedule.

3. ZERO hour will be 1.10.am, 19/6/1918.

4. Brigades concerned to acknowledge.

[signature] Major, R.A.
Brigade Major,
Heavy Artillery, I Corps.

18th June 1918.

Copies to:-
R.A., I Corps.
55th Division.
55th D.A.
S.C., H.A.

C.B.S.O., I Corps.)
7th Brigade, R.G.A.) for
48th Brigade, R.G.A.)information.
22nd Brigade, R.G.A.)

Bde.	No. of 6" hows.	Time.	Task.	Time.	Task.
18th.	4.	ZERO to ZERO plus 5 mins.	Dugouts from S.26.d.48.68 to. S.26.b.57.33.	ZERO plus 5 mins to ZERO plus 20 mins.	Dugouts from S.26.d.48.68 to S.26.b.57.33.
44th.	3.	do.	M.G:A.2.b.98.72.	do.	do.
	3.	do.	M.G:A.3.a.05.82.	do.	do.
	3.	do.	M.G:A.2.b.38.65.	do.	do.
	3.	do.	M.G:A.3.a.40.65.	do.	do.

RATES OF FIRE:-

ZERO to ZERO plus 5 minutes....................RAPID.
ZERO plus 5 minutes to ZERO plus 20 mins.....NORMAL.

AMMUNITION:- H.E. with 106 Fuzes.

SECRET.

I CORPS COUNTER BATTERY ORDER No 85.

1. In support of a Raid to be carried out by the 55th Division in A2 on the night of 18th/19th, Hostile Batteries will be neutralized as under:-

Brigade.	Calibre.	Hostile Batteries.
7th.R.G.A.	1-8" how on each	AX35, AX39.
	1-6" ,, ,, ,,	AX90, AX91.
	2-60 pdrs on each	SD53, SD64, S30b66.05. B7d70.30.
18th.R.G.A.	1-9.2" how on each	SD21, SD23. SB80. AX38.
	2-6" hows on	SD55.
44th.R.G.A.	2-6" hows on	AX57.
46th.R.G.A.	2-60 p'drs on each	SA61, SA62.
	1-60 ,, ,,	SA60.

2. RATES OF FIRE:-

Zero to Zero plus 10 min's = RAPID.

Zero plus 10 min's to Zero plus 20 min's = NORMAL.

,, ,, 20 ,, ,, ,, ,, 25 ,, = SLOW.

3. ZERO HOUR will be 1.10am (One-ten) on the 19th June 1918.

4. PLEASE ACKNOWLEDGE BY WIRE

K. Holmes-Brown.
for. Lt.Col.R.A.,
C. B. S. O. I Corps.

18th June 1918.

Copies to:-

H.Q. R.A. I Corps	(1)	H.Q. 7th.B'de.R.G.A.	(5)
,, H.A. do.	(1)	,, 18th. ,, ,,	(5)
"G" 55th Division.	(1)	,, 44th. ,, ,,	(2)
D.A. ,, ,,	(1)	,, 46th. ,, ,,	(2)
O.C. No 9 Group.F.S.Co	(1)	File.	(2)

Recd. 5.20 pm. 20.6.18.

166th Inf.Bde No G.11/67/4.

Confidential

55TH DIVISION.

I forward herewith for the information of the Major General the statement of the Officer Commanding the 1/5th South Lancashire Regt. regarding the discrepancies in his casualty return submitted after the Raid carried out by his Battalion, and also certain details regarding the missing men.

(a) I am ordering a further inquiry into the reason why, when the Stretcher Bearers were told by the wounded man where one of the other two wounded was lying, they failed to find him and bring him in.

(b) The circumstances surrounding the leaving out of the body of Rifleman JONES though not creditable in the way that no credit can ever be attached to a Unit which leaves its dead or wounded behind in a minor enterprise, are explained and the circumstances being as reported by the O.C. Party, I feel that he was justified in leaving the dead man and bringing in the wounded man, if as he states it was not possible to bring them both in.

(c) I have nothing to state regarding the fourth man who was reported last seen going forward.

The facts as brought out are as a whole, of an unsatisfactory nature, but the most unsatisfactory of all is the failure on the part of the Battalion Commander and of the O.C. Raid to ensure the roll being called on the return of the party and consequently no one knowing until 12 hours afterwards that there were four, and not one man missing. It is not one of the details I went into with the Commanding Officer because that Officer has been planning and carrying out raids for a very long time and ought better than anyone else to have known of the importance of arranging for the calling of the Roll, and that he did not do so is both unthinkable and inexplicable.

I have nothing further to add except to state that I have ordered the Battalion to send out another search party tonight and have made known my dissatisfaction with the facts as disclosed, to the Officer Commanding the Battalion.

A.J. Kelly [signature]

BRIGADIER GENERAL,

20th June, 1918. Commanding 166th Infantry Brigade.

C O P Y.

****

C.O.7. No B/329.

166TH INFANTRY BRIGADE.

Search parties working in NO MAN'S LAND last night found no trace of men missing from Raiding Party. The Search Party contained a Sergeant and 3 Privates from the detachment the men were missing from; they had immediately volunteered for the work.

I have no wish to make excuses for regretable incidents which no one feels more keenly than the Officers and Men of the Raiding Party, but in justice to the latter I would ask permission to draw the attention of the Brigadier General Commanding to the following points.-

i. It is pretty definitely established that the two Men missing from the Left Section did not go forward at all. A shell which landed amongst three of this party wounded one man in the hand; this wounded man saw one of the other two lying in a shellhole saying he was wounded. The wounded man told the Stretcher Bearers where the man was.

ii. The dead man left close to the O.B. Line.- His body was being brought in by a Stretcher Bearer who did exceptionally good work throughout the night. When a man was wounded beside him the man's body was left (after taking his Paybook) and the wounded man was brought in.

iii. The fourth man missing was last seen crossing the wire of the O.B.Line going forward.

The point which I wish to make is that with the exception of the body left close to the O.B.Line all the casualties missing occurred on the way forward, whereas most of the wounded casualties occurred on the way back and they were brought in.

The fact that the area raided comprised about 7,000 sq.yds of ground covered with long grass and several old trenches, plus ditches and shell holes, helps to explain why all the missing were not collected on the return journey.

(sd) C.E.THOMPSON, Lieut-Colonel,
Commanding 5th S. Lan. R.

20/6/1918.

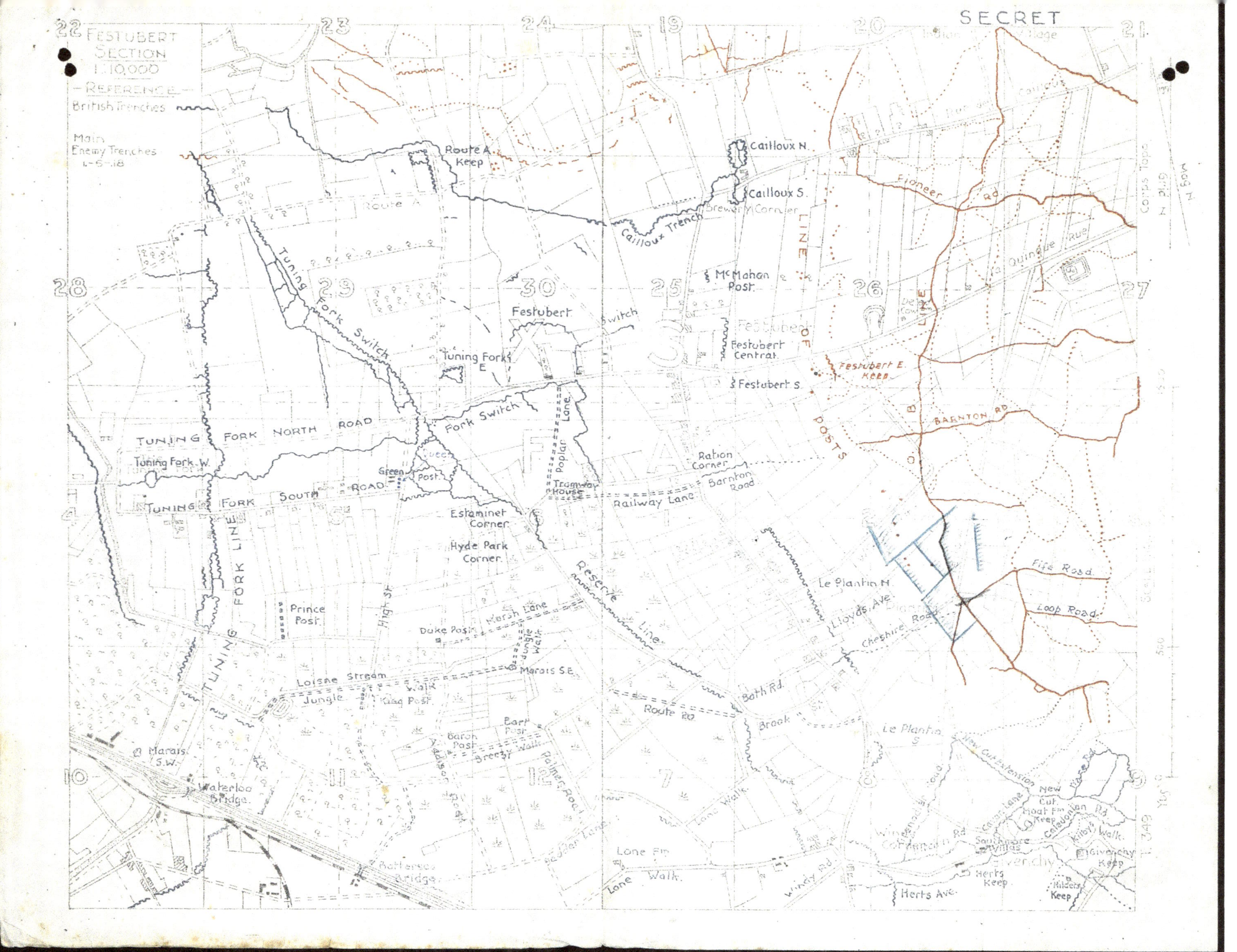

SECRET
FESTUBERT SECTION
1:10,000
REFERENCE
British Trenches
Main Enemy Trenches 1-5-18
Route A Keep
Route A
Cailloux N.
Cailloux S.
Brewery Corner
Cailloux Trench
LINE OF POSTS
McMahon Post
Festubert Central
Festubert S.
Festubert E. Keep
Festubert
Switch
Tuning Fork Switch
Tuning Fork E
Fork Switch
Poplar Lane
Tramway House
Ration Corner
Barnton Road
Railway Lane
BARNTON RD
Pioneer Rd
Quinque Rue
TUNING FORK NORTH ROAD
TUNING FORK SOUTH ROAD
Tuning Fork W.
Queen Post
Green Post
Estaminet Corner
Hyde Park Corner
TUNING FORK LINE
Prince Post
High St
Duke Post
Marsh Lane
Jungle Walk
Marais S.E.
Reserve Line
Le Plantin N.
Lloyds Ave
Cheshire Road
Fife Road
Loop Road
Loisne Stream Walk
Jungle
King Post
Barb Post
Baron Post
Breezy Walk
Addison Road
Palmer Road
Route Rd
Bath Rd
Brook
Le Plantin S
Marais S.W.
Waterloo Bridge
Battersea Bridge
Lone Walk
Lone Fm
Windy Rd
Herts Ave
Herts Keep
New Cut Extension
New Cut
Hoat Fm Keep
Caledonian Rd
Kilby's Walk
Givenchy Keep
Hilders Keep
Givenchy
Corps Topo
Grid N
Mag N

(SPECIAL) 1:10,000 WINGLES.

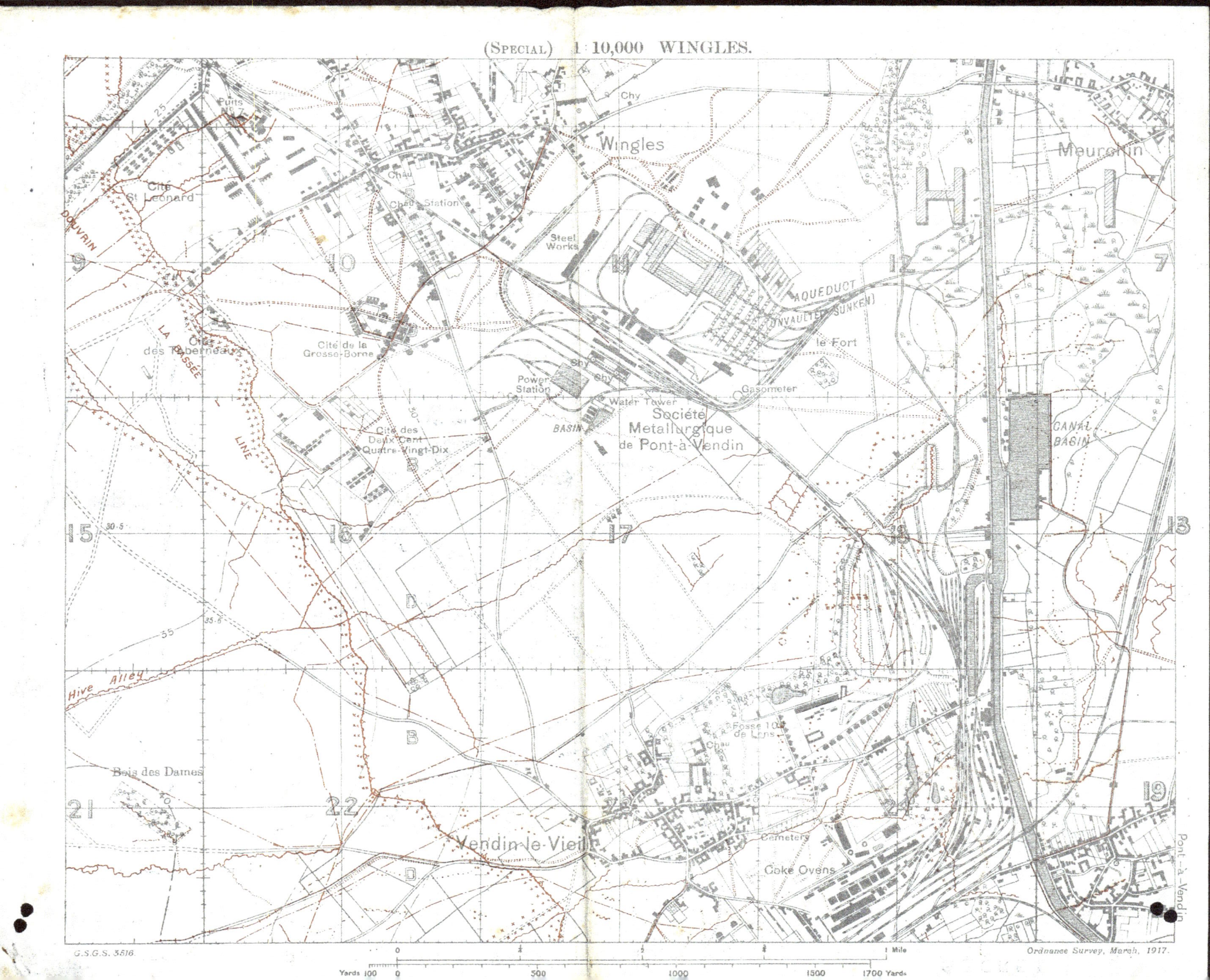

I

List of Honours and Awards gained by

5TH. SOUTH LANCASHIRE REGIMENT

since April 1st. 1918.

Rank.	Name.	Award.	Date of Award.
Major.	W.N. Pilkington, D.S.O. (5th.S.L.R.)	(Bar to (D.S.O.	3.6.18.
Capt.	J.A. Bell, M.C. (R.A.M.C. Attd.)	(Bar to (M.C.	3.6.18.
Lieut.	F.J. Frodsham, (5th.S.L.R.)	M.C.	3.6.18.
Capt.	De La Hay, (C.F., C.E.).	M.C.	3.6.18.

Rank.	Name.	Award.	Date of Award.
Sergt.	Critchley, J.W. (241042).	M.M.	24.5.18.
Sergt.	Carr, J. (240569).	M;M.	-do-
Sergt.	Hughes, J. (240190).	M.M.	-do-
Sergt.	Platt, W.S. (242172).	M.M.	-do-
L/Cpl.	Bishop, F. (50225).	M.M.	-do-
Rfn.	Smith, F. (40529).	M.M.	-do-
Rfn.	Owens, J. (19691).	M.M.	-do-
Rfn.	Hughes, W. (42125).	M.M.	-do-
Rfn.	Cahill, C. (36697).	M.M.	-do-
Cpl.	Holcroft, H. (241694).	D.C.M.	3.6.18.
Sergt.	Jackman, J. (240424).	M.S.M.	24.6.18.

ORIGINAL

5th S-LAN-R. — JULY 1918.

Army Form C. 2118.

WAR DIARY
or
INTELLIGENCE SUMMARY.

(Erase heading not required.)

Instructions regarding War Diaries and Intelligence Summaries are contained in F. S. Regs., Part II. and the Staff Manual respectively. Title pages will be prepared in manuscript.

VR 31

Place	Date	Hour	Summary of Events and Information	Remarks and references to Appendices
In the Field	July 1st	1918	Quiet Day.	
	2		—do—	
	3		—do—	
	4		Relieved by 1/5 KINGS OWN and took over support positions "A" Coy at LONE FARM "B-C+D" Coys in LE PREOL, DEFENCES	
	5th		Quiet Day	
	6		—do—	
	7		—do—	
	8		—do—	
	9th		Relieved by 1/6th KLR and moved to "A" Batt'n "BUSTLE" (alarm) positions until 5 AM 10/7/18 when the Batt'n moved into Camp NO 1 VAUDRICOURT.	
	10th		Day devoted to cleaning of clothes + equipment and re-fitting	
	11		Training	
	12		166 Brigade Horse Show	
	13		VAUDRICOURT shelled by 5.9 HV Guns at about 11 AM - 3 PM - 6 PM and 9 PM 2 O/Rs Killed. Batt'n: spent night in trenches in vicinity of Camp.	
	14		Presentation of medals by GOC 55 Division for awards since April 1st 1918 Honours received by this Battalion (attached).	I Attached list of Awards including those not present at the presentation
	15th		Battalion relieved 1/6th KLR in the left subsector FESTUBERT subsector. Relief complete 3 AM 16th "B+D" Coys in front line. "A+C" in support.	
	16th		Notification received of expected enemy raid on CAILLOUX KEEP. Consequence alteration in dispositions made leaving only 1 NCO + 6 men in KEEP remainder withdrawn to position in rear.	
	16/18th		Normal routine Quiet period.	
	19th		Enemy artillery more active.	

A7092 Wt. W128.9/M1293. 750,000. 1/17. D. D & I. Ltd. Forms/C2118/14.

ORIGINAL

5TH S-LAN-R. WAR DIARY ~~or~~ ~~INTELLIGENCE SUMMARY.~~ — JULY. 1918.

Army Form C. 2118.

Instructions regarding War Diaries and Intelligence Summaries are contained in F. S. Regs., Part II. and the Staff Manual respectively. Title pages will be prepared in manuscript.

(*Erase heading not required.*)

Place	Date	Hour	Summary of Events and Information	Remarks and references to Appendices
In the Field	July	20th	Minor operation carried out by party of D Coy. under 2. Lt DOWNHURST under short artillery Barrage. No enemy were encountered	2 + 3 Orders for operation and report on results
			Battn: relieved by 1/10 K.L.R (SCOTTISH) went into support. Relief completed 1 AM. Support positions all taken over by 3 AM.	
		21/23rd	No special feature. Usual working parties found.	
		24th	Relieved the KOR LAN R in the Right subsector. A + C in front line. B + D in support	
		25	Normal Day	
		26/27	— do —	
		28th	Relieved by 6th K.L.R.s and Battalion moved back to camp. No 2 VAUFRICOURT after taking up 'B' Battn "BUSTLE" (alarm) positions till 5 AM	
		29	Devoted to cleaning up & refitting	
		30	Training	
		31	Training	

[signature] Major Comdg. 5 S Lan R

A7092 Wt. W128 9/M1293 750,000. 1/17. D. D & L. Ltd. Forms/C2118/14.

3

Patrol Operation 2 am
20th July 1918

The patrol (1 officer + 13 OR) assembled, apparently unobserved by the enemy, about 150 yards E N E of the Northern end of CHILLOUX KEEP. The fall of the shells of flank guns of barrage had been carefully observed & the best line of assembly definitely located.

The Artillery barrage came down accurately at 2 am and immediately it lifted the patrol, formed in pairs at intervals of 5 to 10 yards, moved quickly forward and thoroughly searched the ground within the area of the objective. No enemy were found except one or two dead – not recently killed. The patrol did not return until all artillery fire had ceased. The protective barrage had been well defined & was very effective.

Wire was encountered just about the assembly position but it was not a serious obstacle.

It is considered that the enemy

(a) anticipated attack owing to recent artillery fire & had withdrawn forward posts

or

(b) The relative shortness of the dark portion of the night prevented him from putting out the wiring & covering parties located the night before

C E Thompson Lt Col
Commdg 5 S Lan R.

Casualties NIL

A M.G. opened fire from S. of RUE DE CAILLOUX. It was engaged by a Lewis gun in CAILLOUX S. which had been detailed for the purpose. The Lewis gun fired 4 magazines.

FILE

SECRET.

Copy No. 12.

5TH. S. LAN. R. ORDER No. 37.

Ref. Map WILLOW ROAD 1/10.000. 19th. JULY 1918.

1. At ZERO hour on the 20th. JULY a detachment of between 15 and 20 O.R's from "D" Coy., under 2nd.Lt. DEWHURST will attack enemy wiring and covering parties about S.20.c.55.20, with the object of securing a Prisoner.

2. At ZERO the area S.20.c.50.00. - S.20.c.40.10. - S.20.c.50.35. - S.20.c.70.25., will be subjected to a hurricane bombardment from three 18-pounder batteries. At 0 plus 1½ minutes this artillery fire will lift and/or switch clear of the area to enable the patrol of "D" Coy., to rush in and search the ground.
Artillery fire will cease at 0 plus 8 minutes.
Danger spots on front and flanks will be engaged from 0 to 0 plus 8 minutes by supplementary artillery.

3. O.C. "D" Coy., will arrange for 2 Lewis Guns to protect LEFT Flank. Two supplementary 18-pounders will enfilade RUE DE CAILLOUX from 0 to 0 plus 8 minutes.
Position of assembly will be about S.20.c.20.20., but actual position will be decided by O.C. Patrol after observing the practice shoot of the Left Flank Guns of barrage. These left Flank Guns will fire salvos at the following times to-night :-

11-30 p.m. 12 mid-night. 12-30 a.m.

4. Equipment will be as customary for Patrols. Bombs may be carried at the discretion of O.C. "D" Coy.

5. O.C. "D" Coy., will arrange a place of Rendezvous for patrol on its return, where return of each individual will be checked.
O.C. "D" Coy., will ensure each Subordinate Leader knowing thoroughly every soldier under his command.

6. O.C. "D" Coy., will arrange for two men to act as Stretcher Bearers to follow the Patrol, and for a reserve of Stretcher Bearers to be available in CAILLOUX KEEP.

7. ZERO hour 2a.m. 20th. July 1918.

R.H. [signature]
Lieut.,
A/Adjutant, 5th. S. LAN. R.

19.8.17.
Issued at 8 p.m.
Distribution see over.

Copy No. 1.	O.C. "D" Coy.
" " 2.	O.C. "A" "
" " 3.	O.C. "B" "
" " 4.	O.C. "C" "
" " 5.	166th. Infantry Brigade.
" " 6.	Left Group R.A.
" " 7.	1/5th. R. LAN. R.
" " 8.	1/10th. L'pool R.
" " 9.	4th. Leic. R.
" " 10.	166th T.M.B.
" " 11.	Left Group M.G.
" " 12.	File.
" " 13.	War Diary.
" " 14.	Spare.

Vol 32

War Diary

of

1/5 S Lan R.

for period

1st to 31st August

1918.

Z 39

Instructions regarding War Diaries and Intelligence Summaries are contained in F. S. Regs., Part II. and the Staff Manual respectively. Title pages will be prepared in manuscript.

WAR DIARY
or
~~INTELLIGENCE SUMMARY.~~

(*Erase heading not required.*)

AUGUST 1918

Army Form C. 2118.

Place	Date	Hour	Summary of Events and Information	Remarks and references to Appendices
In the Field	AUG 1-2-3 1918		Training in Divisional Reserve.	
	Aug 3rd		Relieved the 6th KLR in Right Subsector (LE PLANTIN)	
	"	4	Normal Day	
		5	—do—	
	"	6	2nd Lt F C WALLINGTON led a successful fighting patrol into O.B.L. He was killed when returning to our lines.	Appendix A.
	"	7	Normal Day	
	"	8	—do—	
	"	9	—do—	
	"	10	—do—	
	"	11	Relieved by 1/10th KLR and Battalion moved back into Support.	
	"	12	Brigade Reserve	
	"	13	—do—	
	"	14	—do—	
	"	15	Relieved by 1/7th KLR and Battalion moved back to DROUVIN CAMP	
	"	16	Training in Divisional Reserve	
	"	17	—do—	
	"	18	—do—	
	"	19	—do—	
	"	20	Relieved the 1/7th KLR in Left Subsector (FESTUBERT)	
	"	21	Normal Day	
	"	22	—do—	
	"	23	—do—	
	"	24	164 Brigade on the RIGHT took the [illegible] and 1/5 KORL on Battn RIGHT [illegible]	
	"	25	Normal Day	
	"	26	—do—	
	"	27	—do—	
	"	28	FESTUBERT EAST KEEP occupied by 'A' Coy and posts advanced to conform with the straightening of the line from CAILLOUX to O.B.L. where the RIGHT Brigade are established	

A7092 Wt. W128 9/M1293. 750,000. 1/17. D. D & L. Ltd. Forms/C2118/14.

Instructions regarding War Diaries and Intelligence Summaries are contained in F. S. Regs., Part II. and the Staff Manual respectively. Title pages will be prepared in manuscript.

WAR DIARY
or
INTELLIGENCE SUMMARY.
(Erase heading not required.)

AUGUST 1918

Army Form C. 2118.

Place	Date	Hour	Summary of Events and Information	Remarks and references to Appendices
	AUG 29 1918		Took over BARNTON Rd from the Battalion on the RIGHT	
	30 "		Two large fighting patrols from B & D Coys went out at 3 am and were engaged by ~~[illegible]~~ snipers and machine gun fire [illegible] enemy as still holding advanced line of posts	
			Relieved by 1/5th KORL and Battalion moved back into Brigade support	
	31 "		Normal Day in support.	

C. E. Thompson
Lt Col Commdg.
5 S. LAN. Regt.

A7092 Wt. W128_9/M1293 750,000. 1/17. D. D & L. Ltd. Forms/C2118/14.

A

2nd. Lieut. DODDS reports :-

At 4a.m. I took up my position. I had with me Sergt. BAKER and six other ranks with a Lewis Gun. There was no sign or sound in the O.B.L.

2nd.Lieut WALLINGTON and party moved forward at 8a.m. I saw them enter the O.B.L. at its junction with LLOYD'S AVENUE and saw them work Northwards about 120 yards.

At 8.40a.m. I saw a good number of Stick Bombs come over where 2nd.Lieut.WALLINGTON'S party had reached. I then saw the party work its way back and out of the O.B.L. to a shell-hole.

As they came out I saw two parties of Bosche, about 10 or 12 each, come over the top - one party from WILLOW ROAD and the other from midway between WILLOW ROAD and LLOYD'S AVENUE.

We opened fire with Lewis Gun and Rifles on the left party and then when 2nd.Lt.WALLINGTON's party had cleared we fired at both parties alternatively. The left party was completely dispersed, and as we concentrated on the 2nd. party, which was chasing WALLINGTON, a third party of Bosche then came over the O.B.L. South of LLOYD'S AVENUE and took up a position about 150 yards from O.B.L. and fired on us.

When I saw that 2nd. Lieut. WALLINGTON and party had got well behind us I withdrew my party. I found Sgt. CARR and all the party, except 2nd. Lieut. WALLINGTON, in the breastworks and heard that 2nd.Lt. WALLINGTON had been killed about 100 yards from our lines.

I sent out two stretchers, one for 2nd.Lt. WALLINGTON and one for Rifleman ANDERSON of my party who had been wounded. 2nd.Lt. WALLINGTON must have been killed by Machine Gun Fire.

The Lewis Gun did great execution, especially amongst the first party of enemy fired on.

From the time of going out until 8.40a.m. we received messages from O.P. that no movement was observed in or behind the O.B.L.

S E C R E T.   P A T R O L   O R D E R.   Copy No.....

Ref: Intelligence Map No.4. WILLOW ROAD.

1. On August 6th. as soon after 8a.m. as possible a Fighting Patrol consisting of 2nd. Lieut. WALLINGTON and four Other Ranks will enter the O.B.L. about its junction with LLOYD'S AVENUE, and search Northwards for any enemy post. Any enemy encountered will be killed or captured and every effort made to secure an identification. Patrol will not search further Northward than A.2.b.32.40.

2. Patrol will have an immediate Supporting Party consisting of One Officer and eight Other Ranks (with a Lewis Gun). This party will take up a position about A.2.d.10.90., and will be prepared either to move to the assistance of the Patrol or to cover its withdrawal. Great care must be taken to keep this party screened from the enemy's view, but the Officer mast take up a position so that he can follow the movements of the Patrol.

In addition two parties will take up positions, one about A.2.d.10.35. and the other about A.2.a.50.55. The function of these parties will be to cover the flanks of the Patrol. They will each consist of one N.C.O. and four Men with a Lewis Gun. If necessary they will open flanking fire to cover the withdrawal of the Patrol. The exact limits of their fire will be pointed out to them on the ground.

The two flanking parties will not withdraw until the Patrol with its immediate support has returned to our lines.

3. The Supporting Party and Flanking Parties will take up their positions just before dawn breaks. The patrol will move out with the supporting party and remain with it about A.2.d.10.90. As soon after 8a.m. as the Patrol Commander decides, the patrol will crawl forward and enter the O.B.L.

4. If the O.B.L. is found to be unoccupied patrol, plus the immediate supporting party, will occupy O.B.L. about A.2.b.43.15., and will lie in wait for enemy moving forward at dusk to occupy his forward posts.

In this event the Lewis Gun at ~~XXXXXXXXXXX~~. A.2.a.50.55. will move across to A.2.d.10.90. and replace the immediate supporting party which is to move forward.

5. "Z" HOUSE O.P. will be in direct communication by wire to the immediate supporting party at A.2.d.10.90.

6. In the event of the fighting patrol being heavilly attacked the artillery will barrage according to the barrage lines marked on attached map. The signal for the barrage will be ONE WHITE VERY LIGHT fired from the O.B.L. due East over enemy lines. On this signal the Signaller with the immediate supporting party will send "COD" to "Z" HOUSE O.P. and gunner will transmit to the batteries.

7. If enemy do not come forward after dusk, the patrol will return to our lines at 11p.m.

8. Any prisoners secured will be sent down at once under escort to Battalion Headquarters.

9. DRESS FOR PATROL. Rifle with bayonet fixed and dimmed with mud, 50 rounds of ammunition in pocket and soft cap worn. The Officers and two Sergeants will carry two bombs each.

10. Password for patrol - "LUCK".

[illegible]JOR,
Comdg: 5th. [illegible]

Headquarters,
1[illegible]th. Infantry Brigade.

[illegible]

Attached are narratives from Sergeant CARR, with 2nd. Lt. [illegible]'s patrol, and the officer in command of the immediate support.

Our casualties were 2nd. Lieut. [illegible] killed and two other ranks wounded, all of whom have been brought into our lines.

From speaking personally to both the Patrol and Supporting Party it is evident that considerable damage was done to the enemy, as he deliberately came over the top bunched, and had no idea that supporting party with a Lewis Gun was in the vicinity.

The patrol and supporting party are being sent down to the Divisional Reception Camp to-night for a rest.

B.E.F.

Major,
Comdg: 5th. S. Lan. R.

A

REPORT BY SERGEANT CARR.

The party consisted of 2nd. Lieut. WALLINGTON, myself and three men.

We left the supporting party at 8a.m. and entered the O.B.L. at its junction with LLOYD'S AVENUE at 8.15a.m., and moved Northwards 150 yards examining shelters. The shelters had the remains of British kit in them, but there were no signs of any German kit.

At about 8.40a.m. a German bomb dropped six yards ahead of me. I was at the head of the party and 2nd.Lt. WALLINGTON was behind me looking towards Boscheland. More bombs fell and 2nd.Lt. WALLINGTON gave the order to go back.

We went back along the O.B.L. and got out where the wire was poor to a shell-hole at about A.2.b.46.00. Here we stayed five minutes and saw two parties of Bosche, 10 or 12 strong each, come over the O.B.L. While here 2nd.Lieut.DODDS' party on our left opened out with Lewis Gun and Rifle fire. The fire must have had good affect as the Bosche were coming over the top and presented a good target.

We retired again to the end of hedge on LLOYD'S AVENUE. As we retired another party appeared from South of LLOYD'S AVENUE and O.B.L. We opened fire from here also and after 10 minutes moved back to the post in LLOYD'S AVENUE. 2nd.Lieut. WALLINGTON was leading and was hit when near the right covering post about 120 yards from LE PLANTIN Breastworks. A sniper was also slightly wounded. 2nd. Lieut. WALLINGTON was brought in to the Bombing Post.

The following congratulatory telegrams have been received by the Battalion :-

From MAJOR GENERAL SIR H. S. JEUDWINE, K.C.B. 20.9.18.

"Well done 5TH. SOUTH LANCASHIRES".

From 5TH. S.LAN.R. to 166th. Infantry Brigade. 20.9.18.

"Many thanks for the General's message.
Please thank the Major General for his kind message".

From 1/10th. LIVERPOOL SCOTTISH. 20.9.18.

"Hearty congratulations on your splendid success. Good old 5TH".

From 5TH.S.LAN.R. to 1/10TH. LIVERPOOL SCOTTISH. 20.9.18.

"Many thanks for your message".

From 1/5th. K.O.R.L.Regt. 20.9.18.

"Hearty congratulations".

From 1/5TH.S.LAN.R. to 1/5TH. K.O.R.L.Regt. 20.9.18.

"Many thanks for your message".

To NAJO (275 Bde. R.F.A) and 166th. Infantry Brigade from 5TH. S.LAN.R. 20.9.18.

"Everyone engaged to-day is very appreciative of fine artillery support aaa Assaulting Companies say it was wonderful".

From NAJO to 5TH. S.LAN.R. 20.9.18.

"Gunners very much bucked by your appreciative message aaa Congratulations on obtaining all objects and holding them".

-----oOo-----

ORIGINAL

5 SLAN R

SEPT 1918

5 S Lan Rgt

Army Form C. 2118.

WAR DIARY
or
~~INTELLIGENCE~~ SUMMARY.

(Erase heading not required.)

Instructions regarding War Diaries and Intelligence Summaries are contained in F. S. Regs., Part II. and the Staff Manual respectively. Title pages will be prepared in manuscript.

Place	Date	Hour	Summary of Events and Information	Remarks and references to Appendices
In the Field	1/9/18		Normal day in Support.	
	2/9/18		Relieved by 5th H.L.R. and Battn. moved back to VAUDRICOURT No. 1 CAMP	
	3/9/18		In Corps Reserve. Normal.	
	4/9/18 to 8/9/18		do.	
	8/9/18		Relieved the 5th H.L.R. in the left subsection – "B" & "D" Coys in the front line, "C" Coy in Support & "A" Coy in Reserve	
	9/9/18		Re-disposing the two forward companies.	
	10/9/18		Normal day.	
	11/9/18		do.	
	12/9/18		Relieved by the 1/5th K.O. (R. Lanc. R.) and Battn. moved into support i.e. VILLAGE LINE.	
	13/9/18		Normal Day.	
	14/9/18		do	
	15/9/18		do	
	16/9/18		Relieved 1/5 K.O. (R. Lanc. R.) in Outpost Line.	
	17/9/18		Quiet day	
	18/9/18		do	
	19/9/18		do Preparing for attack.	
	20/9/18		"B" & "D" Coys attacked (Narrative attached). Relieved by 1/10th H.L.R. and moved back into Brigade Reserve	* I
	21/9/18		Normal day in Reserve.	
	22/9/18		do	
	23/9/18		Relieved by 7th H.L.R. and Brigade moved back to BETHUNE (RUE DE LILLE AREA)	
	24/9/18		Refitting.	

A7092 Wt. W128/9/M1293 750,000. 1/17. D. D & L. Ltd. Forms/C2118/14.

ORIGINAL

5th S. LAN. R
SEPT 1918.

Army Form C. 2118.

WAR DIARY
or
~~INTELLIGENCE SUMMARY.~~

(Erase heading not required.)

Instructions regarding War Diaries and Intelligence Summaries are contained in F. S. Regs., Part II. and the Staff Manual respectively. Title pages will be prepared in manuscript.

Place	Date	Hour	Summary of Events and Information	Remarks and references to Appendices
In the Field	25/9/18		Training	
	26/9/18		do	
	27/9/18		do "A" & "B" Coys. attended Tank Demonstration @ AIX NOULETTE.	
	28/9/18		Training.	
	29/9/18		Relieved 6th K.L.R. ("C" Battn.) in Brigade Reserve.	
	30/9/18		Normal day in Reserve.	

C. E. Thompson
LIEUT. COL.
COMMANDING 5TH BN. S. LAN. R.

A7092 Wt. W128 9/M1293 750,000. 1/17. D. D & L. Ltd. Forms/C2118/14.

8th.SOUTH LANCASHIRE REGIMENT.

OPERATION OF 20th.SEPTEMBER 1918.

Ref: RICHEBOURG
1/10,000.

On the night of 16th/17th.September 1918 the Battalion took over the outpost line of the Brigade on a frontage of 1 mile. At 5-30 a.m. on the 20th.September the Battalion attacked the enemy's outpost system on a frontage of 1,250 yards, advanced to an average depth of 400 yards, captured 39 unwounded and 4 wounded prisoners. A fair number of enemy were killed in the assault (20 is a conservative estimate) and many more casualties were caused him by active sniping and Lewis gun fire after the objectives were gained.

The attack was made with the object of covering the right flank of the 10th.Royal Warwicks (19th.Div.) who were simultaneously attacking THE DISTILLERY (S.17.central) and SHEPHERDS REDOUBT. The Battalion was informed early on the morning of the 18th.September that the attack was to be made and objectives were indicated.

The assault was carried out by 2 Companies plus 1 Section ("B" Company on right, "D" Company plus 1 Section of "C" Company, on left) directly supported by 275 Bde.R.F.A. and 6 guns of 166 L.T.M.B. 276 Bde.R.F.A. and Heavy artillery co-operated in protection of right flank of the attack. The position of assaulting troops at ZERO, the objectives of platoons and the line gained are shewn on the accompanying map. Machine guns of 55th.M.G.Battn. co-operated by putting down a protective barrage and maintaining harassing overhead fire on enemy's lines for several hours during the day. "A" Company (with one sub-section of M.Gs. attached) were given the task of protecting the right flank of the attack. This Company had its attached M.Gs.,and six Lewis guns, disposed on the line S.28.d.9.1. to Cemetery in S.29.a.

The action resolved itself into six separate platoon attacks, each assaulting Company having 1 platoon in hand. The artillery and Stokes mortarsopened at ZERO and lifted from the different objectivesat times varying from Z plus 3′ to Z plus 7′, thereafter creeping forward at the rate of 100 yards in 3 minutes. The infantry advanced at ZERO and closed up to the barrage. The Right Company (B) secured its objectives with little difficulty. The plan of taking the pumping stations from the South worked successfully. Very thorough reconnaissances had been made in the short time available and the assault was carried out with coolness and precision under personal observation of the O.C. Company. 15 prisoners were taken by this Company and at least two enemy were killed. 1 Light M.G. was captured, used against the enemy (3 belts were fired) and brought out of action. The right Company's casualties were 1 officer and 9 O.R. wounded and 1 man (stretcher bearer) missing. The latter had gone over to help right platoon of "D" Company and either got lost and captured, or was killed by hostile M.G./ which was considerable. /fire

The left Company (with the exception of its right platoon) had considerable fighting. The right platoon crossed SPOOK TRENCH and SPOOK DRAIN (120 yards E.of the trench) without opposition, found its PILLBOX objective did not exist, the construction of the PILLBOX having only been begun. They then occupied the line of old emplacements along ditch S. of 23 central. They previously lostdirection through not recognising objective, moved to the right on PILLBOX S.23.d.1.4. which was the left objective of the right Company. They shot down 2 Germans who were observing from the top of this pillbox. They suffered severe casualties from hostile M.G. fire.

The centre platoon, followed by O.C. Company with his reserve platoon reached SPOOK DRAIN about PILLBOX S.23.a.5.0. Considerable fighting took place here, about 7 or 8 Germans being killed and about a dozen prisoners taken. O.C.Company was severely wounded immediately afterwards, but not before he had personally accounted for more than one German. The centre platoon had pushed on quickly, seized the old shelters N.of S.23.central and crossed the track S.W. of PIONEER DUMP. They captured the first pillbox in PIONEER DUMP with 14 prisoners. This platoon was now reduced to 11, two of whom were wounded but carrying on. A Lewis gun was posted on the side of the moat, but the No.1 was shot dead and the platoon came under heavy M.G. fire at close range from another pillbox a short distance in front. Having seen the platoon on his right being rather held up, the O.C. platoon withdrew his men on to the old gun positions North of S.23.Central. He crawled back to the pillbox with 3 men to look for a German machine gun, which he thought he would find useful. They could not find a machine gun but found two Trench mortars on mountings: they destroyed these with Mills bombs.

The left platoon of "D" Company (with 1 Section of "C" Company attached) moved quickly up SERPENT TRENCH close behind our barrage which, excellent throughout, was particularly effective on this flank. The enemy resisted stoutly and bombed vigorously but the assault was made with a dash and determination which carried it well beyond the junction of SERPENT and NORA TRENCHES. Touch was gained with the platoon on the right and with the 10th.Royal Warwicks on the left. The O.C.Platoon was wounded shortly after reaching his objective. Machine gun fire along SERPENT TRENCH was heavy. O.C."C" Company, who had supported the advance of this platoon with Lewis gun fire from the top of dugouts at junction of SERPENT and SOLACE TRENCHES as long as it was possible, took over command of "D" Company when O.C. that Company was wounded. Owing to officer casualties definite information from "D" Company's left platoon had been lacking. Reconnaissance shewed that the position at junction of SERPENT and NORA TRENCHES was fairly secure although touch had temporarily been lost with the platoon on the right. Seven men from this platoon are missing. They were last seen in shell-holes East of NORA TRENCH. Considerable enemy movement was seen in front and was heavily fired on by our men. Shortly before 10 a.m. the enemy heavily shelled SERPENT TRENCH and the Battalion on the left. Our artillery were asked to shell PIONEER DUMP. No attack developed against the Battalion's front but it is not unlikely that one was prevented from developing by the artillery, rifle fire and heavy indirect M.G. fire on to the area N.E. of PIONEER DUMP.

At dusk connection was gained between the two left platoons of "D" Company and an intermediate post established about S.23.b.10.50.

The enemy's artillery retaliation was only moderately heavy. His first S.O.S. signal was seen at ZERO plus 3′, and generally along the line at ZERO plus 5′. His artillery responded quickly and his barrage was down by ZERO+6′ to 7′. The Division on the left put a smoke screen on the left of their objective at ZERO minus 3′. Machine guns of 19th.Division opened fire at this time - our machine guns opened at ZERO minus 1½′, but this did not appear to matter. The enemy barrage was heaviest on the right and left of our line and along the RUE DU MARAIS, which he enfiladed. The Right Company's Headquarters 100 yards E. of the junction of the EITEL ALLEYS was subjected to rather heavy harassing fire at intervals throughout the day, as was also the area about junction of SPOOK DRAIN and SERPENT TRENCH.

ADDENDUM TO NARRATIVE OF OPERATIONS 20th.SEPTEMBER 1918.

In addition to furnishing 1 Section (attached to "D"Company) to garrison the junction of SPOOK DRAIN and SERPENT TRENCH, "C" Company had the remainder of this platoon at the disposal of "D" Company for carrying ammunition etc. up SERPENT TRENCH. They made three journeys under considerable machine gun fire and formed a dump at the junction of SERPENT TRENCH and SPOOK DRAIN.

Another platoon of "C" Company was employed in reinforcing the two left platoons of "D" Company and giving covering L.G. fire from the top of PILLBOXES in SERPENT TRENCH.

A third platoon of "C" Company was employed - 2 Sections joining with remainder of "D" Company's reserve platoon to form a close support in SPOOK DRAIN - 2 Sections in escorting prisoners to Bde.H.Qrs. The latter two sections were subsequently used to link up between the two left platoons of "D" Company.

Consequently there was only one platoon of "C" Company (disposed in ADALBERT ALLEY) which did not become involved in the operation.

23.9.18.

Lieut.Col.
Commanding 5th.[illegible]

As soon as SERPENT TRENCH was gained 166 T.M.Battery rushed up two Stokes mortars to SPOOK DRAIN, the teams carrying forward their ammunition. This was done under considerable machine gun fire.

The Battalion was relieved by 1/10th.LIVERPOOL SCOTTISH on the night 20th/21st.September - completed at 12-20 a.m. 21st.September.

SUMMARY OF CAPTURES.

PRISONERS.	MACHINE GUNS.	TRENCH MORTARS.
43.	2 Light. (brought out of action)	2. (destroyed)

The Battalion's casualties in the operation were:-

	KILLED.	WOUNDED.	MISSING.
OFFS.	-	3.	-
O.R.	6.	37.	2.

22.9.18.

LIEUT.COL.
COMMANDING 5th.Bn.S.LAN.R.

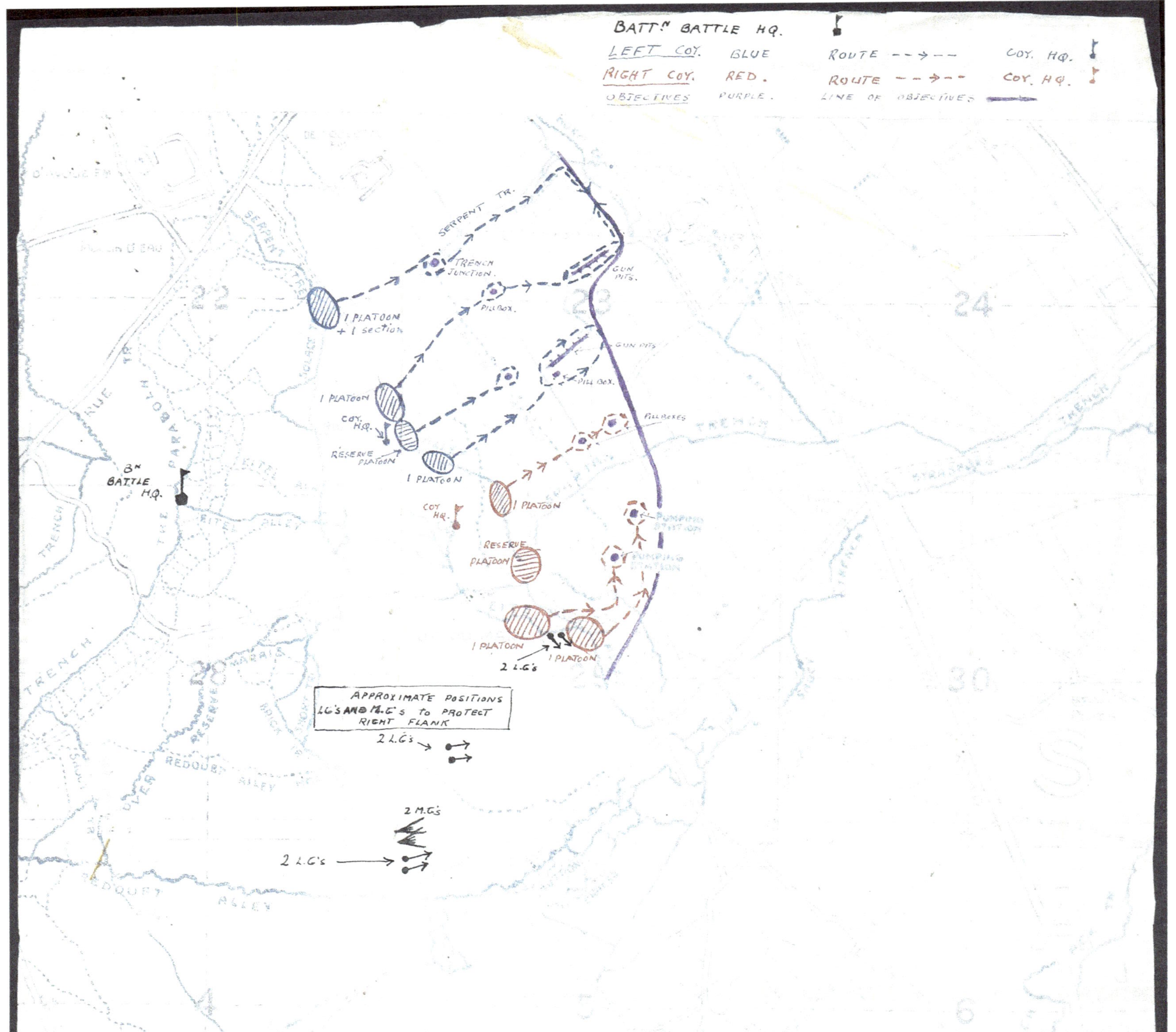

BATTN BATTLE HQ.
LEFT COY. BLUE ROUTE COY. HQ.
RIGHT COY. RED. ROUTE COY. HQ.
OBJECTIVES PURPLE. LINE OF OBJECTIVES
SERPENT TR.
TRENCH JUNCTION.
GUN PITS.
PILLBOX.
GUN PITS
PILL BOX.
PILLBOXES
1 PLATOON + 1 section
1 PLATOON
COY. HQ.
RESERVE PLATOON
1 PLATOON
BN BATTLE HQ.
COY HQ.
1 PLATOON
RESERVE PLATOON
1 PLATOON
1 PLATOON
2 L.G's
APPROXIMATE POSITIONS L.G's AND M.G's to PROTECT RIGHT FLANK
2 L.G's
2 M.G's
2 L.G's
22
23
24
30
TRENCH
PARABOLA TR.
RUE
REDOUBT ALLEY

Vol 34

War Diary

of

1/5 S Lan R

for period

1st to 31st October

1918

2 41

ORIGINAL

Instructions regarding War Diaries and Intelligence Summaries are contained in F. S. Regs., Part II. and the Staff Manual respectively. Title pages will be prepared in manuscript.

WAR DIARY

~~or~~ 5th SOUTH LANCS. REGT.

~~INTELLIGENCE SUMMARY.~~

(Erase heading not required.)

Army Form C. 2118.

Place	Date	Hour	Summary of Events and Information	Remarks and references to Appendices
	1.10.18		Normal day in Reserve.	
	2 " "		Enemy reported withdrawing. Batt moved forward at 18.00 and occupied O.B.L. from INDIAN VILLAGE to YELLOW ROAD.	
	3 " "		At 06.30 Batt. advanced and occupied old German line from BRICKFIELDS to DE TOULOT FARM with B.H.Q. at PARABOLA TRENCH. At 13.00 again moved forward to LA BASSEE – FROMELLES line from LA BOUCHAIRE to DISTILLERY A 6 4 (the main line of resistance) B.H.Q. at LE TILGUT REDOUBT	
	4 " "		Occupied the line SALOME GRAVELIN BHQ at MORQUETTE FARM	
	5 " "		Relieved "A" Batt (1/10th K.L.R.) in support line LABOURSE – FONTAINE and proceeded to consolidate position	
	6 " " 7 " "		General consolidation.	
	8 " "		[illegible] raid by 3 sections of A. Coy unsuccessful owing to newly erected enemy wire	
	9 " "		No change	
	10 " "		Heavy shelling during night and day. Brigade [illegible] our line taken over by 7th K.L.R. (165 Bde) Batt took up position from Road Junction GRANDE RUE to Point about U 9 a 6 4 the right sector of Brigade's new line of resistance.	
	11 " "		Improving positions. Heavy bursts of enemy shelling during day on Batt area.	

A7092 Wt. W128.9/M1293 750,000. 1/17. D. D & L. Ltd. Forms/C2118/14.

Instructions regarding War Diaries and Intelligence Summaries are contained in F. S. Regs., Part II. and the Staff Manual respectively. Title pages will be prepared in manuscript.

WAR DIARY
or
~~INTELLIGENCE SUMMARY.~~

(*Erase heading not required.*)

Army Form C. 2118.

Place	Date	Hour	Summary of Events and Information	Remarks and references to Appendices
	12.10.18		Relieved by 2/5th LANCS FUS and go into Div. Reserve billets at BEUVRY	
	13 " "		Reorganising, Baths etc	
	14 " "		Route march	
	15 " "		Firing on Range (400x) Orders received to be in readiness to move at one hours notice	
	16 " "		00.15 hours received orders to "BUSTLE" and moved forward to FREMAUX FARM at 11.00 hours and at 15 hours again moved to LA PLACE - HOCRON - BASSE RUE with B.H.Q at HOCRON	
	17 " "		Batt crossed CANAL at DON leaving HOCRON at 16.30 hours and arriving at HERRIN at 18.30 hours. B.H.Q. in CURE'S HOUSE	
	18 " "		Again moved forward at 08.45 hours to SECLIN containing about 1000 civilians B.H.Q in RUE LILLE	
	19 " "		Moved to FRETIN @ 18.00 hours B.H.Q in Square.	
	20 " "		Again advanced to CYSOING at 08.30 where Batt awaited orders till 14.00 hours then proceeded to WANNEHEIN. B.H.Q at T23 b 17.25	
	21 " "		At 11.00 hours moved to ESPLECHIN and at 17.30 hours again moved forward and relieved 8th K.L.R in OUTPOST LINE (St MAUR - V10 CENTRAL - V.4 CENTRAL - O33 d and a X ROADS O27 c) 'A' Coy right front 'B' right support 'C' left front 'D' left support B.H.Q at WILLEMEAUX in BREWERY Enemy snipers and shelling briskly	
	22 " "		At 04.30 hours A Coy attacked BARGES CHATEAU O.11 c. 70.90 'C' Coy co-operating. Attack unsuccessful	
	23 " "		Less enemy shelling during day except on St MAUR which at [illegible]	
	24 " "		B.H.Q moved from WILLEMEAUX to MONASTRY at ERE	

A7092 Wt. W128 9/M1293 750,000. 1/17. D. D & L. Ltd. Forms/C2118/14.

ORIGINAL

Instructions regarding War Diaries and Intelligence Summaries are contained in F. S. Regs., Part II. and the Staff Manual respectively. Title pages will be prepared in manuscript.

WAR DIARY
~~or~~
~~INTELLIGENCE SUMMARY.~~
(Erase heading not required.)

Army Form C. 2118.

Place	Date	Hour	Summary of Events and Information	Remarks and references to Appendices
	25.10.18		A good deal of enemy shelling during day. Barrage put down on outpost line at 16.15 hours no enemy attack. B.H.Q. shelled heavily between 16-15 and 17 15 hours	
	26.–.–		Batt relieved in the outpost line by the 1/10th L'pool Scottish Regt Batt moved down to ESPLECHIN in Billets and became C. Batt	
	27.–.–		Normal day in Reserve	
	28.–.–		Normal day in Reserve. Reorganisation of Coys	
	29.–.–		Normal day in Reserve. Training under Coy arrangements	
	30.–.–		Normal day in Reserve. Batt played Brigade HQ at football Result 2-2. Range completed at X Roads near CUSTOM HOUSE	
	31.–.–		Normal day in Reserve. Batt moved into Support at FROIDMONT relieving 1/5th K.O.R.L. Very slight shelling of new B.H.Q.	

C. E. Thompson Lt. Col.
Commanding
5th Bn. [illegible] Lancashire Regt.

A7092 Wt. W128 9/M1293 750,000. 1/17. D. D & L. Ltd. Forms/C2118/14.

CONFIDENTIAL

WAR DIARY

OF

1/5th S LAN R

FOR THE PERIOD

1st - 30th NOVEMBER 1918

Army Form C. 2118.

WAR DIARY
or
~~INTELLIGENCE SUMMARY.~~
(Erase heading not required.)

Instructions regarding War Diaries and Intelligence Summaries are contained in F. S. Regs., Part II. and the Staff Manual respectively. Title pages will be prepared in manuscript.

Place	Date	Hour	Summary of Events and Information	Remarks and references to Appendices
[illegible]	1/11/18		Battn paraded under the [illegible] on field in Western outskirts of ESPLECHIN	
	2/11/18		Normal day in Support. Training under Company arrangements	
	3/11/18		"	
	4/11/18		Slight shelling of guns in rear of "CHATEAU WOOD" during the morning. Training under Coy arrangements. Normal day in Reserve	
	5/11/18		Relieved 1/5 K.O.R.L.R in the outpost line	
	6/11/18		Heavy enemy gas shelling of St MAUR during afternoon. 2 [illegible] fired on Battn HQ & vicinity about 23 30 hours	
	7/11/18		One platoon of B Coy attacked MYSTERY HOUSE at 0840 hours in accordance with attached A/476 and A/480. [illegible] captured	
	8/11/18		Enemy withdrawal commences. Battn moves forward. Bn HQ move to BEAUREGARD FARM – thence to St MAUR thence to CHERCQ. Coys take up positions on West side of River ESCAUT. Heavy enemy MG fire met with at this point. During night rafts and [illegible] bridges thrown across river	
	9/11/18		Battn crosses ESCAUT and pushes on to first objective. Battn continues the advance & pushes on to second objective. Both objectives gained	
	10/11/18		Battn again marches forward on TOURNAI–LEUZE Road [illegible] LEUZE & pushes forward to EASTERN OUTSKIRTS. Relieved by [illegible]. Battn marches back to LEUZE & spends night in billets [illegible] C [illegible]	
	11/11/18		Marches forward to MAULBAIX – Received [illegible] that armistice takes effect from 11 AM. Battn continues to march to LORETTE [illegible] and C & D Coys billet the night at this place A & B Coys on Eastern outskirts	

A7092 Wt. W128 9/M1293 750,000. 1/17. D. D & L. Ltd. Forms/C2118/14.

Instructions regarding War Diaries and Intelligence Summaries are contained in F. S. Regs., Part II. and the Staff Manual respectively. Title pages will be prepared in manuscript.

WAR DIARY
or
~~INTELLIGENCE~~ SUMMARY.
(*Erase heading not required.*)

Army Form C. 2118.

Place	Date	Hour	Summary of Events and Information	Remarks and references to Appendices
In the Field	12/12/18		[illegible] moved to billets at LORETTE. General cleaning up.	
	13/12/18		Baths. Route march. Officers & Sgts football match in afternoon. Sgts won	
	14/12/18		Normal day in billets	
	15/12/18		Route march in the morning. Street in ATH entered by first British troops named by the Belgians RUE DE ~~[struck out]~~ LA ~~BE~~ GRANDE BRETAGNE	
	16/12/18		Officers dance – huge success	
	17/12/18		Normal day in billets	
	18/12/18		Work on railways commenced	
	19/12/18		Normal day in billets	
	20/12/18		Sgts Dance	
	21/12/18		Played the 1/10th L'pool Scottish at football. Score 1–5	
	22/12/18		C.O. & 2nd in Command proceed to BRUSSELS to see King of Belgium enter	
	23/12/18		Normal day in billets	
	24/12/18		Div massed band performance in the square at ATH	
	25/12/18		Played 422 Field Coy R.E. at football [illegible]	
	26/12/18		Normal day in billets	
	27/12/18		Novice Boxing tournament at Brigade	
	28/12/18			
	29/12/18		No 20 Platoon played No 8 – Result – Draw 1–1	
	30/12/18		Normal day in billets	

C E Thompson Lt Col
COMDG 5th S LAN R

A7092 Wt. W1289/M1293. 750,000. 1/17. D. D & L. Ltd. Forms/C2118/14.

War Diary SR 35

of

1/5 S. Lan. R

for period

1st to 31st December

1918.

Z 43

ORIGINAL

Instructions regarding War Diaries and Intelligence Summaries are contained in F. S. Regs., Part II. and the Staff Manual respectively. Title pages will be prepared in manuscript.

WAR DIARY
or
~~INTELLIGENCE SUMMARY.~~
(Erase heading not required.)

5TH SOUTH LANCS REGT
DECEMBER 1918

Army Form C. 2118.

Place	Date	Hour	Summary of Events and Information	Remarks and references to Appendices
IN THE FIELD	1 12/18 to 12 12/18		Normal Days in BILLETS at ATH (BELGIUM)	
	13 12/18		Advanced Billeting Party leaves for new area	
	14 12/18		Normal Day in Billets	
	15 12/18		Battalion moved by march route for new area Arrived BASSILLY staying night there.	
	16 12/18		March resumed. Arrived HONSTAD staying night there.	
	17 12/18		Battalion arrived new area at 14.15 hours – ST JOB – BRUSSELS	
	18 12/18 to 22 12/18		Normal Days in BILLETS.	
	23 12/18		166 Inf Bde played a Belgian Team at FOOTBALL Result 166 Bde – 5 – goals Belgians 4 goals.	
	24 12/18 to 28 12/18		Normal Days in BILLETS.	
	29 12/18		DIVISION played BRUSSELS at Football. Result 55 DIV – 3 goals BRUSSELS 2 goals.	
	30 12/18		Normal Day in BILLETS.	
	31 12/18		Brigade Cross Country Run.	

C. E. Thompson
Lt Col Comdg.
5 S. Lan. Regt

D. D. & L., London, E.C.
(A6540) Wt W5300/P713 750,000 5/18 Sch. 52a Forms/C2118/16.

"B" Company. A/276.

"A","C","D", Coys. 276 Bde.R.F.A.;)
166th.Infantry Brigade.)

1. If the situation continues normal the raid on MYSTERY HOUSE and neighbouring posts will take place at 0840 hours 7th.November 1918.

2. The whole Brigade of artillery will cover the operation. All guns open fire at ZERO.

Two 18-pounder Batteries less one section will engage the objectives. Right hand gun will fire on U.11.b.85.10. The movements of the barrage regulating the advance of your attacking platoon will be as follows;-

At ZERO plus two minutes, two right hand sections switch clear of the area to be assaulted and engage selected targets. At ZERO plus three and a half minutes, the remaining three sections similarly switch in rapid succession from the right, leaving the whole area to be raided clear of artillery fire a few seconds after ZERO plus three and half minutes.

You need not be troubled with other details of artillery programme except that all ranks engaged must realise that targets 500/1000 yards EAST of them will be engaged continuously throughout the operation, the shells going over the heads of assaulting party.

Artillery fire will last until ZERO plus twenty, beginning to die away from ZERO plus fifteen.

3. Reference action of assaulting platoon.

(a) You must take no risk of being seen assembling. If you cannot debauch from the Farm in time, the assembly must be done singly by individuals crawling. This will take a long time.

(b) Platoon Commanders must have small reserve to throw in where needed.

(c) Any post captured complete will be despatched to the rear under two men of the attacking group. These two men to be detailed deforehand. Remainder of group will have orders where to carry on.

(d) Ensure all group ~~xxxxxxxxxx~~ leaders and as many men as possible identify objectives by observation so far as they can be seen.

(e) Impress on all ranks essence of sucess is determination and speed, moving as close to barrage as possible.

(Signed) D.NISBETT, Major,

for Lieut.Col.
Comdg.5th.Bn.S.LAN.R.

6.11.18.

"B" Company. A/480.

"A", "C", and "D" Coys.)
276 Bde.R.F.A.))for information.
Right Gp.R.F.A.))
166th.Inf.Bde.)

---

1. The raid on MYSTERY HOUSE will be carried out by a platoon of "B" Company (about 25 strong) at 0840 hours to-morrow 7th.November., in accordance with instructions in A/476.

2. EQUIPMENT. Rifle, bayonet and S.B.R. - 8 rounds in magazine and one in breach - two or three clips in pocket. Selected men to carry a bomb or two each. One or two men in each attacking group to carry wirecutters.

3. PRISONERS. "B" Company will be responsible for escorting prisoners to BAUREGARD FARM. "A" Company will have a small escort in readiness to bring them on to Battalion H.Q.

4. ADVANCE AID POST. for the operation will be established at BAUREGARD FARM.

5. Two stretcher bearers will accompany raiding party. It will be their duty to see no wounded man is left behind.

6. O.C."B" Company will arrange for a rendezvous for checking return of raiders to ensure quick and accurate information of any casualties incurred.
N.C.O. in command of each attacking group must know well by sight and name each individual under his command.

7. SYNCHRONIZATION. Watches will be synchronized with the Artillery at THESE H.Qrs. at 0400 hours 7th.November.
A watch will then be sent to "B" Company.

(Signed) S.GIBSON, Capt. & Adjt.
5th.Bn.S.LAN.R.

6.11.18.

ETR 53

VR 37

WAR DIARY

4th S. LANC. R.

JANUARY - 1919

Z.44

WAR DIARY 5th S.LAN.R.
For JANUARY 1919.

Army Form C. 2118.

WAR DIARY
or
~~INTELLIGENCE SUMMARY.~~
(Erase heading not required.)

Instructions regarding War Diaries and Intelligence Summaries are contained in F. S. Regs., Part II. and the Staff Manual respectively. Title pages will be prepared in manuscript.

Place	Date	Hour	Summary of Events and Information	Remarks and references to Appendices
FORT JACKO BRUSSELS.	1/1/19 to 10/1/19		Normal days in billets.	
	11/1/19		55th Divl.Cross Country Run.Gained 4th place out of 13 teams.	
	12/1/19 to 16/1/19		Normal days in billets.	
	17/1/19 and 18/1/19		55th Divl.Boxing Tournament held at 'Palais D'Etẽ' BRUSSELS.	
	19/1/19		Normal day in Billets.	
	20/1/19		Finals of 55th Divl.Boxing Tournament.	
	21/1/19 to 25/1/19		Normal days in Billets.	
	26/1/19.		Review of III Corps Troops by S.M.King Albert of the Belgians.	
	27/1/19		Normal day in Billets.	
	28/1/19		Final of Divisional Association Football Competition.7th Kings L,pools 4 goals,166 Inf.Bde.H.Qrs.2 goals.	
	29/1/19		Normal day in billets.	
	30/1/19		Football Match .Runners Up of Divl.Competition. 2/5th L.Fs 4 goals 166 Inf.Bde.H.Qrs.Nil.	
	31/1/19		Normal day in Billets.	

C H Robertson Capt,Commdg.
5th.S.LAN.R.

D. D. & L., London, E.C.
(e340) Wt W5300/P713 750.000 3/18 E 2688 Forms/C2118/16.

19 V838

WAR DIARY

1/5TH S. LANCS. R

FEBRUARY 1919

2.45

Instructions regarding War Diaries and Intelligence Summaries are contained in F. S. Regs., Part II. and the Staff Manual respectively. Title pages will be prepared in manuscript.

WAR DIARY
or
INTELLIGENCE SUMMARY.
(Erase heading not required.)

Army Form C. 2118.

Place	Date	Hour	Summary of Events and Information	Remarks and references to Appendices
	1919.			
BRUSSELS.	Feby.			
	1.		Normal day in billets.	
	2.		-do-	
	3.		-do-	
	4.		-do-	
	5.		-do-	
	6.		-do-	
	7.		-do-	
	8.		-do-	
	9.		-do-	
	10.		-do-	
	11.		-do-	
	12.		5th Army Boxing Competition.	
	13.		-do-	
	14.		-do-	
	15.		Major Marshall took over command of Battalion.	
	16.		3rd Corps Cross Country Run won by Sgt. Dwerryhouse.	
	17.		Normal day in billets.	
	18.		-do-	
	19.		-do-	
	20.		-do-	
	21.		Company knock-out competition won by "D" Coy. Runners-up H.Q., and Transport.	
	22.		Normal day in billets.	
	23.		-do-	
	24.		-do-	
	25.		-do-	
	26.		-do-	
	27.		5th Army-Run, 1st. 6th Camerons, 2nd.-1/5 R.L.R. 3rd. Liverpool Scottish.	
	27.		Liverpool Scottish V 6th Camerons, 3rd Match. Scottish 3 Camerons 2.	
	28.		Normal day in billets.	

C. Marshall
MAJOR, Commanding,
5th South Lancs. Regt.

D. D. & L., London, E.C.
(A6340) Wt W5300/P713 750,000 3/18 E 2688 Forms/C2118/16.

5th. South Lancashire Regiment.

Instructions regarding War Diaries and Intelligence Summaries are contained in F. S. Regs., Part II. and the Staff Manual respectively. Title pages will be prepared in manuscript.

WAR DIARY
or
INTELLIGENCE SUMMARY.
(Erase heading not required.)

Army Form C. 2118.

Vol 39

Place	Date	Hour	Summary of Events and Information	Remarks and references to Appendices
	MARCH.			
"BRUSSELS"	1.		Normal day in billets.	
	2.		--ditto--	
	3.		166 Infantry Brigade leaves - Bn. under command of 165 Infantry Brigade.	
	4.		Normal day in Billets.	
	5.		--ditto--	
	7.		--ditto--	
	8.		--ditto--	
	9.		--ditto--	
	10.		--ditto--	
	11.		--ditto--	
	12.		Cup Final 8th. Bn. M.G.C. V 159 Bde. R.F.A. Signals.	
	13.		Normal day in Billets.	
	14.		--ditto--	
	15.		--ditto--	
	16.		--ditto--	
	17.		--ditto--	
	18.		--ditto--	
	19.		--ditto--	
	20.		--ditto--	
	21.		--ditto--	
	22.		--ditto--	
	23.		--ditto--	
	24.		--ditto--	
	25.		--ditto--	
	26.		--ditto--	
	27.		--ditto--	
	28.		--ditto--	
	29.		Battn. moved to BOULOGNE - entrained at RUYSBROECK.	
	30.		On train to BOULOGNE.	
	31.		Battn. arrived at BOULOGNE.	

C H Robertson
Captain,
Commanding 5th. S. Lan. R.

2.4.1919.

2.46

D. D. & L., London, E.C.
(12340) Wt W5300/P713 750,000 3/18 Sch. 52a Forms/C2118/16.

CONFIDENTIA –

WAR DIARY

OF

166 INF. BDE

FOR PERIOD

1/41 – 3/4/41

10

Army Form C. 2118.

Instructions regarding War Diaries and Intelligence Summaries are contained in F. S. Regs., Part II. and the Staff Manual respectively. Title pages will be prepared in manuscript.

WAR DIARY

or

~~INTELLIGENCE SUMMARY~~. 5th Bn. South Lancs. Regt.

(Erase heading not required.)

April 1919.

Place	Date	Hour	Summary of Events and Information	Remarks and references to Appendices
BOULOGNE.	1/4/19.		Ostrohove Camp taken over - Battn. made up to strength and Command taken over by Lt.Col. Little D.S.O. 190 Officers & 2208 O.Rs despatched to U.K. for Demob.	
	2/4/19.		119. Offrs. 1157 O.Rs. despatched to U.K. for Demob.	
	3/4/19.		204. " 1503 " " " "	
	4/4/19.		160. " 1801 " " " "	
	5/4/19.		79. " 917 " " " "	
	6/4/19.		72. " 869 " " " "	
	7/4/19.		11. " 8 " " " "	
	8/4/19.		87. " 856 " " " "	
	9/4/19.		105. " 649 " " " "	
	10/4/19.		111. " 1125 " " " "	
	11/4/19.		36. " 497 " " " "	
	12/4/19.		15. " 290 " " " "	
	13/4/19.		19. " 5 " " " "	
	14/4/19.		54. " 779 " " " "	
	15/4/19-		36- " 497 " " " "	
	16/4/19-		No sailings.	
	17/4/19.		57. " 701 " " " "	
	18/4/19.		38. " 1900 " " " "	
	19/4/19.		48. " 1253 " " " "	
	20/4/19.		No sailings.	
	21/4/19.		15. " 37 " " " "	
	22/4/19.		13. " 458 " " " "	
	23/4/19.		No sailings.	
	24/4/19.		32. " 1140 " " " "	
	25/4/19.		57. " 750 " " " "	
	26/4/19.		21. " 786 " " " "	
	27/4/19.		No sailings.	
	28/4/19.		44. " 1249 " " " "	
	29/4/19.		21. " 550 " " " "	
	30/4/19.		29. " 597 " " " "	

ORDERLY ROOM 4046 -5 MAY 1919 1/5th S. LANCASHIRE REGT.

Lieut.Colonel.
1/5th Bn. South Lancs. Rgt.

D. D. & L., London, E.C.
(16240) W1 W5300/P713 750,000 5/18 Sch. 52a Forms/C2118/16.

Instructions regarding War Diaries and Intelligence Summaries are contained in F. S. Regs., Part II. and the Staff Manual respectively. Title pages will be prepared in manuscript.

WAR DIARY
or
INTELLIGENCE SUMMARY.
(Erase heading not required.)

Army Form C. 2118.

Place	Date	Hour	Summary of Events and Information			Remarks and references to Appendices
			Officers	O. R's.		
Ostrohove Camp BOULOGNE.	May 1st.		46	1336	Despatched to U.K.	
	" 2		43	2115	" " "	
	" 3		13	587	" " "	
	" 4		74	1469	" " "	
	" 5		52	2199	" " "	
	" 6		25	1137	" " "	
	" 7		3	399	" " "	
	" 8		-	54	" " "	
	" 9		67	241	" " "	
	" 10		50	714	" " " Battalion Sports.	
	" 11		52	1180	" " "	
	" 12		6	72	" " "	
	" 13		No Sailings.			
	" 14		35	1046	" " "	
	" 15		34	738	" " "	
	" 16		35	1970	" " "	
	" 17		28	894	" " "	
	" 18		9	158	" " "	
	" 19		37	583	" " "	
	" 20		48	1176	" " "	
	" 21		33	515	" " "	
	" 22		18	1523	" " "	
	" 23		-	46	" " "	
	" 24		No Sailings.		Divisional Sports.	
	" 25		67	472	" " "	
	" 26		36	573	" " "	
	" 27		55	744	" " "	
	" 28		74	542	" " "	
	" 29		93	1004	" " "	
	" 30		278	854	" " "	
	" 31		63	2199	" " "	

A. J. Stealer [signature]
Major,
Commdg. 1/5 th. Bn. South Lancs. Regt.

1/6/19

D. D. & L., London, E.C.
(A8340) Wt W5300/P713 750,000 3/18 E 2688 Forms/C2118/16.

Army Form C. 2118.

Instructions regarding War Diaries and Intelligence Summaries are contained in F. S. Regs., Part II. and the Staff Manual respectively. Title pages will be prepared in manuscript.

WAR DIARY
or
INTELLIGENCE SUMMARY.
(Erase heading not required.)

Place	Date June	Hour	Summary of Events and Information	Remarks and references to Appendices
OSTROHOVE	1.		44 Officers 11550 O.Ranks for Demob. - Embarked for U.K.	
CAMP.	2.		9 O.Ranks for Demob. and 30 Officers 330 O. Ranks for leave Embarked for U.K.	
BOULOGNE.	3.		49 Officers. 1796 O.Ranks for Demob. and 5 Officers. 701. O. Ranks for Leave embarked for U.K.	
	4.		16 do 613 -do- -do- 4 do- -- -do- -do-	
	5.		10 do 731 -do- -do- 14 do 136 -do- -do-	
	6.		25 do 686 -do- -do- 67 do 573 -do- -do-	
	7.		No Sailings.	
	8.		56 Officers. 2315 -do- -do- 2 do 28 -do- -do-	
	9.		54 do 1260 -do- -do- 11 do 414 -do- -do-	
	10.		8 O.Ranks. for Demob. 10 do 667 -do- -do-	
	11.		1 Officer. 54 O. Ranks. for Leave Embarked for U.K.	
	12.		4 do 265 do for Demob. 19 Officers 201 -do- -do-	
	13.		53 O. Ranks for Demob. 33 do 693 -do- -do-	
	14.		70 Officers. 1851 O.Ranks for Demob. 38 do 593 -do- -do-	
	15.		11 do 899 do do 142 do 249 -do- -do-	
	16.		62 do 879 do do 49 do 149 -do- -do-	
	17.		54 do 918 do do 97 do 639 -do- -do-	
	18.		125 do 2564 do do 5 do 2 -do- -do-	
	19.		41 do 2073 do do -- do 3 -do- -do-	
	20.		26 do 93 do for leave Embarked for U.K.	
	21.		6 do 15 do for Demob. 3 Officers. 3 -do- -do-	
	22.		12 do 603 do do 67 do 561 -do- -do-	
	23.		34 do 888 do do 46 do 206 -do- -do- Acceptance of Allied Peace Terms by Central Powers.	
	24.		20 Officers. 1354. O. Ranks for Demob. 42 do 625 -do- -do- General Holiday.	
	25.		47 do 1156. do do 1 do -- -do- -do-	
	26.		30 do 679. do do 109 do 1345 -do- -do-	
	27.		70 do 2439. do do Embarked for U.K.	
	28.		35 do 1355. do do do PEACE SIGNED.	
	29.		8 do 299 do do 5 Officers 307 -do- -do-	
	30.		7 do 205 do do 1 do 117 -do- -do-	

2/7/19.

C. Lotter [signature]
Lieut.Colonel.
Cm
Cmdg. 1/5th Bn. South Lancs. Rgt.

14/1   1/5 S Lanc Regt 55

Army Form C. 2118.

Instructions regarding War Diaries and Intelligence Summaries are contained in F. S. Regs., Part II. and the Staff Manual respectively. Title pages will be prepared in manuscript.

WAR DIARY
or
INTELLIGENCE SUMMARY.

(Erase heading not required.)

53

Place	Date	Hour	Summary of Events and Information	Remarks and references to Appendices
	July.			
	1.		Passed through Camp & Embarked for U.K. 57 Officers 1395 O.Rs.	
Ostrohove	2.		-do- -do- 25 " 788 "	
Camp.	3.		-do- -do- 93. " 1969. "	
BOULOGNE.	4.		-do- -do- 45. " 1298. "	
	5.		-do- -do- 127 " 3252. "	
	6.		-do- -do- 93. " 2749. "	
	7.		-do- -do- 28. " 1248. "	
	8.		-do- -do- 25. " 474. "	
	9.		-do- -do- 17. " 674 "	
	10.		-do- -do- 19. " 870 "	
	11		-do- -do- 46. " 772 "	
	12.		-do- -do- 69. " 488 "	
	13.		-do- -do- 61. " 1772. "	
	14.		-do- -do- 20 " 1384. " French Peace Celebrations. 1 Coy. took	
	15.		-do- -do- 46. " 865 " Part in Procession.	
	16.		-do- -do- 1. "	
	17.		-do- -do- - " 318."	
	18.		-do- -do- 46. " 1090. "	
	19.		-do- -do- 19. " 759. " British Peace Celebrations. Bn. held Dance	
	20.		-do- -do- 48. " 269. " WhistvDrive & Concert.	
	21.		-do- -do- 15. " 141. "	
	22.		-do- -do- 49. " 875. "	
	23.		-do- -do- 89. " 1495. "	
	24.		-do- -do- 11. " 348. "	
	25.		-do- -do- 1. " 1."	
	26.		-do- -do- - " -	
	27.		-do- -do- 31. " 983. "	
	28.		-do- -do- 30. " 95. "	
	29.		-do- -do- 4. " 170. "	
	30.		-do- -do- 204. " - "	
	31.		-do- -do- 212. " 2234. "	

1/8/19.

C. Lettershol[?]

Cmdg. 1/5th Bn. South Lancashire Lieut.Colonel.
Regt.

D. D. & L., London, E.C. (10340) Wt W5300/P713 750,000 3/18 E 2688 Forms/C2118/16.

9.2